THE NEW
COMPLETE AFGHAN HOUND

The all-time top winning Afghan Hound, succeeding his sire to the honor (*see below*), Ch. Kabik's The Front Runner (Ch. Kabik's The Challenger ex Kabik's Ariel), black and tan dog. Bred by Chris and Marguerite Terrell and Gail Savage. Owned by Mr. and Mrs. William Clot. Handled by Chris Terrell.

Ch. Kabik's The Challenger—"Pepsi"—(Kabik's Standing Ovation ex Kabik's Mindy), multi BIS winner including Westminster 1983 and the Tournament of Champions, 1984. Bred and owned by Chris and Marguerite Terrell.—*Vicky Fox Foto.*

THE NEW COMPLETE

Afghan Hound

by CONSTANCE O. MILLER
and EDWARD M. GILBERT, JR.

ILLUSTRATED
including special drawings by Lois Gossner

FOURTH EDITION
First Printing—1988

230 Park Avenue, New York, NY 10169

Library of Congress Cataloging-in-Publication Data

Miller, Constance O.
   The new complete Afghan hound / by Constance O. Miller and Edward
M. Gilbert, Jr.; illustrated, including special drawings by Lois
Gossner.—4th ed.
      p.   cm.
   Rev. ed. of: The complete Afghan hound. 3rd ed. 1975.
   ISBN 0-87605-001-1
   1. Afghan hounds.   I. Gilbert, Edward M.   II. Miller, Constance
O.   Complete Afghan hound.   III. Title.
SF429.A4M5   1987
636.7'53—dc19
                                                              87-31062
                                                                   CIP

Printed in U.S.A.

*To our families who sacrificed countless
hours of companionship that this book
should become possible*

*This book is also dedicated to the
dignified and aloof "King of Dogs"—the Afghan Hound*

Original oil painting by F. T. Daws (English artist) of Westmill Omar, Ch. Badshah of Ainsdart, Ch. Asri-Havid of Ghazni, and Ch. Sirdar of Ghazni in the Khyber Pass. From the collection of Kay Finch, Crown Crest Kennels. Kay has generously willed this historical painting to the American Kennel Club, to be hung in its New York office.

Puppies of a repeat breeding of Ch. Mecca's Zeus ex Ch. Pandora Xotica of Stormhill.—*Ludwig.*

Contents

Front cover: Ch. Stormhill Domino Masquerade (Rader) and his son Stormhill's Freeze Frame (Frosty), America's first Afghan Hound bred by frozen semen, whelped 8/22/84. Breeders/Owners—Stormhill Kennels, Reg., Dave and Sandy Withington Frei, Woodinville, Washington.—*Photo by Ludwig*

Back cover: Ch. Zuvenda Sandman of Sheimar, bred by Bonnie Peregoy and Karen Martin, and owned by Bonnie Peregoy and Leslie Nelson.

Foreword

to Fourth Edition

WHEN asked to write the Foreword to the new edition of *The New Complete Afghan Hound* I felt honored, but, to be honest, it was nostalgia in disguise. Not long ago we lost two of our old boys. When you have had Afghan Hounds as friends for over twenty years this is not unexpected, it is just part of life; but with the passing of each dog, certain memories become more vivid.

Because Ed Gilbert lives in Southern California, I have known him, his industry and devotion to the breed, primarily through club business. But Conni lives in Northern California, as do I, and we have been friends since long before publication of "The Book," as it is known around here. Our mutual base was the Afghan Hound Club of Northern California, Inc. Its newsletter was the first repository of various kinds of breed-related material that was later to furnish the basis for The Book and make me feel like one of its many godparents.

Our first Afghan Hound, Khim, was a willful soul and probably the smartest one who ever lived with us, but who took great pleasure in embarrassing me in the show ring. At one time I was a little annoyed because neither Conni nor The Book gave quick tips for turning her into the show automaton that I (then) thought it would be nice to have. Nozee, our second dog, guarded us and the house with great zeal, but was able to open doors in ways no dog should be able to do. The Book, again, had no ready answer.

Then came our first litter. We kept the two males, reasoning that when we decided which was "best" the other would be sold. Both boys endeared themselves to us, each in his own way, and both spent the rest of their days with us. The Book was a big help, but one that I took for granted and can appreciate even more in retrospect. Melanie reigned with great dignity, while Lili wagged her tail in circles like a propeller. A carrot will never be peeled in our house that Lili won't come to mind, as they were her favorite treat. We learned about giving carrots to pups, if not from The Book, from Conni's earlier writings—I no longer remember which. Turhan was a stud-fee puppy, and Peanut a "returnee" from our last litter. The Book warned us about contracts and such, but we, like so many trusting souls, had to learn the hard way.

During the bygone days of the benched show, Conni and I, with various friends, spent long hours discussing our mutually beloved breed. She and I spent little or no time discussing the favorite topic of faults, but dwelt at length upon the magnet that drew people to the breed, and the various mini-magnets that kept them there. Much of my continuing overview of the breed was gotten as a working member of the Board of Directors, both local and national. Conni remained ever-present, if not in person, in print, at both the local and national level.

Every fancier that I have known has been touched by owning an Afghan Hound, and found some way of expressing a part of themselves through the medium of their dogs. Such expression need be no more than taking time out from tedious duty to make a relaxing contact with another living being.

Memories of friends, a particular dog show or circuit, club meetings and parties, triumphs and disappointments flood into my mind. There are thoughts of whelping litters, and of holding a tiny newborn puppy and wondering what lies ahead. The Book was always there—not just to inform, to supply pedigrees, pictures of relatives, and lists of statistics that I might happen to need—but also to support and to sustain all of us fanciers who could read, and who owned dogs that could not. That is its enduring quality.

Ours is a breed that has undergone much turmoil since the time of The Book's publication. A rise to quick popularity brings as many problems as pluses. The Book has been there as a helpful guide, but could not foresee all eventualities. The new edition is much needed; not because of any insufficiency of the last one, but because the plot is a continuing one and now there is much more of the story that needs to be told. For those of us who have lived through these years, the update provides a much needed perspective about those turbulent times. For those who have only recently entered the breed, or are just planning to do so, the update provides the latest and most complete history to be found between two covers.

By virtue of having acquired this book, you, the reader, obviously share my interest in Afghan Hounds, and either own or will soon own one (or more) of these special dogs. This book will tell you (and I take this opportunity to echo the sentiments) to enjoy your relationship with your friend and companion and understand your Afghan

10

Hound for what it is. Do not let outside forces drag you into the world of showing, or of breeding, or of living vicariously through your dogs, past the point of genuine enjoyment for you both. That is not what owning an Afghan Hound is all about. Each dog that I have owned, or known, was a treasure in its own right, and to be cherished as such. Just having had some of those characters to live with has been the most rewarding experience of all.

—Joanne R. Montesano

Mrs. Montesano served the Afghan Hound Club of America as Corresponding Secretary (1979-82), President (1983-84), and Board Member (1985).

Ch. Zuvenda Renegade of Esfahan, F.Ch., stretched out. Razzle was 1979 Afghan Hound Club of America National Specialty BOB winner. Owner, Karen Wagner.

Preface

WHERE can I find information on the Afghan Hound? How many times has the breeder and exhibitor of the Afghan Hound asked or heard this question? For years, the only available work was Hubbard's *The Afghan Hound* which was printed in England. This book, as Hubbard states, is "merely a small handbook on the breed for those who are interested in it. . . ."

The authors undertook the task of writing *The Complete Afghan Hound* in order to supply the urgent need for a standard reference book on the breed. This book is an attempt to compile a comprehensive story in regard to the Afghan Hound's history, conformation, breeding, feeding, grooming, training and exhibiting. This is not a rehash of old cliches; it is the product of painstaking research into the past in order to compile an accurate story of the Afghan Hound.

No attempt has been made to cover general information pertaining to all breeds in regard to feeding and breeding, but rather to discuss these topics as they relate to the Afghan Hound. In other words, the general subject of dog nutrition can be found in books on feeding dogs, but the peculiar problem of the finicky-eating Afghan Hound is covered herein.

This book has been copiously illustrated to inform the newcomer to the breed and to show the old timer where we have been. The drawings in Chapters 3 and 7 were made specifically for this book by Lois Gossner. All the illustrations will enable us to know better where we are going.

The authors received the help and aid of many people throughout the world. This group included dog fanciers, non-dog fanciers, and Afghan Hound breeders and exhibitors. Their help is greatly appreciated. In particular, the officers and members, both past and present, of the Afghan Hound Club of America provided individual aid and encouragement.

The late Mr. Elsworth Howell was an invaluable ally. His contributions were many and the books he helped produce will stand as a lasting monument for many years to come.

One of the purposes of this book is to preserve and protect the Afghan Hound as a breed for those people lucky enough to appreciate his traits. This is also one of the purposes of the parent club and the various regional Afghan Hound clubs. In order to obtain the address of the Afghan Hound club nearest to you, write to the current secretary of the AHCA. The name and address of the current secretary is listed quarterly in *Pure-Bred Dogs—American Kennel Gazette* under The American Kennel Club—Member Clubs.

To those who answered our letters, often providing a link in the chain, and the various helpers and contributors to this effort, the thanks of the authors are hereby extended. The authors also thank the librarians, museum curators, and the various scholarly research organizations. Finally, thanks are due to the breeders: without their interest nothing could have been written. But most of all, thanks go to the Afghan Hound—King of Dogs.

Ch. Cavu's Flying Circus (Ch. Cavu's Oyster Rockefeller ex Zafara Zenobia), black mask gray brindle, multiple BIS winner. BOB at 1987 AHCA National Specialty. Bred and owned by Betsy Hufnagel.—*Fox & Cook Photography.*

Ch. Crown Crest Topaz (Ch. Ophaal of Crown Crest ex Ch. Crown Crest Tae-Joan), black-masked red dog, sire of 14 champions, bred by Kay Finch, owned by Gordon W. and Constance O. Miller. Original oil painting from Mrs. Miller's collection by artist Lois Gossner.

1

Meet the
Afghan Hound

THE official breed standard (approved by the American Kennel Club, September 14, 1948) of the Afghan Hound Club of America opens with the following preamble:

> "The Afghan Hound is an aristocrat, his whole appearance one of dignity and aloofness with no trace of plainness or coarseness. He has a straight front, proudly carried head, eyes gazing into the distance as if in memory of ages past. The striking characteristics of the breed—exotic or "Eastern" expression, long silky topknot, peculiar coat pattern, very prominent hip bones, large feet, and impression of a somewhat exaggerated bend in the stifle due to profuse trouserings—stand out clearly, giving the Afghan Hound the appearance of what he is, a king of dogs, that has held true to tradition throughout the ages."

This short essence of the "hound" as he should be at maturity means much to the dedicated breeder and knowledgeable judge. But to the passerby who glimpses his first Afghan Hound, the dog presents a bizarre and strange effect, even prompting children to occasionally ask, "Is it a dog?" When told it is an Afghan Hound, there is probably no retort as common or as irritating as the oftheard, "An African what?" With his haughty air and unusual coat pattern, the hound makes a pronounced impact and rarely goes unnoticed in any surroundings. Response to the sight of the hound is instantaneous; viewers are either strongly and immediately attracted to the dog's elegance and "different" beauty, or just as strongly repelled by its strangeness and "comical" aspect. The dog itself is quite apt to reply in kind, being determined to pick his own friends. His reactions to strangers can be most unpredictable.

The Afghan Hound puppy is quite a different matter as no dog goes through such marked transitions during one lifetime, both in temperament and in physical appearance. Born flat-nosed, wrinkly-faced, short-haired, and rat-like, it would take an expert to pick an Afghan Hound puppy from a nest of mongrels of similar size. The breed pattern takes form very slowly. By three months of age, the legs have lengthened to approximately the same length as the body, and the sheen of short hair has been replaced by a dense puppy fluff. The coat begins to lengthen, blurring the outline of the dog's form from toes to tail. "Monkey whiskers" frequently sprout from the sides of a still short and broad muzzle. Accompanying this outlandish appearance is a similarly outlandish puppy personality often thoroughly abandoned in wild, carefree play and knockdown exuberant demonstrations of affection to owners and littermates.

The prospective buyer who expects to find more than a faint hint of the flowing-coated, sedate and elegant hound in a pup is certain to be not only disappointed, but fairly skeptical of the parentage of these bewhiskered apparitions. The puppyhood state is an integral part of the hound's unique development. As the frame lengthens and the coating bursts forth, the yearling who has not yet broken "saddle," nor gained firm control of his limbs, is apt to be more reminiscent of a misbegotten sheep dog than of any Afghan Hound-to-be. With the shedding of much facial hair and the development of a natural short-haired saddle running from withers to tip of tail, comes the emergence of an inscrutable "Oriental" attitude and restrained dignity. In maturity, the "foolish Prince" becomes a responsible King.

American dog fanciers were given this early description of the breed in an article, "The Dog of the Mystic East" by Miss Jean C. Manson in the June 1929 *American Kennel Gazette:*

"From about three months of age, the Afghan puppy is a most wonderful youngster, all legs and the most lovely soft fur. More like down, and all eyes, just like Teddy Bears. From babyhood, they are most wonderfully gentle, never snatching food and in every way they are most lovable. They make charming pets and are so distinguished looking, stately and graceful that the most fastidious fancier would consider them an ornamental asset. There is something so foreign about his appearance—something perhaps a little outlandish—that the dog brings to mind the splendor of the mysterious East. Instinctively, one associates him with Eastern magnificence, stately palaces, gardens, and courtyards . . . and native attendants to grant their wishes. . . . In spite of this aristocratic appearance and look of reserve, these dogs are the very reverse of unapproachable and are, indeed, most docile and affectionate. A kind word and pat are never forgotten. A rebuff will be taken to heart with great distress."

Modern use of the hounds in fashion illustrations and current emphasis on coat beauty lead outsiders to think of the dog as purely ornamental. Intimate knowledge of these dogs gives clear lie to this concept, and evidences of his amazing mental and physical versatility are astonishing and plentiful. A rare combination of fierce hunting abilities and conversely, gentle herding instincts, endeared him to tribesmen and royalty in turn. His marked physical adaptability to extremes of climatic conditions provided him with the endurance to thrive where other dogs would have perished. His natural wit and independence of thought enabled him to survive with or without the guidance of man as successive civilizations rose and fell. He was as much at home in a tent as in a palace.

Legends place the Afghan Hound in a fantastic variety of situations. Widely quoted claims by the Afghan people place him on the Ark with Noah, as the only representative of the *Canidae.* Archaeological devotees stress his resemblance to some of the ancient Greyhound-type dogs appearing on Egyptian tombs dating back to 3000 B.C. Another student of the lore of antiquity insists the Afghan is the "monkey-faced dog" mentioned in papyrus documents of 4000 B.C. found on the Sinai Peninsula. More recent interpretations of Chinese manuscripts place the hound in the company of Genghiz Khan and before that time as one of the most primitive of all dogs running with the earliest nomadic tribes that roamed the Steppes of Asia. One of the first Westerners to export the hounds from Afghanistan lays claim for the breed's pre-Christian history on the basis of some ancient and colossal rock carvings from the Balkh area of Afghanistan.

Tales, reeking with the incense and romantic mystery of the Bagdadian Mid East, infer that the Afghan Hound jealously guarded harems of beautiful concubines, and was the pampered pet of Kings' daughters. The Afghan peoples, in rare reference to the breed in native writings, referred to the hound as having been a zealous herder of flocks of sheep, a courier, guard and mascot for war-lords of the tenth century A.D.; and as an animal that primarily made his reputation as a hunting dog *extraordinaire* in the company of tribal chieftains and kings. From India comes an amazing eye-witness ac-

The writings at the top and bottom of this Afghan stamp have the same meaning. Under "1962" is the Mohammedan year 1341, and the left hand side reads "Tazi Hound."

count of the hounds functioning as independent, unbidden garrison sentries.

Some of the earliest claims of the versatility and value of the hound are not supported by example. To write a breed book, one might expect that all that is required is a practical knowledge of the breed and an aggregation of articles containing references to the breed and its history. Close scrutiny of the many scattered writings on the Afghan Hound of today and yesteryear, however, brings disappointing evidence that a large part of the literature from books and magazines is nothing but repetition or plagiarism, with amazing embellishments, of a few statements. Many of these statements are of dubious authenticity but accompanied the hounds as they left Afghanistan in the late 1800s and became an inseparable part of the breed's history. When all has been considered in light of present-day knowledge, a distinctly uneasy feeling remains that the basic questions asked most often by the fancy are yet to be solved to the satisfaction of anyone. Such questions are: Where and when did the Afghan Hound originate? What are the differences and the relationship of the Afghan Hound to other sight-hound breeds? What "type" hound is typical of the best of the native Afghan Hound?

In answering such questions, probably the simplest reply is the old Eastern statement on the breed, "No man knoweth whence they came, but there they are and there they stay." In California, the Kato Indians have a story about creation that states: "Negaicho, the creator, the Great Traveler, was walking around creating, and he took along a dog." Many Afghan Hound owners are content with a similar thought: God had a dog, and it was an Afghan Hound. But, as the nature of human beings is to look for explanations, we will attempt to explore what is and what is not known of our breed's colorful past in a concerted effort to discover what an Afghan Hound is.

18

2

Tracing the
Afghan's Background

ARCHAEOLOGISTS tell us that dogs were among
man's first domesticated animals, in a relationship that preceded
earliest recorded history. Unfortunately the structural details that
separate wild dogs from domesticated dogs are extremely subtle, and
the true story of where or when man sought the services of dogs
remains conjecture. We know only that in antiquity, the dog had
become practically universal, roaming the globe in a wide variety of
shapes and sizes.

Kennel club grouping and common sense place the Afghan
Hound with the "Greyhounds," a generic term for a family of unusually long-limbed, long-muzzled, swift dogs that overtake and
quickly dispatch game by means of sharp eyesight as opposed to
trailing a ground scent. The Afghan Hound fits the group easily
but can also follow a spoor with considerable talent.

Gazehounds (those which hunt by sight), ranging from the stately
36-inch Irish Wolfhound to the terrier-sized Whippet, are known
for their lean, oval-shaped bodies and "tucked up" narrow loins
within a range of lighter to heavier frames. In structure the Afghan
is intermediate, possessing larger feet, more breadth of body, and
less streamlining than other greyhounds of comparable size. Among
the coursing breeds the Afghan is not, nor was he meant to be, the
leader in sheer straightaway speed. But, as a jumper and broken field
runner, he is without peer, being built for the rigors of actual prolonged field combat with a wide variety of game under difficult

5000-year-old Stamp Seals from Tepe Gawra illustrating Greyhound type dogs.

ground conditions. His ability to wheel, dodge, and leap obstacles must be seen to be believed.

There is conclusive proof that a greyhound type, long-jawed and long-limbed, was among the very earliest of the recorded domestic dogs. At Tepe Garwa, a few miles northeast of Mosul in north Iraq, an ancient stamp seal considered to be over 5,000 years old was excavated with the likeness of just such a hound on it. A pre-Sumerian skull from the same site was shown to be remarkably similar to that of the Salukis that inhabit the area today. But archaeologists rarely find the soft fleshy parts that are needed for meaningful precise breed identification. Aside from the sheer size, it is primarily the differences seen in ears, tails and coats that clearly distinguish the various greyhound breeds.

The majority of today's greyhounds carry an intermediate or "rose ear," small in size, that folds back against the side of the head. Only the Ibizan Hound, from the Balaeric Islands off Spain, still exhibits a large archaic upright hound ear. Among the gazehounds, the Afghan Hound and the closely related hounds of Persia and Arabia alone have retained the pendent "lop" ear so common in short-legged scent hounds and other canine groups.

Sighthound coats range from the smooth velvet of the Greyhound proper through the harsh roughness of the English Deerhounds and Wolfhounds to the soft wavy coat of the Borzoi. The Arabian Saluki is basically a smooth-coated hound, but there is a highly prized "fringed" variety characterized by its exquisite, heavily plumed tail and thick furnishings on ears and toes. Despite the extreme and deliberate development of long, thick coats on modern Afghan Hounds, a study of the breed in Afghanistan indicated that in coating the hounds begin where the Saluki leaves off, and the Afghan's hunting dog is casually accepted in a wide variety of coat types from smooth-haired to shaggy or corded.

20

In searching for valid breed differences between the Saluki and the Afghan Hound, one finds himself on loose ground. While the Afghan is said to have lower-set ears, a shorter, higher-held tail and more prominent hipbones, in actuality there is great overlapping of these characteristics in the two breeds. With such muddy breed boundaries, most early writers preferred to lump the Saluki and the Afghan together as Oriental greyhounds. Yet a fair amount is known of the history of the Saluki, and the question of just how much of this history can be rightly claimed by the Afghan Hound remains unanswered. A newspaper clipping from Kabul, Afghanistan, dated 8 August 1962, written by Gulbaz, clearly illustrates the overlapping coat characteristics:

> "The greyhound or 'Tazi' as it is called all over Afghanistan . . . There are three popular breeds of this dog. One is called 'Bakhmull' meaning 'velvet' because it has a long silky coat which covers the whole body including the ears. Another is called 'Luchak' or smoothcoated, and the third one is 'Kalagh' (rhyming with 'blast') which has long silky hairs on its ears and legs, but the rest of the body is smoothcoated."

This same article depicts the Afghan shepherd's dog as somewhat similar in the range of size, colors, and coat varieties to the native greyhounds. But the massive-headed "sheepdogs" are decidedly different in build, showing a marked affinity to the powerful and brutish Tibetan Mastiff.

The Afghan Hound as a breed is reputed to be heavier-boned and less delicate than the Saluki, but the breeds vary greatly within themselves. Such diversity is definitely not random, but to a marked extent follows geographical patterns. The lowland Afghans of south and west Afghanistan, towards Iran or Baluchistan, lean towards the sparse coat and the lean and racy build of the adjacent Saluki types. But the Afghan Hounds of the rugged mountain country of the formidable Hindu Kush range tend to be shorter, more powerfully built, and often considerably shaggier-coated. As a matter of fact, only in these mountain areas surrounding the ancient city of Kabul has our modern concept of full-coated hounds with flying topknots been reported in considerable numbers. It is the mysterious development of the "mountain type" of hound that remains historically perplexing. The discovery of these great shaggy dogs has touched off a never-ending controversy as to which is the senior sight hound, the coated Afghan Hound or the short-haired Saluki type.

A Pack of Hounds: copy in tempera of an Egyptian wall painting dated in the XVIII Dynasty from the tomb of Rekh-mi-Rē in Thebes.

The Metropolitan Museum of Art

In the absence of paleontological evidence, it is necessary to turn to ancient art renderings for clues to superficial breed differences. Dog types, including greyhounds, are found in Egyptian dynastic art tracing back to the third millenium before Christ. This does not mean that such dogs were necessarily indigenous to Egypt as the bulk of osteological evidence points to prior importation from other areas, but we are greatly indebted to Pharaonic scribes for their picturesque renderings of animals known to them. Tomb paintings include greyhounds adorned with elaborate jeweled collars, framed with falcons, gazelle, and other symbols of the chase. These leggy, pointed-jawed Egyptian greyhounds were in contrast to pendulous-lipped, heavy-bodied, huge mastiffs and short-legged hounds of Dachshund proportions. The Pharaoh's greyhounds varied in details of ears and tails, with the very earliest representations illustrating the upright ear. Strangely enough, no "rose-eared" hounds are to be seen, but the "lop" ear becomes increasingly evident in succeeding dynasties. The tails of these greyhounds vary from the short, tight screw tails of today's Basenji through the high curled loops typical of the Afghan Hound to unimpressive limp ropes.

Persian Greyhound: bas relief in bronze by Cellini (1500–72).

Alinari photo, courtesy Fratelli Alinari

In the tomb of Rekh-mi-Rē of the 18th dynasty (ca. 1450 B.C.), there is a panel depicting a pack of hounds, all lop-eared, with short hair lines on the tails. Most of the tails hang limp, but at least one waves high and fairly well curled. The tomb writings tell that these hounds were a tribute gift from Upper Nubia. The giving of gift dogs was common practice then as it is today. In this manner, ancient dog types quickly spread throughout the world. It is stretching things to connect the long-coated Afghan Hound directly with the dogs of ancient Egypt for, excluding a few short hair lines on the tails, the latter were completely smooth.

Many centuries later in the sixth century B.C., evidence of hounds with some featherings occurs, on a hydria of Athenian fabric and a Hellenistic amphora of the same era. Once into the Christian era, a magnificent feather-tailed dog called a "Persian Greyhound" caught the imagination of European and Oriental artisans. In the 16th century A.D., a marvelous bronze medallion of a graceful beauty was done by Benvenuto Cellini, and similar hounds are to be found in the delicate brushwork of the Chinese, dating to well over a thousand years ago.

The terms Persian Greyhound or Persian Gazellehound appear rather frequently in canine literature, usually with reference to a fringe-tailed Saluki, but also to a passable light-coated Afghan Hound. Note the prominent hipbones and sturdy bone structure so obvious in the photograph of the Cellini bronze on page 22. The

23

Persian Greyhound is pivotal in the two breeds, being basically smoothcoated, but trimmed with handsome ear fringes and a gracefully ringed plume tail. Featherings to a greater or lesser degree are found on legs, chest, feet, and tail and sometimes shoulders in the pattern seen on today's Setters. The plume-tailed hounds are known to have ranged with man from Arabia, north through Iraq, from Iran into Turkestan, and to whatever far-away fields the trade routes would carry them, even into China.

There is little doubt that the Persian Greyhound is a sub-species of the Saluki, for in all recorded time Persians have called this hound *sag-i Tazi* which translates, "dog from Arabia." There is also little doubt that there are connections between these dogs and Afghan Hounds, if for no other reason than that the Afghan name for their own hunting hound is also *Tazi*.

Artistic representations of the smooth Saluki or the plume-tailed Persian hound are found in many sources. Unfortunately to date absolutely no authenticated representation of an even passably coated Afghan Hound has been found, dating prior to 1800 A.D. To make matters worse, one of the distinguishing characteristics of the Afghan Hound is the fact that his tail is not supposed to be bushy.

The absence of pictorial evidence, however, to support the claim that a long-coated Afghan Hound existed in antiquity, could be due to the historical circumstances surrounding the country of the breed's major development. It is helpful to study Afghanistan with map in hand. Since the beginning of man's migrations for food, wealth and power, the land-locked country now known as Afghanistan has been in the middle of the major overland routes from Greece and Persia to India and China. These routes were formed by ancient tribes of hungry nomads who came from the great Asiatic steppes following the seasonal grasses with huge flocks of sheep and goats, living a transitory existence in tent-camps. The northern region of Afghanistan was once a part of ancient Bactria and came under the swords of Alexander the Great, Darius, Genghiz Khan and Tamerlane, whose powerful armies cut wide swaths from Persia to India, both coming and going. Residues of the armies remained to occupy the regions of miscellaneous tribes, thereby planting foreign cultures into the ancient soils. In consequence, Afghanistan grew as a loose-knit nation of multiple, highly confusing, and often mobile, layers of changing ethnic groups, desperately clinging to their own identity. Such tribesmen often cannot tell you the names of their grandparents, yet seriously claim direct descent from Timur (Tamerlane). Wandering nomads rarely left tangible messages to posterity, and neither did warring armies. Some accounts of these periods of conquest do appear in ancient Persian and Chinese literature, but rarely mention dogs.

24

In the seventh century A.D., the overwhelming Islamic religion flooded Afghanistan from the west. Mohammed, determined to strengthen the "one God only" thesis, waged holy wars and dictated grave penalties against the raising of heathen images. Simple drawings of animals concocted idol worship. The dog, which had been revered in previous Zoroastrian times, was suddenly regarded as an unclean object of loathing. The priceless Saluki and Tazi escaped a large part of this stigma, but such religious barriers prevented the preservation of any clear picture of the dogs in Moslem countries. Older evidences may well have been destroyed at this time in Mohammedan idol-breaking frenzies.

The development of the independent country of Afghanistan has been marked by constant skirmishes with the neighboring countries and bloody internal tribal power struggles. In recent centuries, the country has been considered "out of bounds" for strangers and a hostile land of mystery. From 1839 to 1921 England established a "protectorate" which was strongly resented by the tribal chiefs. In 1973 a military coup ushered in a republic, and in 1979 Russian troops invaded.

With scant information available from Afghanistan, the arguments over "which came first, the Saluki or the Afghan Hound?" resolve into two points of view with seemingly logical hypotheses on both sides. Proponents of the coated hounds point to evidence which says the original domestication of herd animals took place in the extensive steppe region of central Asia which includes Mongolia, the Black Sea area, south Russia, north Afghanistan, Iran and Iraq. Due to the severity of the steppe winters, they contend, it would have been essential for these sheep, goats, cattle and horses to have thick woolly coats for protection against freezing. When these animals were transported to the warmer climates of Egypt and Arabia, their heavy coats would have been useful in cloth-making and thus would have been preserved.

According to this reasoning, it is plausible to assume that the hunting dogs of the most primitive inhabitants of the steppe region would have had similarly long and heavy coats, but that unlike their bovine, ovine and caprine neighbors, these hounds would have found no use for their thick hair in the valley of the Nile. Thus a new breed with a short and sleek coat would have been developed for comfort in warmer temperatures.

This argument is hardly congenial to those who credit the Saluki as being the most primitive canine type. Their contention is that the smooth-coated hound could have been carried through Afghanistan and traded in China where evidence exists of Saluki types dating back to the tenth century A.D. Supporters of this theory claim that a blending of one of the "royal hounds" with any one of a number of native types could have supplied the ingredients that differentiate the mountain hound from the Saluki. The similarities between the massive Tibetan Mastiff which is thick and long-coated with a fair length of bushy tail curled over its back and the brutish Afghan shepherd's dog are mentioned. The inference is that a bit of this type of influence could well have drastically changed a poor shivering Saluki into a dog better suited to the terrain. Other debaters point to the better-tempered woolly shepherd's dog of south Russia as a possible relation of the Afghan Hound. Some of these shepherd's dogs are quite graceful and agile and are known to have played a part in the development of the Borzoi. And so the argument runs on . . .

The herding instinct, whether primeval or acquired through blood blending, is not to be glossed over. Verified reports of the regal hound being used with sheep come directly from Afghanistan. Modern fanciers have noticed some Afghan Hounds' tendency to be heel biters and follow round-up procedures at play. Dr. Betsy Porter in England was quite struck by a spontaneous demonstration of herding by one of her champion Afghan Hounds during the Second World War. She was in the habit of taking the dog with her on hospital duties, and then allowing him to run home alongside of the car for the last five miles. One day, when going past a dairy yard with about 30 cows in it, her hound suddenly jumped the fence and herded the cows. He worked them into a small circle and then ran down the field to retrieve a stray. After working it back to the herd, the dog moved the bunch to the corner of the pasture. When satisfied with his work, he jumped back across the fence and continued on his way home.

We seriously doubt that the "which came first" arguments can ever be resolved. The very concept of "breed" is man made for his own purposes. Only through physical restraint and human selection, or through absolute geographical isolation, can any breed be kept pure. There is, however, one valid reason for contemplating the origin of the coated Afghan Hound. Only if the Afghan Hound is actually the primeval type believed by some are we correct in accepting the various different types of hounds in Afghanistan as being true varieties of one ancient breed. But, if the opponents of the theory are correct and the breed is a more recent mixture of two or more ancient dog types, we must accept the fact that only the precarious mixture seen in the best hounds constitutes the true desired modern "breed," with all other types being degenerates pointing back to the delicate Saluki or the stocky peasant herd-and-guard dog types. As such borderline specimens frequently occur in modern

26

litters, it might be wise not to rely too heavily on the concept of the "ancient Afghan Hound" until one can be located. Instead, we might better work to carefully preserve the best of the hounds described and seen in the 19th and 20th centuries.

Early written accounts of hounds that could conceivably be true coated Afghan Hounds are extremely scarce. A few were found by the amazingly diligent searching of Jackson Sanford who published the results of his studies in the *Afghan Hound Club of America Bulletin* of March 1942. In the article entitled, "Are Afghans the Oldest Breed?," Mr. Sanford attempted to trace a logical history of the hound back to the oldest known *Canidae*, or pre-dog forms. While some of his conclusions such as ". . . the Afghan or its immediate ancestor inhabited the steppes of central Asia no less than 100,000 years ago," do seem premature on the basis of available evidence, he did unearth a reference that could just possibly refer to very early Afghan Hounds. Sanford postulated that the Yucchi peoples brought the dog from Central Asia into northern Afghanistan about 126 B.C., basing this on a quotation from a Chinese manuscript of the era describing the Yucchi as follows:

"They are of the race that inhabits the Land of the Frozen Earth. They are keepers of herds, breeders of horses, and drinkers of mare's milk. Their sheep and horses are herded together . . . At night . . . their dogs stand watch by the common herd . . . These dogs are as large as the foals in the herd, black and exceedingly fierce; the hair on them is long and, on the ear, is of such texture that the women shear them as sheep, and make from the ear-wool a felt, which is the material of their finest headgear . . . When they hunt no animal stands before the ferocity of the dogs, and the mounted huntsmen are hard pressed to keep in view of the pack."

While such passages can be applied almost as easily to the fierce Tibetan Mastiffs of Mongolia, nevertheless, black is a known color of the Afghan Hound. The shaggy Asiatic horses of that era were scarcely larger than a good-sized pony, therefore the size of a "foal" (new born colt) is well within the size range of the hound.

Sanford has also supplied a more specific description from the time of Tamerlane, in the 14th century A.D., of dogs that could, conceivably, be related to Afghan Hounds:

"Now you should be informed that the people of this land beyond the river (Oxus) have a race of hounds as large as young colts, which excited the interest of the Tartars to no small degree . . . When we first saw them in no case could we come up with any. They looked down at us from the strongholds of their mountain master, a thousand feet above and eluded us. They amazed us by the (three words undecipherable) with which they eluded the arrows we sped at them . . . At night they would come in silence, like great cats, and (having been trained in this art by their roguish masters), they would loose the horses' tethers and lead them away. One such fell victim to Dojhur's arrow, and we examined the beast with amazement. Except on the foreface, the hair on these dogs . . . is long and tangled. The ears are abundantly hairy and drooping, as are none of other beasts. The Chinese surgeons examined the dog; they say that its stomach is under the great-rib. The captives from Herat had seen such dogs in the hills to the Westward. The mountain chieftains, they say, are wont to hunt with these hounds, and to this end, they train them leopards and falcons, as do the Franks, to work with the dogs . . . When these dogs run, no man nor beast can come abreast; or so it is said . . ."

While Sanford logically looked to the steppes of Asia for the birthplace of the breed, others have cited different opinions. One speculation that appered in the American Kennel Club's official *Complete Dog Book* until recent revision eliminated it, read:

"It was near Jebel Musa, or the Mountain of Moses, on that small peninsula called Sinai, between the Gulf of Suez and the Gulf of Aqaba, that the breed now known as the Afghan Hound first became a recognizable type of dog."

The basis for this statement fell directly on a translation of a certain papyrus document, attributed to 3,000 B.C. The connection between the document and the Afghan Hound stemmed from the translation of the word *cynocephalus* into "monkey-faced hound" by one Major H. Blackstone. Illustrations on nearby tombs of associated age depicted a dog-like form with a head suggestive of a baboon. However, later experts generally agree that while the Afghan Hound could possibly have been known in the area, the word *cynocephalus* should be more accurately translated as "dog-faced monkey" and rightly refers to the gelada monkey, or baboon. Such monkey remains have been found in mummified form within the tombs, and were sacred pets in the time of the New Kingdom of Egypt. Evidence of *cynocephali* as being other than dog-faced baboons is lacking in scientific circles.

The picture "Dog and Monkey, From Tomb No. 50" on Page 29 is from *The Tomb of Siphtah*, Theodore Davis, London, 1908, which states: "In the first tomb opened (No. 50), the chamber was about 19

Dog and Monkey, from Tomb No. 50, photo from *The Tomb of Siphtah*, Theodore Davis, London, 1908.

feet long by 6-8 feet broad. The shaft, 12 feet deep by about 4 feet square, was full of rubbish, some of which had penetrated into the room. It had been almost completely plundered, only a few fragments of wood remaining from the coffin. Propped up against the eastern wall was a large dog, quite perfect although stripped of its wrappings, and a monkey still partially wrapped. This type of dog is described by Daressy and Gaillard in the Cairo Catalogue (*Faune de l'Anc. Egypte* (1), 29,501). Unfortunately we could find no trace of the owner of the tomb."

Written clues to the breed that actually come from Afghanistan are the rarest of all. After acquiring an Afghan Hound of his own in 1956, a Lt. Col. Kullmar of the American Embassy in Kabul, made an attempt to attach local history to the breed. He sought out a native Afghan General who was willing to search the historical archives. The General supplied the following notes:

"The Tazi Dog . . . According to Afghan history, the Tazi dog first became popular and well known in the time of Sultan Mahmud Ghaznawe (note: Mahmud is known as a particularly able and energetic ruler. He deposed his younger brother, Ismail, and ascended the throne in 988. He invaded India no less than twelve times before his death in 1030. In addition to his military campaigns, he was known as a patron of learning). Mahmud admired the Tazi and always carried a pack of them with his army, using them as couriers, guards and hunters. He considered them to be symbols of luck and victory. Following one of his Indian campaigns, he named a location in eastern Afghanistan (between Ghazni and Kandahar) for the breed and this area is still known today as Tazi."

The General added, "There are two types of Tazi found in Afghanistan; the long-haired (called the most pure and the most valued) and the short-haired. The long-haired Tazi lives in the north and northwestern parts of Afghanistan. The short-haired Tazi lives principally in the eastern, southern and western parts of the country."

As a name for these long-coated hounds, "tazi" only compounds confusion in attempting to unravel the origin of the breed. In all parts of Afghanistan "tazi" clearly differentiates the respected greyhound from the despised common dogs. Various reputable sources within Afghanistan have translated *"tazi"* into "fast," "sprinter" and even "white" on one occasion with reference to the hounds.

The various Afghan dialects are basically of Persian derivative but often stray far from classical Persian counterparts. In modern Iran, as well as in Persian literature dating back at least as far as Firdausi's Ghaznavid tenth century epic poem, *Shah Nama,* "tazi" has been accepted as meaning "from Arabia." Middle Eastern historians have been unable to suggest any faintly similar Persian words that can be tied to either "speed" or "white," but sources in Afghanistan continue to ignore any possible connection between their canine "tazi" and Arabia. When queried on this inconsistency, official Afghan correspondence reaffirmed the translation of "tazi" as "sprinter" despite the fact that Persian greyhounds of Iran, up to and certainly including the huge white heavily-feathered Kirghiz greyhounds of Turkestan, are all known as "tazi" (with reference to Arabian background) within their respective borders.

Dr. Van Beek, of the Smithsonian Institute, considers the word "tazi" to have come from the ancient seacoast city of Taiz, in Yemen, Arabia. Merchants of bygone eras travelled the entire Far and Middle East, plying their trades along oceans and through the tributary networks of rivers and lakes. One such passage was the Indus River in today's Pakistan with northern tributaries flowing directly into northeast Afghanistan. Men from the port of Taiz, and their wares, including the distinctive Arabian horses and hounds, became *taiz-i* (from Taiz) which easily shortened to "tazi." The word Tazi is also found in the *Tadjiks* (pronounced "taziks"), a widespread tribal population in north Afghanistan and south Russia, who were originally said to have emigrated from Arabia during the Moslem conquest era.

We would seem to have a definite source link between the Arabian Saluki and the Afghan Hound in the word "tazi," but care must be taken before running too far with this assumption. In studying the ethnic hodge-podge of north Afghanistan and its migratory tribes, Dr. Schurmann, University of California, with other ethnologists, stumbled onto tribes of obvious Mongol features who had completely abandoned their ancient Mongol mother tongue in favor of local Persian or Tadjik dialects. Such "lost" tribes could well have unwittingly picked up the word "tazi" believing it to mean "fast," and pinned it onto long-haired hounds that they had possessed for previous centuries. Following such lines of conjecture, it is as possible that early Oriental migratory groups with rugged, rough-coated dogs adopted not only dialects from the West but also incorporated qualities from native hounds as well, gradually forming new breeds well-suited to the prevailing terrain.

A mention of the hounds is found in *An Account of the Kingdom of Caubul, and Its Dependencies,* published in 1815 by the Hon. Mountstuart Elphinstone. This tome is heavy with descriptions of the countryside, the peoples, customs, and history of Afghanistan. The author writes: "The dogs of Afghanistan deserve to be mentioned. The Greyhounds are excellent; they are bred in great numbers, particularly among the pastoral tribes, who are much attached to hunting . . ." Elphinstone gave these hounds no name other than "greyhounds," but of more than passing interest is his mention of "tauzee" horses seen in the Balkh region, quite unlike the common rough Afghan horses and obviously related to more elegant Arab breeds. Regarding the *Dooraunee* peoples, tent-living nomads following flocks of sheep and goats, Elphinstone remarked that, "Almost every man has a horse and a great number of them keep greyhounds." At no time does he mention any other type of herding dog.

Modern fanciers prefer to think of the Afghan Hound, not as the property of crude, tent-living herdsmen, but as the prized sporting possession of ruling chieftains. Elphinstone does not disappoint them: "They were received by the chief's brother, who had just come in from hunting. He was a fair good-looking young man, with a rude but becoming dress, a bow and quiver at his back, a hare's scut in his turban and two fine greyhounds following him." Elphinstone frequently dwells on the great passion of the Afghans from all stations of life for hunting and hawking. It would have been most helpful had he donated an extra sentence or two to his greyhounds rather than to the table-settings. His lack of words leaves one with the suspicion that the dogs he saw might not have been greatly different from the greyhounds of England.

Before the 20th century, compilers of all-breed books were vaguely aware of the "eastern greyhounds" and made rudimentary, but often confused, attempts to catalogue them. Richardson, in *Dogs: Their Origin and Varieties,* published in 1857, writes of two distinct varieties of Persian Greyhounds. The latter one sounds suspiciously like a coated Afghan Hound. The first variety, with the usual tail and ear featherings, is described as being tan in color and a "most powerful creature frequently exceeding thirty inches in height at the shoulder, (but) the other variety is furnished all over the body with long silky hair of the length of five to eight inches, according to the purity of the blood, and the ears are feathered like those of a Spaniel. The latter dog seldom exceeds twenty-eight inches in height, and is far less powerful than the preceding. His color is usually black relieved with tan."

With decided opinions on the temperaments of the varieties, he continues: "The Persian greyhound differs from all the varieties of rough greyhounds in his hair, it being soft silky texture like a Spaniel. In dispositions the varieties present a striking difference—the black (bicolor) variety being very docile and gentle as a Spaniel, and the tan fierce and untouchable . . . the tan variety is a match for the caracul or Persian lynx and can kill that very formidable animal single-handedly. The black is fit only for hare coursing."

Sir Harry Lumsden, who was with the English Army in Kandahar during the Indian Mutiny of 1857, was not greatly impressed by these hounds as he wrote in his biography, "The dogs of Afghanistan used for sporting purposes are three sorts: the greyhound (Afghan Hound), Pomer and Khundi. The first are not formed for speed and would have little chance on a course with a second-rate English dog, but they are said to have some endurance and, when trained, are used to assist charughs (hawks) in catching deer, to mob wild hog, and to course hare, fox, etc. . ."

A Frenchman, Count Henry de Bylandt, wrote a monumental but seldom seen work, *Les Races de Chiens,* in 1894. By the third edition, published in 1904 in four languages, de Bylandt included a chapter jointly titled "Afghan Greyhound—Persian Greyhound" with illustrations and a standard of sorts, based primarily on the Persian type. A head portrait of an "Ideal Afghan Greyhound," sketched by Mr. L. Beckman, shows a hound with profuse ear coating, no topknot, and a white blaze from nostrils to eye level. A few of the interesting points from this description follow:

"Ideal Afghan Greyhound, from a sketch by Mr. L. Beckmann," from *Les Races de Chiens* by Count Henry de Bylandt, 1904.

General appearance—A rather big dog, but delicate and elegant.

Eyes—Mild, intelligent, dark brown, like a gazelle.

Legs—Fine, straight, clean and nervous.

Tail—Of medium length, carried hanging like a sabre, slightly feathered.

Coat—Smooth and very soft; on the ears and tail much longer, covered with wavy, silky hair; sometimes entirely smoothcoated.

Color—Self-colored black and the different shades of fawn, sometimes dirty white.

Height at shoulder—Between 23½ and 29½ inches.

Weight—60 and 70 pounds.

From *Les Races de Chiens* by Count Henry de Bylandt, 1904, by Arthur Wardle. Shazada and an unknown name, Rampur. This illustration first appeared in *The Field* in 1895, so identified.

During the Indian wars that opened Afghanistan to foreign influences, several Englishmen on duty with the attachments found themselves completely captivated by the unusual hounds seen hunting with the native horsemen or disappearing into the forbidden native encampments. A Major Mackenzie was able to procure several such hounds and took them to Switzerland where he set up residence. Two of his hounds were used to illustrate *British Dogs,* written by W. D. Drury in 1903, under the "Barukhzy and Allied Eastern Greyhounds" chapter. The plate shows "Muckmul and Mooroo II." One hound is lying down with the other standing alongside. They are just passable Afghan Hounds. There is some coat on body and legs, with a suggestion of feathering on the toes, but absolutely no top-knot at all. The tails are a proper length with a good ring on the end. It is unwise to gauge heights of dogs from pictures devoid of objects for comparison, but these appear to be leggy animals of Saluki proportions. Major Mackenzie's letters to author Drury inspired the breed chapter and just happened to include some of the best known and most abused quotations ever circulated within the breed. Major Mackenzie writes in part:

> "The sporting dog of Afghanistan, sometimes called the Cabul dog, has been named the Barukhzy Hound from being chiefly used by sporting sirdars of the royal Barukhzy family. It comes from Balkh, the northeastern province of Afghanistan, where it is believed that dogs of this variety entered the Ark with Noah. That it is an old variety (probably the oldest domesticated breed in existence) is proved by very ancient rock-carvings within the caves of Balkh of dogs exactly like the Barukhzy Hound of today. On some of these carvings, of colossal size, are inscriptions of much later date that were written by invaders under Alexander the Great."

The breed is strongly indebted to Major Mackenzie for much of the information that later writers repeated and embellished, occasionally with credit to Mackenzie, but more often as "new finds." Mackenzie's now famous mention of "rock-carvings" at Balkh has a rather substantial ring to it, but the subsequent and fantastic development of this story, with dates receding further into the past with each telling, leads one to question even the original statement in light of the fact that absolutely no trace of these carvings has been scientifically authenticated.

In search of evidence of early Afghan Hounds in the country of their development, extensive correspondence has been exchanged between the authors and the Afghan Government, including the Minister of Culture and various Museum Directors, as well as with the French Embassy in Afghanistan and a wide array of authorities

34

Le Roi Chasseur: copy of the Kakrak original.
J. Hackin photo, courtesy D.A.F.A.

from several countries who have explored the Middle and Near East. Without exception they have expressed disbelief in Mackenzie's "rock-carvings," stating that the Balkh area is without caves of any sort.

Most archaeological work in Afghanistan has been directed by the French *Delegation Archaeologique Française en Afghanistan* (D.A.F.A.). All finds, no matter how small, have been completely photographed, cataloged, and described in multiple D.A.F.A. volumes. Senior living members of the D.A.F.A. maintain that the only possible representation of a "levrier Afghan" (Afghan greyhound) that has ever been reported in Afghanistan was found and photographed in 1928 by Monsignor J. Hackin of the D.A.F.A., and appeared in Tome III on an illustration entitled "Le Roi Chasseur" or "The King's Hunter." Mrs. W. S. Macdonald (secretary of the AHCA) has graciously translated the accompanying text from the French as follows:

"A Princely Personage, shown full face (long description of costume follows). Beneath the throne appears, turned in profile to the left,

35

the mouth open and his outstretched muzzle slightly lifted, a dog rendered in grey blue, in whom we do not hesitate to recognize as an authentic Afghan Hound. Two arrows are affixed between the dog and the column that supports to the right the broken pediment . . ." (Note: The area at the right that looks suspiciously like a dog's hind leg, is merely flaked off plaster.)

This painting with its peculiar little dog is dated between 450 and 700 A.D. and located in Kakrak, well to the south of Balkh and northeast of Kabul. Mackenzie's mention of superimposed Hellenistic inscriptions on his cave-renderings completely negates any connection between them and the younger Kakrak paintings, should one be able to overlook the other apparent discrepancies.

Mackenzie also makes the earliest known reference to these dogs as having been on the Ark with Noah. There seems little doubt that this story is told in good faith by the Afghan peoples. With the acceptance of the Islamic beliefs came the teaching of the Koran. Many of the writings of the Koran are based on the more ancient Jewish Pentateuch or Books of Moses. The story of the Flood is one of these. There are modern tribes in Afghanistan which firmly claim to be direct descendants of Noah and his sons. Perhaps, in regard to the hound, it would be wisest to interpret the story to mean that the Afghan Hound, in some form or other, has been indigenous to that country for as long as can be remembered. This belief is also useful in furnishing religious grounds for lifting the hound well above the level of the common dog.

Major Mackenzie also relates the famous leopard-killer story of how Koosh singlehandedly killed a nearly full-grown leopard attempting to carry away the bitch Mooroo II. He used this story to illustrate his contention that while these hounds may appear timid, they are actually very courageous. He ascribes their seeming timidity to the fact that the bitches are kept in seclusion by the women of the tribes except when required to hunt. He does not explain how this would affect the temperament of the males. His description of the dogs, which pre-dates any Standard, is informative:

"They usually hunt in couples, bitch and dog. The bitch attacks the hinder parts; while the quarry is thus distracted, the dog, which has great power of jaw and neck, seizes and tears the throat. Their scent, speed and endurance are remarkable; they track or run to sight equally well. Their long toes, being carefully protected with tufts of hair, are serviceable on both sand and rock. Their height varies from 24 to 30 inches; their weight from 45 to 70 lbs. Usually they are of a fawn or bluish-mouse color, but always of a darker shade on the back, which is smooth and velvety."

36

A Meenah of Jajurh with Afghan Hound (1813) from "Letters Written in a Mahratta Camp during the Year 1809" by Thomas D. Broughton.
Courtesy Gerald Massey

Major Mackenzie's own hounds would seem to be the best representatives of the breed in his day, principally because there are so few pictures for comparison. In his excellent *Afghan Handbook*, however, Clifford Hubbard managed to obtain and include a rare plate called, "A Meenah of Jajurh with His Afghan Hound," dated 1813, and taken from Broughton's "Letters Written in a Mahratta Camp during the Year 1809." This small dark hound, about 24 inches at the withers according to Hubbard's guess, with lighter-colored underparts, is really quite heavily coated, with good top-knot and long coat except for a tapering at the pasterns, over very large furred feet. The existence of such a fine picture from the early 1800s relieves us of the necessity of accepting Major Mackenzie's rather scraggly, smooth-skulled hounds as being the best specimens known to date. Visitors to Afghanistan constantly repeat that the natives will rarely part with really good stock, and it is quite possible that Major Mackenzie knew of far handsomer hounds than he was able to take out of the country.

The now rare *Hutchinson's Dog Encyclopedia* furnished another famous tale of dogs said to be Afghan Hounds which were located with the Army at the Indian Frontier. These dogs were grotesquely described as being, "large extraordinary-looking creatures . . . in size and shape they somewhat resemble a large Greyhound, but such slight resemblance is dispelled by the tufts with which they are all adorned; some having tufted ears, others tufted feet and others again possessing tufted tails." The author of the tale, writing under the

37

name of "Mali" calls them "Baluchi Hounds" and marveled at the sight of these dogs patrolling the fort in pairs, seemingly without human direction: "Between a deep ditch and wall of the fort is a narrow path. Throughout the night, this path is patrolled by successive couples of dogs. Immediately one couple has completed the circuit of the walls and arrived back at the main gate, another couple starts out. When it is remembered that these extraordinary hounds have never had any training whatsoever, that their duties are absolutely self-imposed—for no human being has the slightest control over them—the perfection of their organization and the smoothness with which they carry out their tasks makes man gasp."

Modern history of the breed took on new significance during the time a Major Amps from England was stationed in the Kabul area shortly after the Afghan War of 1919. He and his wife, Mary, developed a lasting interest in the breed and became influential in the future of these hounds with their "Ghazni" Kennels, established in the hill country of Afghanistan at an elevation of 6,000 feet. Their Sirdar and Khan of Ghazni left lasting lineage effects to be found in the pedigrees of most American hounds. Much of our current knowledge about the hounds has been left by Mrs. Amps, a prolific writer on behalf of her beloved breed. Her many letters to editors of newspapers, magazines and books furnish the basis of the Afghan Hound chapters in most of the English books on dogs in the 20th century. When occasionally challenged by other importers on her concept of the "correct type" of hound, she spared no words in spearing her opponents to the wall with facts and quotes, establishing herself very shortly as *the* authority on the breed. It is possible that her words went a bit further than her actual knowledge, but her sincerity and genuine admiration for the breed cannot be questioned.

Mrs. Amps wrote of the great difficulties in acquiring these hounds after becoming intrigued by their unusual appearance as they accompanied native hunting groups. She found it absolutely necessary to enlist the aid of influential Afghan officials before gaining access to the hostile Afghan villages, and even then the natives were reluctant to admit to having such hounds. It was not unusual to have the dogs, recently purchased from the natives, stealthily re-stolen by their original owners who relished having the price of a good hound despite the risk involved in retrieving it from the 10-foot high walled compound. Good bitches, said Mrs. Amps, were the most difficult to come by.

She took great relish in blasting some of the myths surrounding the breed. She saw the legend of bitches being used to guard the harems as nonsense: "The hounds of Afghanistan were all hard-working hunters, regardless of sex." She also concluded that the hounds were fed very rarely by their native owners, for at sundown each new acquisition would become resistive and try to get out of the compound gates, presumably in search of food. Once used to regular feedings inside the fort, however, they settled down quietly after the evening meal. The even temper of the dogs surprised and certainly pleased the Ampses, who often had 20 to 30 hounds in the same enclosure with very little fighting or resentment of any new-comers by the group. A high appreciation of the breed's temperament pervades all of Mrs. Amps's writings, as she repeatedly cautions against turning these sensitive and affectionate hounds into kennel dwellers.

In A. Croxton Smith's *Hounds and Dogs* (1932), Mrs. Amps gives a fascinating detailed description of Afghan Hounds trained to work with hawks:

"One of the oldest forms of hunting, which is often portrayed in old Persian and Moghul manuscripts, is still being carried on in the remoter parts of Afghanistan. The quarry, a small very swift deer called Ahu Dashti, is hunted by Afghan Hound with the aid of hawks. . . . The young birds and Afghan puppies are kept together, the young hounds being fed on the flesh of deer whenever possible. The food of the young hawks is placed each day between the horns of a stuffed deer; later a string is attached to the head and it is drawn across the floor, the young bird flapping after it. As soon as they are able to fly, they are released and called to this lure. As the training progresses, they are flown at a young kid, and when they seize it, the animal is killed and they are fed on the flesh. When fully-grown the hounds are loosed after a fawn and the hawks flown at it. The training completed, hawks and hounds are taken to the hills. Immediately when the deer is spotted, the birds are unhooded and released, and they descend above the head of the unfortunate beast and, by flapping about it, impede its progress sufficiently to enable the hounds to overtake it and pull it down. The Ahu Dashti or chinkara, as it is known in Indian, is so swift that it is said that, 'The day a chinkara is born, a man may catch it; the second day a swift hound; but the third, no one but Allah.' "

Major Amps spread proof of these hounds' remarkable hunting abilities when he took four of them along with him to visit the Maharajah of Patiala in India. Greyhound coursing events were in progress and the Maharajah asked that the Afghan Hounds be allowed to participate. Major Amps agreed, although well aware that the flat grassy parade grounds where the coursing meet was held was a far cry from the rough stony country his hounds were accustomed to. He was dubious about their performance in comparison to the Greyhounds, but his shaggy mountain hounds acquitted themselves surprisingly well. While somewhat slower on the straightaway, they proved extraordinarily quick on the turns, and illustrated unbridled enthusiasm for the sport that astonished some of the jaded spectators. Major Amps had no doubt that if the test had taken place over rougher country, his hounds being built for the maximum staying power under the most arduous of hunting conditions, the Afghans would have had the distinct advantage over the Greyhounds. The Maharajah was enough impressed to purchase a number of the mountain hounds from Major Amps for his royal kennel.

A provocative note from Major Amps brought out his opinion that the tribesmen living in the plains near India often crossed the Afghan Hound with the Saluki to reduce the coat so that the dogs could better withstand the intense heat of the flat summer plains. This brings up the question as to whether the lesser-coated hounds found in Afghanistan, especially those that most strongly resembled Salukis, were, in fact, a fair percentage of Saluki crossed with coated Afghan Hound stock. The truth of this hypothesis is not and probably will not be known, but several such lesser coated dogs have played important parts in modern Afghan Hound pedigrees.

During the 1920s and 1930s, a fair number of these hounds slipped through the borders of Afghanistan. Evidence from descriptive notes and from the few available pictures indicate that the exports were a diverse crew with respect to size, leg-to-body ratio, coat pattern, texture, quantity and color, and attitude and temperament. The tendency was for various exporters to claim that their own hounds were, according to native standards, the only correct type.

The bulk of early Afghan Hounds that arrived on American shores came by way of a generation or two in Great Britain, or in a few cases, from India. But in 1934 "Saki of Paghman" and "Tazi of Beg Tute" were exported to America directly from Afghanistan with foreign correspondent Laurance Peters of Seattle, Washington. They were registered with the American Kennel Club in the days when such direct imports from the East were acceptable. This is no longer true; any hounds coming directly from Afghanistan to America today function only as fascinating curiosities, ineligible for registration. Fearing that it is being looted of one of its national treasures, Afghanistan now prohibits the exportation of these hounds except under very special circumstances.

In 1950, Walter Fairservis, Jr. led an American archaeological group into Baluchistan and Afghanistan. While in Kabul he fell heir to an Afghan puppy whose parents had been given to the

40

Persian Ambassador's wife by the King of Afghanistan. The puppy, named "Besyar Hob" (meaning "very good" in Persian), was brought by the Fairservis family to the United States and, in 1952, was exhibited unregistered at the Afghan Hound Club of America Specialty Show. In a letter to the then AHCA President, Charlotte Coffey, Mrs. Fairservis told what she knew of these precious hounds:

"Afghan Hounds are privileged (unlike the despised dogs) and sleep in a kennel. Their masters provide them with crude coats of felt or goat skin to protect their short-haired backs in the cold mountain winters. They are led on light chains or leather thongs. Though they have been prized and cared for above other dogs for untold generations, we never saw any signs of warm friendship between the dogs and their masters.

"They are not bred for any particular traits, lest it be speed and general vigor.

"The diet of Afghan Hounds over there is largely 'nan,' an unleavened whole wheat bread, and meat. Their appetites are not as unlimited as the carrion eating pie-dogs, but they could not possibly be called fussy eaters. There is little clean food left for dogs in the East; consequently, only those with the strongest constitutions can survive."

Besyar Hob was coated in the chaps-and-bolero pattern of feathering rather than in long pants. Mrs. Fairservis wrote that they never saw any really long-coated hounds but had heard of a few. They were gratified to find that the sullen temperament of the Eastern hounds they knew was not innate, as their own puppy grew up gay, gentle, and highly intelligent, sharing a home with loving owners.

An interesting note on native hounds appeared in the Canadian *Our Dogs* in 1947 wherein Juliette de Bairacli Levy, noted hound fancier and author of *The Herbal Book for the Dog*, told of a conversation with a Mr. R. Dalby, recently returned from Afghanistan:

"The best time (according to Mr. Dalby) to see Afghan Hounds in any numbers in their native land is at the feast of the goats. At this time, vast numbers of goats are brought down from the mountains to the plains, and most of the herding is done by Afghan Hounds. The hounds are decorated for the occasion, with necklaces of beads, especially the native blue stone lapis lazuli which is held to bring good fortune—or with garlands of flowers."

Mr. Dalby also states that many of the Afghan Hounds in the interior had cropped ears as a precaution against dog-fights. As regards the hound's diet, Mr. Dalby mentioned that when meat was in short supply, the hunting hounds were fed large quantities of figs and dates.

Despite stringent regulations against the exportation of hounds from Afghanistan, specimens did continue to cross the border and find their way west in one manner or another. Most of these hounds were said to have come from the "King's Kennel" for the kings of Afghanistan for many generations kept large packs of these hounds for sportive hunts. At times, these hounds were given as gifts to foreigners in residence, such as ambassadors who had found royal favor. Most of these hounds did not leave the country but were handed from consul to consul or from friend to friend in the turnover of officials coming to and going from the country.

A royal pair of bitches was brought to California from Afghanistan in 1960 by Melvin Gade who obtained them from a resident Army officer. The mother and daughter were of a black-and-tan color pattern, but with bright silver-colored feet and trim. Mr. Gade managed to get his beloved pair of hounds out of the country by means of official intervention. Hoping to circumvent some of the shipping expense of heavy wooden or metal dog crates, he had large leather crates made especially for the hounds. The plan backfired when guards decided to make export charges on the huge crate according to the square inch rather than to the usual pound weight. On the ocean liner the hounds, unaccustomed to dog food, were kept alive with galley scraps and hamburgers, buns and all. On their arrival in California, the hounds were thin and unapproachable by strangers. They were inclined to scream in panic when left alone in the family car but were very affectionate with their owners. These two bitches, moreover, conformed to our visions of the beautiful Afghan Hound, having lovely full-length coats which hang in rich silken waves. They were both small, about 24 inches in height, and weighed barely 40 pounds apiece, but had elegant carriage, long refined muzzles, and dark, exotic, almond-shaped eyes under profuse silken topknots. Within six months, however, whether due to a drastic change of climate, diet, or to the onset of the troublesome female seasons, both bitches had lost much of their luxuriant coats. The Gades were most disappointed at not being able to register their lovely pets with the AKC.

We suspect that the only point we have made in this chapter is that what is actually known about these intriguing hounds of Afghanistan is quite limited, both here and in the Middle East. As one Afghan exchange student who owned a pair of these hounds in Afghanistan commented when attending a regional Afghan Hound club meeting, "There is very little I can tell you, for not only have you people bothered to find out more about these hounds than we would ever do, but you see a good many more of them right within your own club group than I could hope to show you in Afghanistan."

3

Early Afghan Hounds in England

PRIOR to 1907 there were no important Afghan Hounds in England. A few "hounds from Afghanistan" had been entered in the Foreign Dog Class, but none caught the fancy of either the judges or the public. In truth, these hounds were far below the modern sub-standard of a bad Afghan Hound. They ranged from "Shahzada" labeled a Barukhzy Hound, through "Khelat," whose resemblance to an Old English Sheepdog caused sheepdog fanciers to seriously consider him for stud, to "Afghan Bob" who could have easily passed for a third rate Irish Setter, right to his tail.

The Foreign Dog Class perked up smartly in 1907 with the sudden appearance of Mrs. M. C. Barff's Zardin, who immediately astonished the English dog world with his arresting and haughty demeanor, combined with an impressive size and a unique profusion and pattern of coat. Mr. A. Croxton Smith, noted canine authority of the times, wrote of Zardin in *Sporting Dogs*, ". . . All of us who looked on him realized that we were in the presence of a very fine animal, whether he embodied the correct type or not." Other experts pronounced him the "finest Oriental Greyhound ever seen in England." Zardin was never defeated in the Foreign Dog Class, and was later presented to Queen Alexandra.

Zardin, originally found in Seistan, Persia just west of Afghanistan, was exhibited in India while enroute to England, where for nationalist reasons he became an Afghan Hound. In October of 1906, an *Indian Kennel Gazette* article described him in minute detail (*Kennel Review* 8/48): "Zardin is a light-coloured hound, almost white, with a black muzzle. He has a very long, punishing jaw of peculiar power and level mouth; his head resembles that of a Deerhound, but with skull oval and prominent occiput, surmounted by a top-knot; ears fairly large, well feathered, and hanging to the side of the head rather than carried to front. He has a keen, dark eye, and little or no stop. A long, strong, clean neck, fairly well arched, running in a nice curve to shoulder, which is long and sloping and well laid back; his back is strong, loin powerful and slightly arched. He, as well as all this class of hound, falls away towards the stern, which is set on low, almost destitute of hair, and usually carried low. He is well ribbed, tucked up under loin; forelegs straight and strong and covered with hair; great length between elbow (which is straight) and ankle. The forefeet are long, fairly broad and covered with long hair. Not too narrow in brisket, which is deep, with good girth of chest. Hind quarters very powerful, furnished with plenty of muscle; great length between hip and hock, which is low and strong, a fair bend of stifle, hind feet not so long as forefeet, but fairly wide and well protected with hair. The hind quarters, flanks, ribs and forequarters are well clothed with protective hair, thick and fine in texture, showing some undercoat. The coat on the back is shorter."

This observing note quoted Zardin's height as being "about 28 inches, or nearly so." A 1907 English newspaper account of him stated that Mrs. Barff thought him to be about five years old, and that he stood at least 26 inches at the shoulder. Unfortunately weight figures are not given.

We have one small quarrel with the Indian article which says that Zardin's tail (stern) was "usually carried low." His photograph in *Turner's Kennel Encyclopedia,* and the portrait done by Arthur Wardle on his arrival in England show a rather short, loosely curled tail, carried well above the back level, and feathered on the under side. To illustrate Zardin we have selected both the photograph and a copy of the portrait by Arthur Wardle. The latter shows a hound of the true working sort with torn coat under chest and lower legs, but jagged fur thick enough to promise the good length of coat that materialized after a year of good British care. Beneath the torn coat Wardle faithfully portrayed the hound's strong leg bones, huge feet and powerful frame, which cannot be seen in later photographs due to his profuse coat.

The term "Afghan Hound" gained sudden meaning with Zardin, and when talk of forming a breed standard arose, he automatically became the model. In 1912 such a standard was written, but at that time standards were private ventures as the British Kennel Club did not take on the responsibility of approving and filing breed standards until 1948. During the First World War, all copies of the

Zardin—Persian Greyhound—5 years old, found in Quetta, India before his importation to England. Photo from *Turner's Kennel Encyclopedia*.

Zardin 1907

From a photograph of the original painting by A. Wardle.

Miss Jean Manson and Eng. Ch. Ranee, cream, and Kanee, fawn with a black mask, both bitches, taken at Crufts in 1924 (daughters of Rajah and Begum). Courtesy, Charlotte Coffey.

Maj. and Mrs. Bell-Murray with foundation stock. L. to r.: Ooty (dog), pale fawn with a black mask; Begum (bitch), cream; Pushum; Baluch (dog); Kanee; Straker; and Eng. Ch. Ranee.

1912 standard simply vanished. For that reason we included the lengthy Indian description of Zardin as clues to the lost Standard's wording. Two tag ends of the 1912 standard turned up in *The New Book of the Dog,* by E. C. Ash, in the form of parenthetical additions to a later standard which is also obsolete: "1912 standard—colour: silver fawn and golden. Height: 24 to 30 inches—weight 50 to 60 lbs." Zardin's name remains basic in the breed, but unfortunately it has never been located on any old pedigrees. He touches the breed as a shadowy and lost ideal and as a model for a vanished standard.

The difficult years of the First World War brought a necessary pause in breed activity. In 1921 when Miss Jean Manson arrived in England, together with Maj. Bell-Murray and a select group of 12 Afghan Hounds from the border of Baluchistan and Afghanistan, the next breed chapter opens.

Miss Manson glimpsed her first Afghan Hound when out riding near Quetta (Baluchistan) and was enchanted by the sight of the distant graceful hound loping alongside her mounted master. Miss Manson caught up with the native and after firm dickering managed to purchase the hound. She named her Begum, meaning "queen," because of the bitch's courtly house manners. According to Jean Manson, Begum was "white in color, with large brown eyes and a perfect body and carriage." The hound and woman were inseparable. Once when riding through a native bazaar, Begum caught scent of her original owner of more than two years past. She dashed from Miss Manson's side, through the thick crowd of faces to greet him with frantic whines of joy. Jean Manson was thoroughly impressed with her dog's beauty, manners and uncanny intelligence.

For four long years Miss Manson searched for a suitable mate for Begum, finally locating a handsome male she christened "Rajah." This male came with a hunter's reputation and was therefore coveted by the natives. He was repeatedly stolen, once returning after an absence of two months, thoroughly disguised in red paint, dragging broken ropes behind him. With the aid of Maj. Bell-Murray, Miss Manson was able to send Rajah, Begum, their offspring, and a few additionally procured hounds to Cove Kennels in Scotland. Once in Britain these 12 imports became known as the "Bell-Murray hounds."

Dissimilarities between the "Bell-Murray hounds" and the earlier Zardin must be mentioned. The new imports for the most part were racy in build, with some males reaching a full 32″ at the shoulder. Their coats, so impressive to Miss Manson, who actually had seen very few specimens of the breed, were scarcely more than exaggerations of a Persian Greyhound's coat. Typical hounds from Begum and Rajah were frilly on shoulder, thighs and sometimes on ribs, with feather between toes and on ears. Top-knots were vestigial. These Bell-Murray hounds, however, play supporting roles in subsequent breed chapters.

In 1925 various owners of these hounds formed the Afghan Hound Club under a standard reading remarkably like the Indian description of Zardin, found in *Pedigree Dogs,* edited by C. C. Sanderson in 1927 with a breed chapter by Evelyn Denyer, then Hon. Sec. of the Afghan Hound Club. The "Denyer standard" was quite short-lived in England, but happened to be around long enough to serve as a basis for the early American standard that held until 1948.

Standard (obsolete) of the Afghan Hound Club of Britain (inactive)

Head—Skull oval with prominent occiput. Jaw long and punishing, mouth level, ears long, eyes dark, little or no stop.

Neck—Long, strong, arched and running in a curve to shoulder.

Shoulder—Long and sloping—well laid-back.

Back—Strong, loin powerful and slightly arched, falling away towards stern.

Forelegs—Straight and strong—great length between elbow (which is straight) and ankle.

Forefeet—Very large, both in length and breadth, toes well arched and the feet covered with long thick hair, fine in texture.

Brisket—Deep and not too narrow.

Hindquarters—Powerful, well muscled, great length between hip and hock, which is low and strong. Fair bend in stifle.

Body—Well ribbed and tucked up under loins.

Coat—Hindquarters, flanks, ribs and forequarters well covered with long thick hair, very fine in texture. Ears and all four feet well feathered. Head surmounted with top-knot of long silky hair.

General appearance—Strong and active looking, a combination of speed and power with a graceful outline.

Height (to shoulder)—Dogs about 28 inches; bitches 25–26 inches.

High in Kabul, Afghanistan, a counterpoint to the Bell-Murray theme was shaping as Maj. and Mrs. Amps, stationed in the mountain country, discovered hounds of a rather different sort. Late in 1925 Mary Amps brought a small group of her "Ghazni hounds" to England, immediately proclaiming them to be the first "true Afghan Hounds since Zardin." She used the press effectively in side-by-side layouts emphasizing the general resemblance in coat and outline between Zardin and her favorite, Sirdar of Ghazni. Pictures did not tell the whole story, however, as Sirdar was a mere 24 inches at the

Eng. Ch. Sirdar of Ghazni, red with a black mask, earned his title in 1927 and was owned by Mr. and Mrs. Amps. This drawing was made from photographs.

shoulder. Mrs. Amps insisted that he might have grown taller had his legs not been broken in puppyhood and badly set, but this hardly seems reasonable as Sirdar was famed for his grand gait, showing no trace of foreshortened or uneven legs. The great Sirdar was certainly not a large hound, but he was a mighty one, carrying more hair than had been dreamed of since Zardin. His esteemed kennel mate, the powerful, leopard-killing Khan of Ghazni, was of an even sturdier build and similarly coated.

A head-on clash between Mary Amps and Maj. Bell-Murray was inevitable, and it appeared publicly in the *Letters to the Editor* pages of the canine journals. Both called each other's dogs "imposters." Maj. Bell-Murray remarked that he had not been enough impressed by the "Ghazni hounds" to bother buying one when he saw them in Peshawar. He claimed that his hounds had lost much of their coating in the damp British climate. Mrs. Amps rejoined that none of her hounds had been for sale, and furthermore, that they were growing better coats in England than they had before. A nasty battle opened with Maj. Bell-Murray wielding the weapon of size against Mrs. Amps's shield of coat. Mrs. Amps admitted that Sirdar was "a bit on the small side" but otherwise excellent, and that

49

she had seen but one quality Afghan hound in Afghanistan that measured over 28 inches.

Mrs. Amps won the early skirmishes, convincing the "authorities" that she had the superior hounds and better background and knowledge of both the breed and the country of Afghanistan. Judge A. Croxton Smith in *Sporting Dogs* wrote with a noticeable trace of awe: ". . . Mrs. Amps . . . brought over the counterpart (of Zardin) except for size in Sirdar of Ghazni, a dog that came as a revelation. In structure and movement and all the attributes that we expect from a really good dog he excelled. . . . It is no wonder that this dog carried everything before him and that he made a great impression on the breed."

In 1962 an English judge, Ursula Rees, revitalized faded interest in clear definition of "Bell-Murray" and "Ghazni" types in a published critique. She intimated that while she had no special preference for either of the two original types and enjoyed a well-balanced blend of the two, what disturbed her was seeing entirely too many hounds which were not harmonious and displayed distinct clashes of type. She averred, furthermore, that due to inherent differences in structure, the two types called for very different handling in the ring. This startling opinion brought frantic agitation from older fanciers, as novices, quite reasonably, wanted to know just what Judge Rees was talking about.

Studies of old photographs and clippings abetted by consultation with various senior English and Continental breeders have inspired the composite illustrations of the so-called "desert" and "mountain" types of pioneer Afghan Hounds. Major structural differences between the two types lie in variation in bone length, substance and in the outline of the dog's carriage. The desert hounds, like Ranee, were of the long fine-bone type, distinctly racy and Saluki-like. Their heads were very long, practically without stop, with sharp, slanted eyes. In outline, these racy dogs stood over a lot of ground. Despite well laid-back shoulders, forequarters were set to the front of the dog rather than well beneath him. This facilitated an effortless, prancing action, seen so frequently in the Saluki and often accompanied by rather upright pasterns and tight feet. Rear legs, also very long, placed well behind the hound. Loins were long and very mobile. At their best, these desert hounds were magnificently noble, elegant and graceful, and extremely fast.

As is the case with slim-line breeds, the lesser specimens fell heir to one or more faults in a predictable pattern. Overfine heads turned weak and "snipey-jawed." Bodies too often were extremely narrow, completely lacking in adequate forechest, with such poorly developed front ribs that elbows practically came together, forcing the

50

Above: "Desert" type; below: "Mountain" type, composite drawings by Lois Gossner, based on photographs.

feet to turn outward for sufficient base of balance. Such skimpy bodies were accompanied by thin loins and, not infrequently, by weak hindquarters to match. These dogs were far more attractive when viewed in profile than from the front or the rear. One breeder recalls that these fine-boned hounds, unfortunately, had a bad tendency to rickets.

The "mountain hounds," as exemplified by Sirdar and Khan of Ghazni, were sturdily built, well-boned hounds, packing a fair

51

amount of weight to the inch, and showing considerably less of the greyhound-look of being poised for flight. Their heavier bone and foreign type was evident from topknot to stern. Heads were long, but broader and deeper of skull than the Bell-Murray hounds with more noticeable stop and eyes set rather level. Their firm, broad forebreasts carried fuller briskets and heavy ribbing that curved upward to meet short tight loins and wide hindquarters. In body silhouette, the mountain hound stood with his legs well beneath his body, poised to spring in any direction. Front legs, set well under the shoulders, accompanied sloping pasterns and large feet. Rear legs, bent at stifle, placed more under the body than behind it. Such leg positioning gave a look of special compactness to the frame. At their best, these sturdy little mountain hounds carried unusually erect necks and tails and radiated power and remarkable agility. The heavier construction of these hounds, however, produced the more common weaknesses of the mountain type. When built to excess, headpieces turned gross, and stops became more pronounced. Necks tended to be short and thick. Bodies were apt to barrel and interfere with elbow action, sometimes to the point where the feet were forced to toe-in.

In coating, the scantily-clad Bell-Murrays boasted of lovely silken textures. The heavier-clad mountain hounds, with good topknots and fair to good leg and side coats, tended to a thick stand-off type of cotton texture. These mountain hounds had excellent definition of saddles, but were inclined to frilly tails.

Aside from structural differences, from the mountain hounds, the desert hounds were more skittish, headstrong and aloof, quite inclined to resent advances from·strangers. The mountain hounds, with their milder expression, were more tolerant of human beings, with Sirdar showing definite signs of amiability on short acquaintance. In subsequent imports, a possible link between the heavy-coated mountain type and more docile tempers is seen, as noted by Mrs. Drinkwater who deeply valued the sweet disposition of her very heavily coated import, Lakki Marwat, in days when dangerously temperamental Afghans were no rarity.

Now that we have carefully placed "Bell-Murray" and "Ghazni" Afghans into their respective boxes, we shall open the lids and let them right out again. It is neither true nor fair to infer that all the Bell-Murray imports, or that all the Ghazni hounds, fitted snugly into separate colonies. Maj. Bell-Murray and Mrs. Amps preferred to perpetuate a concept of two distinct Afghan Hound types, with one supposedly "right" and the other "wrong." In a public letter to

Begum, bitch.

Pushum, bitch: foundation brindle for Afghans in America.

Major Bell-Murray, Mrs. Amps hinted that her Khan could supply precisely what his Afghans lacked. Khan, from the Oxus area of Afghanistan, where a sturdy type was admired, was considered, even by Mrs. Amps, to be on the heavy side compared to Sirdar's finer quality.

Within the Bell-Murray group, at least two hounds were several steps towards the stockier mountain-type by virtue of broader chest, heavier bones and thicker coat. Jean Manson's white bitch, Begum, was one of these. Found in Quetta, India, it is provocative to note that Zardin sired one litter in that very region before being shipped to England. This leaves open the possibility that Begum may, actually, have been a descendant of his. Jean Manson's awareness of Begum's "perfect body and carriage" suggests the direction she basically admired. Also, the thickly-built and rather dowdy brindle bitch Pushum proved of special value. Only when Pushum is in the background of the Bell-Murrays do even fair coats appear, and some semblance of substance in the males. Additionally, she is the one clear route of brindle-genes up to modern times. When bred to Ooty (Zorawar ex Dil), Pushum produced three offspring of note. Her son, Ch. Buckmal, a 32 inch, remarkably intelligent, faintly brindled and well-coated hound, was England's first male champion Afghan. Pushum's dark brindle daughter, Daghai, was the dam of Ch. Taj Mahip of Kaf, the grandsire of the famous English and American Ch. Badshah of Ainsdart. Her other daughter, Oolu, produced Ch. Shadi. As a matter of record, these three English champions coming down from Pushum, plus the very first English bitch champion, Ranee

Head study of Ranee (Rajah ex Begum), first champion bitch in England, 1927.

(Rajah ex Begum) make up the entire roster of undiluted Bell-Murray champions. They also constitute four out of five of the first English champion Afghans, the fifth being Ch. Sirdar of Ghazni.

On the other side of the fence, we see that while Sirdar and Khan were each of one type, the Ghazni *bitches* were of a mixed lot. Roshni of Ghazni (Jack ex Jane) was a fawn of statuesque proportions, being lengthy in neck, tail and legs, very deep in chest and practically devoid of coat. Mrs. Amps explained these features by claiming that the mountain bitches characteristically carried far less coat than did the males. This claim is open to speculation, as we recall that the heaviest coated of the Bell-Murrays was a bitch and see what happened when light-coated Ghazni bitches were bred to Sirdar. From such a breeding Roshni of Ghazni produced the well-known Ch. Asri-Havid of Ghazni. "Rif," as he was known to his owner, Phyllis Robson, was notable as England's first Best-in-Show Afghan and first black-and-tan champion in the breed. His photo, seen in Hubbard's *Afghan Hound Handbook,* proves him to have had an extremely long, refined head, keen Oriental eye, and a startling lack of coat on his lower legs and feet. His overall appearance seemed to reflect a blend of types rather than direct inheritance of the Sirdar strain.

Ghazni, as an uncluttered strain, came to a close just a few short years after the demise of pure Bell-Murrays. Sirdar achieved long-lasting fame and his title in 1927. Taking the sceptre from him in 1929 was the previously mentioned Ch. Asri-Havid of Ghazni, then another son, Ch. Ashna of Ghazni, whose dam was Shireen of Ghazni, and in 1931, a very lovely, coated daughter came to the fore,

54

Ch. Marika of Baberbagh whose dam was Sada of Ghazni, a daughter of Khan of Ghazni. The dynasty concluded with Ch. Westmill Ben Havid (Ch. Asri-Havid of Ghazni ex Elsa of Ghazni) in 1934. These names are important in the background of later English and American breedings.

Just before the close of the 1920s, a few fanciers with elegant Bell-Murray bitches cast envious glances at the Sirdar coat, character and accumulating fame, and chanced a quicker route to a more Zardin-like Afghan by breeding their bitches directly to Sirdar. Within a few short years most of the English championships fell to progeny from blendings of Sirdar, or of one of his sons, to a Bell-Murray type bitch. Judge Rees certainly would have had reason to be critical of the lack of harmony of many of the structurally mixed-up results, and of the wild extremes created by this breeding combination. Only the name "from Afghanistan" held the breed together; judges could rarely agree on a standard of quality. As the supremacy of the pioneer strains was ended, some breeders chose to establish new types from the various local stocks. Others, unsatisfied with the available possibilities, imported fresh blood.

Mrs. E. E. Drinkwater's early Afghans in England: l. to r., Eng. Ch. Sirfreda (bitch), golden; Aswakarna of Geufron (dog); Eng. Ch. Kisagotami of Geufron (bitch), cream; Eng. Ch. Agha Lala of Geufron (dog), red with black points; Eng. Ch. Mahaprajapati of Geufron (bitch), fawn with black points; and Karnikara of Geufron (bitch).

Mrs. Olive Couper's Ardmore Anthony, a small white hound from India, was mated to her Ch. Garrymhor Souriya (Ch. Ashna of Ghazni ex Ch. Alfreda) to produce Garrymhor hounds frequently appearing on later English and American pedigrees. Souriya's dam, Ch. Alfreda, classifies as an import of sorts, being out of the eastern-born Shahzada and Afroz.

At Mrs. Drinkwater's Geufron kennels, Ch. Alfreda's daughter, Ch. Sirfreda, combined well with Lakki Marwat, an extremely heavily-coated, dark-eyed, ginger colored hound of the compact type, imported from the Orient by Col. Marriott. When combined with Geufron bitches of Bell-Murray and Ghazni backgrounds, Lakki Marwat produced some of the most fantastically coated hounds of the era in Ch. Kisagotami of Geufron and the American Ch. Lakshmi of Geufron-Cawtaba, both bitches.

Such breeders, well aware of the questionable backgrounds and breeding potentiality of these hounds, tended to use them sparingly for immediate flashes of stock improvement, with long-range breeding plans for recovering any lost type. These very heavy coats were more often than not of inferior, coarse and woolly textures. The appearance of heavy coats in conjunction with coarse bone structure and short, thick heads was no less prevalent in new Eastern imports. Later breedings were constant struggles to blend the two types into a single form approaching the illusive balance found in the great Zardin. Unfortunately, one generation of happy success was frequently followed by disappointing reversions to extreme types.

By 1933, the Afghan Hound Association was formed and had its own standard, a document decidedly more extensive and detailed than the early, terse description of Zardin. The first A.H.A. president was Mrs. Mary Amps and the Chairman was Mrs. Phyllis Robson. The standard emerged as a compromise attempt to include the best of both types of hounds and yet point towards the ideal of the early Zardin. Mrs. Amps's insistence that the compact, close-coupled dog was the only correct type was accepted, but the size stipulation was in favor of the larger Bell-Murrays. This standard covered the breed until 1946.

Standard of Points—obsolete

Head—Skull long and not too narrow, prominent occiput. Foreface long, punishing jaws, and little stop, mouth level. Nose usually black, liver no disqualification in lighter colored dogs. Eyes, dark preferred; golden colour no disqualification. Ears long, heavily feathered and carried close to the head, which is surmounted by a long top-knot of hair.

Neck—Long, strong, with proud carriage of the head.

Shoulders—Long and sloping, well set back, well muscled and strong.

Back—Well muscled the whole length, falling slightly away to the stern. Loin straight, broad, and rather short. Hip joints rather prominent and wide; a fair spring of ribs and good depth of chest.

Forelegs—Straight, well-boned, elbows rather straight.

Feet—Large. Toes very long, well-arched, and heavily feathered.

Hindquarters—Powerful and long, with plenty of bend to hock and stifle, and well under the dog.

Tail—Set on low and carried "gaily," with a ring at the end; sparsely feathered.

Coat—Long, of very fine texture on the ribs, fore and hindquarters and flanks. From the shoulders backward along the top of the back, the hair is short and close. Hair long from the eyes backward, with a distinct silky top-knot; on foreface hair is short as on the back. Ears and legs well feathered.

Any color.

Height—Dogs 27 to 29 inches. Bitches 2 to 3 inches smaller.

The whole appearance of the dog should give the impression of strength and activity, combining speed with power.

The object of the dog is to hunt its quarry over very rough and mountainous ground, in a country of crags and ravines. For this, a compact and well-coupled dog is necessary rather than a long-loined racing dog whose first quality is speed.

Expression—Dignified, aloof and intelligent. In motion his head and tail are carried high; springy gait.

From the time The Kennel Club awarded the breed individual status in 1927 until the curtailment of shows during WWII, 38 Afghan Hounds became champions. This number may seem small to Americans, unfamiliar with the British system, wherein a dog must defeat even champions in attendance to win the necessary three Challenge Certificates, under different judges, to qualify for its title. One reigning champion may, and often does, accumulate many such certificates, shutting out the young class winners. The C.C.s are awarded only at a few large entry shows. Small English dog shows are frequent, taken seriously by entrants, but champions are not permitted to enter, and wins do not count towards championships. These shows are comparable to American all-breed "matches," and as a result of their system, there is a smaller percentage of champions among the total number of shown Afghans in England than there is in the United States.

Readers might like to know something of the colors of the early hounds. The great majority from all camps were some shade of red or cream, with or without masks. The Bell-Murrays, excepting

Pushum, tended to very faded coloration. The three pre-WWII brindle champions (a legacy of Pushum) included Ch. Badshah of Ainsdart, later sold to America. During the breeding lull of WWII, these brindle genes were completely lost on the Isle and had to be re-introduced from the United States in the 1960s. Black-and-tan genes arrived with the Ghazni hounds, Sirdar and "Roshni," both red themselves, but carrying the factor. Mrs. Amps brought back a few black Afghans directly from Afghanistan, but the black Afghan made no appearance on the championship roster until after the war in 1948 with Ch. Netheroyd Turkuman Camelthorn. There were no blue or gray champions up to 1959, but Mrs. Amps wrote that her red-fawn Khan of Ghazni and his son, Mustavfi of Ghazni, sired a few rare, gray pups. Khan was said to have come from a tribe near the Oxus that coveted the gray coloration, and when hounds other than gray were born, they were tossed out into the greedy arms of less finicky natives.

Newspaper clippings from the 1930s illustrate Afghan Hounds at the shows with peculiar half-coats, like sheep sheared half-way up and half-way down with thick wool patches sticking out from thighs to hocks and from shoulders to mid-lower legs. These hounds appear tiny-footed and flat-headed from lack of foot fur and topknots. Such pictures have bred the false assumption that the handsome full-coated Afghan is a modern item, but Sirdar and Khan were fair coated, as were some of their offspring. Ch. Westmill Tamasar, born in 1932 of about equal Ghazni and Bell-Murray stock including Pushum, and illustrated in Brian Vesey-Fitzgerald's *The Book of the Dog*, is a gray-brindle hound which has an adequate coat, huge hairy paws, and a good length of mandarin whiskers. His coat, his long, lean muzzle and his exquisite structural balance would place him favorably in today's competition. The factors for full coat and all-over breed quality were there, but the selection and the retention of the desired characteristics from such a background served a mighty challenge to the breeders.

The next world war hit England in 1939 and brought a halt to dog shows and breeding activities. The staunch British carried on as best they could, mindful of the Kennel Club edict that "No bitch should be mated unless it is for the express purpose of keeping in existence a line of blood of great use to the future of the breed." The warning was well taken. Women who did not bear arms for Britain did volunteer work and fought on the homefront to keep themselves and a few beloved hounds from starvation. Dogs were not allowed in the Public Air Raid Shelters, and England's quickly formed Canine Defense League devised a system whereby dog lovers made their homes available refuge to strangers with dogs. Red-white-and-blue tags on fenceposts and in windows indicated such homes.

Gas masks were designed for dogs, but without success, for the "average dog takes no more kindly to a mask than he does to a discarded salmon can wedged on his muzzle." Luminous leads and collars were designed by the "League" to allow dogs to exercise and still be seen by motorists and pedestrians in the nightly blackouts.

Many beloved hounds were reluctantly sold or "lent" to friends in countries that were not under air bombardment. America was indebted to the war years for dogs like Ch. Rana of Chaman of Royal Irish and Ch. Sardar Khan el Kabal, which might never have left England under normal circumstances. In 1941 a "refugee" on the S.S. Ville D'Anvers was Tajana Glamour Girl of Chaman, bound for Marion Florsheim's kennel where her valuable bloodlines could be protected. Ties of sympathy between American and British fanciers were tightened during this period.

In 1946 a small group of fanciers regrouped with their aging breeding stock in hopes of rebuilding the breed. Dissatisfaction was voiced with the pre-war Standard, and several dedicated people set about working on revisions. They included Dr. Betsy Porter (Kabul Kennel), Mrs. E. E. Drinkwater (Geufron Kennel), Mrs. Barbara Rothwell-Fielding (Kuranda Kennel), Mrs. Howard Gibson (Ackam Kennel), Miss Marjorie Matthews (Westover Kennel), and Phyllis Robson the columnist. That year a new official standard was recognized by the British Kennel Club, one not greatly different from its predecessor, but attempting to delineate details in clearer order. There was a new stress on the "Oriental" character of the hound's triangular eye; the tail was to be carried as if "raised in action," instead of "gaily," and ears and legs that had merely to be "feathered" in the past, were now to be "coated," except for the pastern joints.

With the shortage of litters from the year 1939 on, the post-war Afghan population of 1946 was a mixture of immature youngsters and aging, war-raised adult dogs. The first post-war champion was the eight-year-old Mitzou of Acklam. With a fresh Standard, plentiful supplies of meat and dog food, and a nucleus of persistent fanciers, England planted and harvested an impressive crop of Afghan Hounds. Names such as Khorrassan, Bletchingly, Netheroyd, Turkuman, Carloway and others rose to share the bounty. In a few short years, through the cooperative efforts of the fanciers, much of the globe was again being supplied with quality Afghan Hounds from England.

Current British Afghan Hound Standard
(Adopted in 1946, accepted by the British Kennel Club in 1948)

Characteristics—The Afghan Hound should be dignified and aloof with a certain keen fierceness. The Eastern or Oriental expression is typical of the breed. The Afghan looks at and through one.

General appearance—The gait of the Afghan Hound should be smooth and springy with a style of high order. The whole appearance of the dog should give the impression of strength and dignity combining speed and power. The head must be held proudly.

Head and skull—Skull long, not too narrow, with prominent occiput. Foreface long with punishing jaws and slight stop. The skull well balanced and surmounted by a long topknot. Nose preferably black but liver is no fault in light-coloured dogs.

Eyes—Should be dark but golden colour is not debarred. Nearly triangular, slanting slightly upwards from the inner corner to the outer.

Ears—Set low and well back, carried close to the head. Covered with long silky hair.

Mouth—Level.

Neck—Long and strong with proud carriage of the head.

Forequarters—Shoulders long and sloping, well set back, well muscled and strong without being loaded. Forelegs straight and well boned, straight with shoulders, elbows held in.

Body—Back level, of moderate length, well muscled and falling slightly away to the tail. Loins straight, broad and rather short. A fair spring of ribs and good depth of chest.

Hindquarters—Powerful, with well bent and well turned stifles. Hip-bones rather prominent and wide apart. Great length between hips and hocks and a comparatively short distance between hocks and feet. The dew-claws may be removed or allowed to remain at the discretion of the breeder.

Feet—Forefeet strong and very large both in length and breadth, and covered with long thick hair, toes arched. Pasterns long and springy, especially in front, and the pads well down on the ground. Hind feet long, but not quite so broad as the forefeet, and covered with long thick hair.

Tail—Not too short. Set on low with a ring at the end. Raised in action. Sparsely feathered.

Coat—Long and very fine texture on ribs, fore and hindquarters and flanks. From the shoulders backwards and along the saddle the

60

hair should be short and close in mature dogs. Hair long from the forehead backward on the head, with a distinct silky topknot; on the foreface the hair is short, as on the back. Ears and legs well coated. Pasterns can be bare. Coat must be allowed to develop naturally.

Colour—All colours are acceptable.

Weight and size—Ideal height; dogs 27–29 inches, bitches 2–3 inches smaller.

Faults—Any appearance of coarseness. Skull too wide and foreface too short. Weak underjaw. Large round or full eyes. Neck should never be too short or thick. Back too long or too short.

Asra of Ghazni (Eng. Ch. Sirdar of Ghazni ex Shireen of Ghazni), cream bitch imported from England and the foundation of Q. A. Shaw McKean's Prides Hill Kennel in Massachusetts. Dam of 7 champions.

The AMERICAN
KENNEL GAZETTE

Vol. 44, No. 3
Per Year $4

March 31, 1927
Per Copy 50 Ce

Reproduction of a photograph loaned by Miss Jean C. Manson

AFGHAN HOUNDS

Cover of *The American Kennel Gazette,* March 3, 1927.

Courtesy, *American Kennel Club.*

62

4

The Afghan Hound
Comes to America

"To own one is to love one! The Afghan Hound gains daily in popularity. The oldest known breed of domestic dog. Wonderful companions and house dogs. Charming dispositions, gentle, equally amiable to children and other dogs. Easily trained for any sport. Immune to either intense heat or cold. Prices range from $150 to $1000."

In June, 1929, the ad above first appeared in the *American Kennel Gazette* at a time when there was a scarce handful of Afghan Hounds in the whole United States. Fully 99 and 44/100% of American dog fanciers had not the vaguest notion that an "Afghan" was anything other than a remote Asiatic native or an inanimate knitted coverlet.

The Afghan Hound had definitely made its noble presence felt in England well before this, though, and by 1926, a few of Miss Manson's hounds had arrived on the Eastern seaboard, creating little attention and leaving no lasting pedigree effects. This advertisement referred to "de Flandre" hounds of "Sirdar" lineage imported by Edward Abrams and seen occasionally at Eastern shows during 1930 and 1931. The fortunate but few fanciers who were aware of this exciting breed were sublimely optimistic about its potential, but judges and the general public considered the dogs freakish and only paused to smirk at them. What the breed needed was a good Madison Avenue type of press agent, and some really outstanding specimens to point up the virtues of the somewhat bizarre breed to a curious American public.

63

Pertinent American history of the breed begins in 1931 with a Hollywood story starring Zeppo, the youngest of the zany Marx brothers. When in England on film location, Zeppo and his wife were completely fascinated by a fleeting sight of these hounds and agreed that they should take a pair for breeding back to California. Fortunately they approached Phyllis Robson, then Editor of the English *Dog World,* who also owned the famous Eng. Ch. Asri-Havid of Ghazni. Mr. and Mrs. Marx left the selection in her hands, stipulating only that they preferred a pair of light-colored hounds with good coats. Asra of Ghazni (litter sister of Ch. Ashna of Ghazni) sired by the great Sirdar ex Shireen of Ghazni, was the first selection. The Search for a suitable male ended at the Westmill kennel where Mr. and Mrs. Marx were both delighted by young Westmill Omar, a dark cream male by Danenda of Ghazni ex Surkh of Ghazni. By today's standards Omar was barely fair coated, and the solid cream-colored Asra was considerably less so, but both had the lively character and wonderful upstanding carriage, finely chiseled head and keen dark eyes that characterized so many of their finest get.

Zeppo Marx brought Omar and Asra to California in the Spring of 1931, but by the close of that year the Marx family had again been forced to leave Hollywood for an extended movie tour and thought it kindest to turn their charming pets over to George Thomas, respected judge and dealer in valuable dogs. Fully aware of their value, Thomas determined to keep them himself until he could find someone who would properly appreciate the unique hounds. In his care Omar and Asra mated and awaited their first litter. Shortly before the pups arrived, George Thomas and his two Afghans returned to Massachusetts. On impulse he called a friend, the highly respected breeder of Wire Fox Terriers, Q. A. Shaw McKean, suggesting that he have a look at his new "prizes." McKean was instantly captivated by Omar and Asra, begging to buy them on the spot. Thomas finally agreed, but only under the condition that he be able to remain breeder and owner of the unborn litter.

McKean took Omar and Asra to the spacious Prides Hill kennels in Prides Crossing, Mass., gave them the run of his home and was amazed at their droll and lively outdoor antics contrasted with their marvelous unobtrusiveness in the house. In Q. A. Shaw McKean the Afghan Hound had found the energetic, wise and experienced press agent the breed so badly needed! The astute McKean concocted long range plans for his exciting new acquisitions, worried that the single pair had limited breeding possibilities: another stud of a different, but not too different, bloodline was needed. As George Thomas was soon to leave for Europe on a judging and dog-buying trip McKean

64

Eng. & Am. Ch. Badshah of Ainsdart (Eng. Ch. Sirdar of Ainsdart ex Ku-Mari of Kaf), pale brindle dog, America's first Best in Show Afghan. Sire of 17 champions. Owned by Q. A. Shaw McKean.

requested that he look out for a suitable second stud. Eventually George Thomas cabled that he had found *the* right dog, and confident of his friend's educated judgment, McKean said "Buy." Thus in 1934 the acclaimed young English Champion Badshah of Ainsdart arrived on American shores. For good measure Thomas also bought Badshah's litter brother, Tufan of Ainsdart. It is a rare American pedigree that does not trace directly back to one or both of these pioneer sires.

Badshah, familiarly known as "Loppie," leaped into McKean's heart and stayed there. A good-sized, pale brindle Afghan, the color of smoke, Loppie's unquenchable spirit shone from his fierce Oriental eyes and showed in his proudly carried head and highly curved tail. A direct son of Sirdar of Ghazni, Badshah's dam was Ku Mari of Kaf, a typical Bell-Murray bitch, giving McKean his desired bit of outcross blood while protecting the Sirdar legacy. Badshah was quite sparsely coated, especially on the legs, but this was easily ignored in sight of his remarkable free-floating stride and energetic breed character.

Shaw McKean first exhibited his fine English Champion at the North Shore Kennel Club in Hamilton, Mass. on Aug. 25th, 1934,

65

where "Loppie" startled the canine world into sharp awareness of the Afghan by shooting straight through to become America's first Best in Show Afghan Hound. Badshah, one of those wily hounds who knew the secret of opening latches and vaulting fences, had the run of the McKean estate, but he was most happy to be within adoring distance of his new American master. On Badshah's death in 1940 McKean fondly recalled the hound's superb expression and his rare combination of great substance and refinement. Said McKean, "In head points he was a class above any Afghan that I have ever seen. He was a beautiful moving animal, with tremendous speed and spring, and could take a six-foot jump without breaking stride." The great smoky-brindle sire was buried in the orchard where he best loved to run, at the close of his tenth year.

After acquiring Badshah, McKean set about educating in earnest the dog owning public about Afghans. Articles authored by him appeared in dog journals. Special Prides Hill folders were freely circulated. In this manner the older breed stories told in England, plus a few new ones, became part of the American breed image. Other writers spun fresh yarns from the basic substance of McKean's loom. There was no time to back up and check to see what was made of true cloth and what was synthetic. Once the public became better acquainted with the breed and its glamorous background the enchanting hounds could sell themselves at close contact.

Part of McKean's strategy was to show his hounds *en masse* at the New England shows, and as Omar and Asra had two litters before Badshah arrived, the classes were sizeable. There are those who scoff at dogs who win championships by defeating only their own kennel-mates, but in a newly introduced breed there is much to be said for this scheme. A gathering of several lively Afghan Hounds is considerably more impressive than a single specimen. This device also forced the judges to really inspect and familiarize themselves with the unique hounds in order to make reasonable merit judgments. From a practical view, the tactics gave McKean young champions who might never have "finished" without the home kennel competition. With young champions on hand McKean was able to make "package deals" with a champion and a selected mate to serve as foundation stock for fanciers with awakening interest in the exotic new breed.

Despite the fact that the Afghan Hound was revered as a sporting dog extraordinary in Afghanistan and India, from the moment that Omar and Badshah reached America, the breed received its billing as a show dog extraordinary capable of winning Best in Shows and great glory for proud owners. Certainly his fascinating history and reputed hunting prowess added to the breed's stature, but one is hard put to find hunting Afghans that left strong marks on the American branch of the breed. There has always been an unusually large percentage of the total Afghan Hound population under exhibition at the shows with marked and enviable success in winning top honors.

The American Kennel Club had accepted Afghan Hound registrations from 1926 under a Standard that was said to have been furnished by The Afghan Hound Club of England. The breed was placed in the Sporting Group as the Hound Group was not given separate status until 1937.

Original American Standard

Superseded in 1948 by the current Standard

Head—Narrow, conforming to that of a greyhound but more powerful; skull oval, with prominent occiput; jaws long and punishing; mouth level, not overshot nor undershot; ears long; eyes dark; little or no stop.

Neck—Long, strong, arched and running in a curve to the shoulder, which should be long and sloping and well laid back.

Body—Strong powerful loin, and slightly arched, falling away towards the stern, well ribbed and tucked up under loins; should be that of a hound and have ample length; the tail set not too high on body, similar to greyhound, having a curve at the end, but on no account a bushy tail.

Legs—Forelegs straight and strong, great length between elbow and ankle, elbows well tucked in; forefeet very large both in length and breadth, toes well arched and the feet covered with long thick hair, fine in texture; pasterns long and pads well down on ground.

Brisket—Deep and not too narrow.

Hindquarters—Powerful, well muscled, great length between hip and hock, this is one of the main features of the hound; fair bend of stifle.

Hind feet—Broad but not as long as forefeet; toes arched; feet covered in long, thick hair.

Coat—Hindquarters, flanks, ribs and forequarters well covered with silky, thick hair, very fine in texture; ears and all four feet well feathered; head surmounted with top-knot of long silky hair.

General appearance—Strong, alert, and active; looking a combination of speed and power, with a graceful outline.

Height—Dogs about 27 inches, bitches 25 inches.

Weight—About 60 pounds.

Ch. Tufan of Ainsdart, Badshah's brother, sire of 10 champions. Owned by Amelia White.

Ch. Amanullah of Kandahar (Ch. Badshah of Ainsdart ex Zahera of Prides Hill), cream dog, most successful show Afghan of the '30s with 9 Bests in Show. Owned by Amelia White.

Despite the marked similarity between this terse standard and the contemporaneous but short-lived "Denyer Standard" based on the Indian description of Zardin, there are curious features in the American document not easily attributed to any known source. Differences in the criteria for head shape, coat and size are superficial, but where the American Standard requests a body that "should be that of a hound and have ample length" was inconsistent with the English ideal that the Afghan Hound was more compact than the other Greyhound types. This loose American Standard did hold court, however, often quite uncomfortably, until 1948.

Ch. Kabul of Prides Hill, from the second Omar-Asra litter, became the first Afghan Hound champion in America in October of 1934. From George Thomas's first Omar and Asra litter, a bitch, Barberryhill Illusive, had been sold directly to the Sealyham breeder, Bayard Warren, a close neighbor of Shaw McKean. On early maturity Mr. Warren bred this bitch to Badshah of Ainsdart, precisely in line with what McKean planned for his own Omar-Asra daughters. At the 1935 Westminster show several "Barberryhill" Afghans issued a friendly challenge to a large McKean entry. Badshah took the breed, and his young daughter, Barberryhill Dolly, captured the bitch points as a quiet forecast to the great future ahead of her.

By 1935 Afghans were spreading to other states. In New Mexico, Miss Amelia White, encouraged by a wise kennel manager, Alex Scott, sensed greatness and climatic suitability in the furry hounds. She obtained Badshah's brother, the cream Tufan of Ainsdart, a bitch, Kali of Prides Hill, and a promising young puppy sired by Badshah ex Zahera of Prides Hill (an Omar-Asra daughter) named Amanullah of Kandahar. This singular young puppy soon put "Kandahar" Afghans on the list of immortals.

Without intending to slight "Tufan" we must emphasize the Omar-Asra-Badshah triple play. These dogs were mated together repeatedly, forming a cornerstone of American breeding. Asra of Ghazni produced some 43 puppies with various studs, including three breedings to Omar, according to McKean's own words. Known affectionately as "Bibbles," Asra left Prides Hill to live with Muriel Boger (Doreborn) where she produced her later litters, dying at the age of 14, the Grande Dame of Afghans. The Badshah-Zahera of Prides Hill combination produced 53 pups for Shaw McKean, Margaret Nison, and later for Dr. and Mrs. Combs (Arthea).

With this much early breeding of a hound of limited demand it is fortunate that these experienced dog fanciers did not panic at the threat of over population and were able to keep surplus hounds from the hands of unscrupulous dog merchants. McKean calmly advertised having over 50 hounds at Prides Hill—with over 40 of them for sale. There were good entries at the prestige New England shows courtesy of McKean and Warren. The southwest classes were patronized by Miss White's Kandahar hounds and the Kingway dogs of Mrs. Porter of Colorado. By the close of 1936 and following Kabul of Prides Hill, Badshah of Ainsdart, Barberryhill Dolly, Kundah of Prides Hill and Barberryhill Charlie were Eastern champions, and in the Southwest Amanullah of Kandahar and Tufan of Ainsdart had completed their title requirements.

Undoubtedly the most successful show Afghan of the 1930s was Ch. Amanullah of Kandahar who picked off groups and Best in Shows like bones from a plate. Not only in the Southwest did he reign supreme, but as breed winner at Westminster he bested all Eastern competition. By 1940 Amanullah had amassed a record of nine Best in Shows. Part of Amanullah's success was directly attributed to his superlative handling and conditioning by Alex Scott, who intimately understood the hound character. A large, spectacular, well-trained, cream hound with a long impressive head, Amanullah had that show-spark that induced him to "perform" with great animation the moment he sensed human eyes turned his way.

Word of the graceful beauty of the first bitch champion, Barberryhill Dolly, raced cross-country to character actor, Charlie Ruggles, in Hollywood, also a noted dog fancier. As quick as transportation could be arranged Dolly was installed in the Ruggles's ultra-luxurious kennel of canine stars.

At this point, letting Dolly sit in Charlie Ruggles's kennel, which is just what she did do, we might digress to the influx of other imports found on the West Coast. Undoubtedly the most exciting, but least known, were Tazi of Beg Tute and Saki of Paghman, transported directly from Afghanistan to Port Blakely, Washington, by Laurance Peters, foreign news correspondent. Having stepped over an animated Afghan Hound "rug" in Kabul in the French Consul's office in 1932, Peters determined to own such a dog someday. In 1934, again in Afghanistan, and with Mrs. Peters, he made a family project of acquiring a brace of the memorable hounds. While certain that there were many fine hounds hidden away in the native villages, he had a time locating them. The natives preferred not to part with their hounds and rather than antagonize the foreign visitors by outright refusal they politely insisted, "Yesterday we had many fine hounds, but last night they all died." The Peters were also frustrated by their Moslem guide and interpreter who disapproved of all dogs and, with an interpreter's advantage, encouraged the natives to deny having hounds. When Peters realized the conspiracy, he enlisted the aid of a friendly Afghan soldier who smoothed relations for a hound

Tazi of Beg Tute, fawn dog, imported from Afghanistan in 1934 by Mr. & Mrs. L. Peters. Picture taken in Afghanistan. Courtesy Mrs. L. Peters.

purchase. But even to their countrymen the natives maintained that "The females all died the night before." At the village of Beg Tute, Mr. Peters was allowed to select a male hound. He was immediately attracted to a small wild-eyed, fawn colored dog, who stood out by alienating himself from the friendly pack to sulk suspiciously in the background. Peters selected the independent young male, and then spent two hours with the natives chasing the panicky hound. Once captured, Tazi of Beg Tute lived in terror under the Peters's bed, completely unapproachable. When they finally decided that they might have to give him up or trade him for a real Oriental rug, he suddenly calmed down, became obedient, affectionate and eventually Americanized, although he always preferred the sound of Persian words. In disgust, the Moslem servant vanished when the dog moved into the hotel.

Procuring a female was a real task. Almost ready to give up the search, one day they pessimistically asked about Tazi bitches at the small village of Paghman. A wily native offered them a tattered and forlorn looking tiny gray female. Knowing that the native was trying to put something over on them, but under her sad haunting gaze and the fear that they might never find another, they made the purchase. In spite of the fact that her coat was always poor and she had no desire to be a show girl, Saki of Paghman developed great charm and proved to have brood bitch potential when mated to Tazi. Among their offspring was the handsome black Ch. Jac-A-Leen's Shab and the slate gray Blue Mist of Egypt which transferred the exotic Maltese Blue coloration from Saki to the later famous Ch. Felt's Thief of Bagdad.

71

Ch. Barberryhill Charlie (Ch. Badshah of Ainsdart ex Barberryhill Illusive), dog, winning Best in Show at Los Angeles Kennel Club, 1937.

Ch. Barberryhill Dolly (Ch. Badshah of Ainsdart ex Barberryhill Illusive), bitch, and Ch. Umberto (Amanullah ex Sheila Beg), dog, imported from India for Venita Oakie's Oakvardon Kennel. Dolly and Umberto were both Best in Show winners.

In Southern California Mrs. Caroline Hall Richmond was the owner of an imported bitch, Fatima, born in India in 1928. In 1936 a litter was registered from Fatima, sired by Ch. Tufan of Ainsdart. From this union, Fatima's Daughter Peri, Fatima's Daughter Kushdil and Fatima's Son Tufan Khan won championships in 1937. Despite great acknowledged quality these hounds were not further campaigned by Mrs. Richmond, who apparently was not really bitten by the Show Bug. Ch. Fatima's Daughter Peri is behind the maternal side of the exotic, nearly-white Ch. Felt's Allah Baba, acclaimed by some breeder-judges as one of the most nearly perfect Afghan Hounds ever seen. Ch. Fatima's Son Tufan Khan, bred to Ch. Dura of Prides Hill, sired some of Dr. Marxmiller's "Dellire" champions in the late 1930s.

R. W. Samson of Redwood City, California, was exhibiting as contemporaries of the Fatima-get his English imports, Ch. Garrymhor Kishtwar and bitches, Garrymhor Khasa (who became a champion) and Jalalabad Kara, as his basic "Kuhsan" Afghans. He later imported the lovely English Mounha of Kuhsan, and when her championship was made, sold her to Mrs. Porter's Kingway kennels where she blended well with Ch. Niliyo of Prides Hill.

The remainder of the West Coast competition was made up of Prides Hill and related stock. Venita Vardon Oakie, beauteous wife of comedian Jack Oakie, developed a rapport with the Arabian Nights hounds and in 1936 was showing a Tufan daughter, Morgiana of Kandahar, in the classes with the Samson and Richmond entries. At this time Ch. Barberryhill Dolly arrived in the West. She won a few honors under the Ruggles banner, but as a sensitive girl not always in an outgoing mood, she was considered unreliable and left in the kennel temporarily forgotten.

Samson's Kishtwar was the Special of the day, above fighting in the class preliminaries, ready to battle the Hound groups, which he topped frequently. With his thick, short, all-over coat Kishtwar looked like a saddled puppy. His head was unlike the typical Prides Hill muzzle, being deeper and more blunt in profile, but with good length.

Suddenly Athos Nilson hit California with Ch. Barberryhill Charlie, Dolly's litter brother. At his first appearance in the west Charlie topped the Hound Group and became the first Best in Show Afghan in California at the Los Angeles Kennel Club in 1937. Charlie rolled up a quick record of western wins at the expense of Kishtwar, and in friendly rivalry Mr. Samson sent for the third champion of the Badshah-Barberryhill Illusive litter, Ch. Barberryhill Phillip, who did not equal Charlie's show career but did leave a definite mark on Kushan pedigrees through an intermix with the English bitches.

Late in 1937 Ch. Barberryhill Dolly, shamefully wasted in the vast Ruggles kennels, went to Venita Vardon Oakie, who lavished understanding care on the lovely hound. In return, with great devotion for Venita, Dolly gained self-assurance and found new favor with the judges, who had always appreciated her graceful femininity and excellent gait. Handled by Russell Zimmerman, with Venita standing close by, Dolly began to collect groups regularly. At home, Dolly was Mrs. Oakie's beloved companion and inspiration for the great Oakvardon Afghan kennel that was to rival Prides Hill in size.

Umberto was imported from India for Oakvardon, winning his championship in 1938 and adding distinction to the Oakvardon stud force. From Ireland came Hanuman of Enriallic. Dolly began to hit her best stride and under the guidance of Phyllis Ranier, at the Del Monte Kennel Club show in 1940, became the first Best in Show bitch in California and the second in the United States at the age of six years old. Rather than retiring on the honor, Dolly again stood alone in the charmed circle twice the following year.

Oakvardon was enriched by two English hounds, Westmill Razuran and the English Champion bitch, Westmill Natanz. The black-masked, light red Natanz was then six years old and carried a full and decidedly wavy coat. She was a granddaughter of Ch. Tufan of Ainsdart through a breeding made before he was exported to the United States, and also of the famous heavy-coated import Lakki Marwat. Natanz had a wonderfully sweet personality and a lovely gait, like a purposeful feather. The judges liked her immediately. When shown at Fresno and Ventura with no class competition, she won her needed points by taking both Best in Shows. With Ch. Umberto also hitting the top all-breed honors in 1941, Oakvardon boasted of three Best in Show hounds that year and the broadest base of quality bloodlines in America. Venita Vardon Oakie became a highly respected judge, and a totally devoted friend of the breed until her untimely death in 1948.

In the Ohio area during 1938, Frank Andrews, Dr. Combs and Frank Weithoff (Kerrin Kennels) and a few others with Prides Hill stock formed the nucleus of a breed club. The previous year the Afghan Hound Club of America had its embryo formation, but became noted only for its complete inactivity. Midwestern fanciers agreed to form a splinter group of greater vigor. On October 9, 1938, the enthusiastic Midwest Afghan Hound Club held America's first Afghan Hound Specialty in conjunction with the Detroit Specialties group. Out of an entry of 12 hounds, Best of Breed went to Garrymhor Pearie, an imported English bitch owned by Miss Nancy Andrews.

In a mild sort of a way, by 1939 the Afghan Hound had arrived in

Venita Vardon Oakie and some puppies from her Oakvardon Kennel. *Ludwig photo*

America. There was little danger of the breed rivaling the German Shepherd in popularity, but registrations had climbed to 148 in that year. Afghan Hound devotees were determined, experienced, and could be found throughout the country. As a prestige item the breed was getting good space in fashion magazines and Hollywood publicity shots.

From the beginning, the number of types of the breed which existed in Afghanistan had served as a natural obstacle to producing uniformity of character, and the early English outcrossings did little to help this situation. In America, however, selective line breeding of Omar, Asra, Badshah and Tufan had produced a certain degree of uniformity which was mainly threatened by the arrival of the new imports. Prides Hill hounds were certainly not all identical, nor did they lack room for improvement, but the assets of a long chiseled head and the agile, purposeful action of the original group had been retained in the best specimens of this kennel.

At this time in America, coats were moderate to poor, but especially in comparison to the lushness of contemporary English winners. George Thomas had told McKean to "show your dogs fit and strong and forget about too many ruffles." This became the Prides Hill creed, and the kennel produced hounds that were marvels of structural soundness. As spokesman for the breed, McKean

75

emphasized breed character and action over physical embellishments.

As cream hounds, totally devoid of black hairs, Omar and Asra had poor skin pigment with light noseleathers and eye rims. Among their offspring and those of Badshah and Tufan were colored pups with large white facial blazes and high white stockings, frequently studded with freckles of color.

The Standard was beautifully unspecific on surface details. Criticisms and penalties were weakly advanced on the grounds of general unattractiveness. Blazed champions and those with practically no coat at all from elbow to the ground were not unusual, as some judges felt that the graces of showmanship and an impressive gait could be better appreciated when not hidden by an excessive coat. Surprisingly enough, through the stockpiling of Sirdar genes, some pretty fair coats with lovely, silken textures appeared from time to time as they did on Dolly and on Ch. Rudiki of Prides Hill.

Each import tended to be a surprise and sometimes a bit of a shocker. In 1939 Mrs. Austin of Catawba Pekingeses brought out her fantastically coated English import, the lovely cream Ch. Lakshmi of Geufron-Catawba, which startled the breeders and judges on the East Coast. That year Lakshmi became the first Best in Show bitch in America. To some, she was a drippy-coated freak, but others realized that she was a sample of things to come in the breed.

The heavier-coated English dogs continued to seep into America, always being mixed with the existing Yankee stock. A race for physical superiority was begun as the newer imports advanced coat potential, bringing leg coat and rich topknots, as well as deeper pigment in skin and fur. Such aims had the effect of softening the set type of Omar and Badshah, and some dogs, valued greatly for their impressive coats and rich coloring, were penalized only slightly for less than elegant muzzles, crooked legs, puny bodies and unsound gaits.

By 1940 the practically defunct Afghan Hound Club of America had pulled its inactive shreds together and applied for membership with the American Kennel Club. Q. A. Shaw McKean was elected President, Mrs. Robert Boger, secretary, and Dr. Beck the first delegate to the A.K.C. Mrs. Boger opened a column in the American Kennel Gazette and remained the breed correspondent for the next nine years. The subject of standard revision came up immediately as the existing one was under fire for its omissions. Judges and breeders complained that it gave no guidance on the finer points of the breed. The obvious need for a more detailed standard was

Ch. Lakshmi of Geufron-Catawba (Yudhajit of Geufron ex Tarawali of Geufron), cream bitch, imported from England. America's first Best in Show Afghan Hound bitch, owned by Mrs. James Austin.

quickly acknowledged, but talk of any specific changes was followed by immediate bickering.

The characteristic American Afghan Hound head, with the slight Roman rise and piercing Oriental almond eye was not detailed in the standard, but had gained acceptance as a model of strength and Eastern beauty from Westmill Omar and Badshah. McKean wanted this spelled out in the standard. He also believed the high tail carriage to be significant, having read an account of hunters supposedly following Afghan Hounds through the brush by means of their high tails. This is certainly one of the more questionable myths in the breed image, as sparsely fringed tails would scarcely make good "flags" considering the get-away speed of an Afghan, and the breed is certainly not suited to brush hunting, but Badshah's extremely high tail and McKean's beliefs encouraged acceptance of the model of the tall tail in the breed.

Through notation of the most pleasing aspects of the more successful dogs, a gradually detailed portrait of external breed character slowly developed, but did not gain unanimous acceptance. McKean's own sensitivity regarding pigment was obvious in the Gazette articles in which he denied any importance to nose or eye rim color. He claimed that the fierce, dark eye, which happened to be prevalent at Prides Hill, was of far greater value. Breeders plagued with light-eyed hounds, with dark masking and strong skin pigmentation, were understandably in discord with McKean. Unattractive blazes and the occasional occurrence of parti-colored

77

Afghans put other breeders on the defensive. The fancy was unanimously against the unsound, the coarse or the puny dog, but could not agree on the boundaries of coarseness or size.

In 1941 the AHCA reviewed a copy of a trial standard submitted by Mrs. Porter to the *Bulletin*. At the February meeting of that year the members declared a ban on all *trimming of Afghan Hounds,* and the Gazette carried the following admonition: "The Afghans' whiskers are a characteristic of the breed, and he sheds his coat naturally where it should be shed, without benefit of the plucking knife. Let us leave him as he is!!" In those days an undersufficiency of hair was far more troublesome than any surplus, as indicated by Mrs. Boger's note to the effect that, "There should be a shed-off place at the pastern or knee joint on the front legs although dogs carrying the heavy coat down to the feet should not be unduly penalized." Revision of the standard was accompanied by a perpetual grumble growing louder when it was known that the English breed fancy had long ago abandoned the standard that roughly corresponded to the American document.

One inexplicable sentence of the standard calling for the body to have ample length caused concern. As a result of the indefinite phrasing, wide variation of ratio of back length to leg length was tolerated in the breed while some breeders strongly advocated a more compact hound. Marion Florsheim, writing an influential breed column in *Kennel Review,* pointed to the current English Standard which stated that the Afghan Hounds were "compact and well-coupled, agile, built for jumping and leaping endurance. Not the long-loined racing dog whose first quality is horizontal speed." From England then, came a statement, to the effect that the Afghan's height should about equal his length. As such a hound was balanced regardless of size, discouraging extremes of either body type, the concept of the square Afghan came into being. Acceptance was not wholehearted, as one writer maintained, "Ample length is open to personal interpretation, but it doesn't seem to mean 'square' no matter how one looks at it." In the midst of the furor, Mr. McKean suggested that the Standard revisions be shelved "for the duration" as America was being touched by the strife in Europe and had larger problems to worry about.

We are rushing past too many influential hounds and must back up a bit. In August of 1937 at Prides Hill Kennels a litter by Badshah ex Ch. Shireen of Prides Hill produced a noteworthy male pup christened Rudiki of Prides Hill. When Shaw McKean introduced the majestic Rudiki in the Fall of 1938, the dog was immediately acclaimed the finest Prides Hill specimen to date. After a

Ch. Rudiki of Prides Hill (Ch. Badshah of Ainsdart ex Ch. Shireen of Prides Hill), dog, owned by Marion Florsheim. A multi-BIS winner and the sire of 31 champions.

quick round of Eastern shows, McKean rested his young champion and awaited coat maturity. A year later he took Rudiki to the West Coast where the sparkling dog etched his name at the top of many a hound group and in the memories of those who viewed him at the California shows. Some still recall his beautifully chiseled head in the tradition of Badshah, but black-masked on a clear gold background. So exquisite was his muzzle that his portrait signaled the Afghan Hound column in the *Gazette* at the debut of the column in 1940 and remained until 1965. With his fine, silken, red-gold coat, an amazingly noble carriage and attractive gait, a grand career was prophesied for Rudiki.

The Afghan Hound Club of America held its first Specialty show in 1940, judged by Dr. Eugene Beck, who chose Ch. Tanyah Sahib of CyAnn from the kennel of Cyrus Rickel, noted multi-breed judge, as top winner. This dog, from the breeding of Ch. Amanullah of Kandahar to Kali of Prides Hill, went on to Group three as the Specialty was held in conjunction with the North Westchester all-breed show. In 1941, the Specialty, held at the same site, was judged by Dr. Combs who placed Dr. Gertrude Kinsey's young Champion bitch, Hazar (Ch. Agha Kush ex Westmill Taree) at the top of the breed.

Many fanciers with acknowledged success in other breeds were magnetically attracted to the Afghan rings. Ch. Kerrin Fachamo

Ch. Tanyah Sahib of Cy-Ann (Ch. Amanullah of Kandahar ex Kali of Prides Hill), dog, owned by Cyrus Rickel, Best of Breed at the first Afghan Hound Club of America Specialty in 1940.

Ch. Garrymhor Zabardast of Arken (Garrymhor Ghalan Nubi ex Ranai of Istalif), imported from England. A Top Producer of the pre-1948 era, sire of 20 champions.

Ch. Rudika of Blakeen (Ch. Rudiki of Prides Hill ex Zahera of Ainsdart), bitch, multi-BIS winner and dam of six champions.

Int. Ch. Rana of Chaman of Royal Irish (Ch. Westmill Bayezid Ansari ex Safiya), dog imported from England by Mr. and Mrs. A. J. Baron, owned by Marion Foster Florsheim. Multiple BIS winner and sire of 11 champions.

(Ch. Badshah of Ainsdart ex Zahera of Prides Hill) was a well-known Best in Show winner from the Weithoff's midwest kennel better known for fine "Kerrin Collies." Another Collie breeder, Lillian Miller, from the state of Washington stopped at Kerrin for a look at the Collies and adopted a promising Afghan named Kerrin Fachamur. Once back in Washington, her young male found practically no class competition but won honors for the breed by frequently topping Northwest groups and garnered the Best in Show award at Seattle in 1941. Ch. Kerrin Fachamur bred to Zar Sunni of Tazi forged a link between the Laurance Peters imports and basic American stock.

Charles Wernsman, long respected for Arken Collies, fostered a tribe of "Arken Afghans" based on Ku Mari Khyaam of Arken (Badshah ex Zahera of Prides Hill) and the imported English sire Ch. Garrymhor Zabardast of Arken. Zabardast was an upstanding hound with a magnificent head and Oriental expression and did some impressive winning. His great claim to fame was as the Arken stud. He and Sara (Ku Mari Khyaam of Arken) combined to raise a dynasty of famous black-masked red Arken hounds. Their first litter produced six notable champions: Bul Bul, Sultan, Pocono Persica, Mogul, Maharanee and Rajah. Miss Whelan, owner of Ch. Maharanee of Arken C.D.X. and Best in Show Ch. Mogul of Arken,

C.D., firmly believed that Afghans were as bright as they were beautiful and well proved her contention.

Ch. Rajah of Arken, a hound of magnificently sound gait and strong temperament remained at Arken, becoming the only Afghan Hound to ever win the Parent Club Specialty three times, in 1942, 1943 and 1944. The breeding was repeated with additional success. Quality Arken hounds stud the back lines of many fine American pedigrees.

In 1939, Rana of Chaman came from the war-threatened Scottish kennel of Molly Sharpe to the safety of America. The Royal Irish suffix was added by his importers, Mr. and Mrs. A. J. Baron. As an immediate group winner from the classes, Rana was acquired by Marion Foster Florsheim. Marion swiftly completed his title and a round of group wins, culminating in Rana's first BIS at National Capital Kennel Club in 1942.

Shortly before Mrs. Florsheim entered the breed with Rana, Mrs. Hayes Blake Hoyt of Blakeen Poodle fame, had been attracted to Shaw McKean's Rudiki whom she obtained together with a few select bitches to found Blakeen Afghans. Rudiki's success rivaled the Blakeen Poodles, and it was not unusual to find Rudiki and a Blakeen Poodle vying for top honors. Afghans at Blakeen were successful, but not lasting. Mrs. Hoyt retained a great fondness for the breed but by the end of 1941 the Afghan area of Blakeen was disbanded. Mrs. Hoyt had acquired an exceptionally lovely stud-fee puppy bitch (sired by Rudiki ex Lasca Klana) named Rudika of Blakeen. Rudiki, together with his gorgeous daughter Rudika, passed to the eager arms of Marion Florsheim joining Rana as the foundation of Five Mile Afghans in Connecticut.

World War II was diminishing the dog fancy in America by 1942. Gasoline and meat supplies were limited by ration cards. Dogs subsisted on commercial kibble and canned foods, sometimes of dubious quality. Suggestions for supplementing wartime diets included fish heads, breakfast cereals and incubator eggs.

As conscription took many of the men from their homes, kennel-keeping became the woman's responsibility. By clever and persistent efforts by dog lovers shows were not completely curtailed but were given over to the raising of monies for wartime charities. Defense stamps were given in lieu of trophies. Traveling on rationed gas was the biggest headache, and the 1945 AHCA Specialty was cancelled through fairness to those who could not make the trip.

In 1942, Dogs For Defense established the K9 Corps, enlisting dogs volunteered by selfless owners wishing to contribute to the effort in all possible ways. One of the few bench show champions in the K9 Corps was Ch. Kerrin Fayunga, Afghan Hound. Mrs.

Ku Mari Khyaam of Arken (Ch. Badshah of Ainsdart ex Zahera of Prides Hill, bitch, owned by Charles Wernsman. Top producing bitch of the pre-1948 era. Dam of 12 champions.

Ch. Rajah of Arken (Ch. Garrymhor Zabardast of Arken ex Ku Mari Khyaam of Arken), bred and owned by Charles Wernsman.

Weithoff's Yunga was one of few Afghans in the Corps, serving with distinction, but never returning home as he succumbed to a hero's case of jaundice shortly before his time of discharge.

The Corps soon became more selective, accepting only specific breeds of value in particular duties. The Afghan Hound was not one of the desired ones. Some suspected that the Afghan had proved temperamentally unfit for Army life, but a later bulletin declared that breeds were dropped for a variety of reasons, one being their lack of availability as the rare breeds could not be procured in large numbers if the request should arise. The few Afghans in the K9 Corps did not become national heroes but managed to get their eye-catching selves into many of the Corps' publicity shots.

Dr. Marxmiller's Afghan, Red Ryder, a mascot of a Naval Bomber Squadron, was killed aloft in action on a South Pacific mission.

The Afghan Hound played its largest war effort role through raising impressive sums of money for charity. The AHCA Match Show of 1942 was held on the grand Florsheim estate in the form of a carnival which had a huge turnout of spectators who contributed over $350 to the United Nations War Relief. Incidentally, the Match was won by Mrs. Froelich's young Zannette of Elcoza, who later took her place on the line of Afghan greats.

As an aviatrix who ferried planes from field to field for Civilian Defense, Marion Florsheim managed to use her Afghans in her job. Ch. Rana, in a pair of long polka-dot pants, acted as Master of Ceremonies at the plush Calling All Dogs charity show. A Florsheim Afghan puppy named Freckles became a raffle prize to help raise money for the Bundles for Britain War Relief effort. Marion also penned an influential column in *Kennel Review*, passing on news from all over the United States, England and Canada. In addition to ferrying the planes, she was able to campaign champions Rudiki and Rana throughout the Eastern seaboard, Canada, and inland to Indiana and the deep South. Between them the two dogs racked up impressive quantities of top all-breed wins. These travels produced widespread puppy purchases and stud uses among fanciers able to glimpse these ambassadors of the breed. Rudiki was certainly the most popular Afghan stud in the United States during the war era.

Marion Florsheim's interests and duties multiplied. She was able to retain her beloved Rudiki and a few hounds at Five Mile, but most of her puppies and other hounds went to other fanciers. In 1945 Helen Bamberger of Salt Lake City, acquired Ch. Rana, spreading his stud effect over the Western United States.

Rudiki's daughter, Ch. Rudika of Blakeen, produced a small litter sired by Ch. Rana, containing Mrs. Bamberger's Ch. Zumerrud of Five Mile, Mrs. Gudgeon's Ch. Asri-Havid of Five Mile, and Ch.

84

Yenghiz-Khan of Five Mile, campaigned some time by Mrs. Flor-sheim before he also was sold. The gorgeous Rudika moved to the home of Charles Costabile in Texas on a co-ownership and spent flying time commuting between Texas and Connecticut. Rudika was the top winning show bitch of the war years and those immediately following.

During 1943 and 1944 Afghan registrations understandably dropped to the pre-war level of 1940. But by the end of 1945, war pressure relaxed and registrations leaped from 134 in 1944 to 526 in 1946, a peak that was not passed again until 1957. Breeders frantically raced to put long-range breeding programs back on a schedule. Budding fanciers, eager for fun after the solemn war years, embraced the dog game as a delightful weekend recreation.

Ch. Ali Khyber, the first of the really extravagantly-coated, American bred Afghans, arose during the war years, making a record that was not clearly realized until after the national emergency. By the end of 1944, fanciers who avidly followed the *Gazette,* suspected that this young Rudiki son was running away with the honors in the New England states. Owned by Leah and "Macky" McConaha, the successful Khyber (pronounced, Keeber) was the family pet as was his mother, Pommel Rock Kashan.

The Pommel Rock hounds, imported property of Mrs. Lynde Selden, had quietly arrived in the United States during the late 1930s. Pommel Rock Kashan, whelped in America, had inherited some of the particularly heavy-coated genes developed through selection in England, coming down from Ch. Garrymhor Yenghiz-Khan (Ardmore Anthony ex Ch. Garrymhor Souriya). The mating of Pommel Rock Kashan to Rudiki represented a strong outcross from the Prides Hill type, unleashing a fantastic and heretofore unseen type of thick and long, stand-off-the-body coating that was to characterize Ali Khyber and many of his future get. Fortunately, Ali Khyber inherited refined chiseling of head from his sire.

Ali Khyber, born in 1941, had amassed 10 all-breed American Best In Shows by the end of 1947, cracking the record set by Ch. Amanullah of Kandahar a decade before. As a great sire Khyber founded Leah McConaha's Khanhasset Afghans and a formidable dynasty leading directly through the modern names of Majara and other offshoots noted for the great coats. The finest Prides Hill coats tended to be of a silky texture and were a slow growing proposition at their best on mature hounds, but coming down from Khyber, thick, full coats often grew at fantastic rates, creating puppy champions, but also on occasion fell off far more rapidly. In breeding combinations representing both types of coat, fantastically heavy and long coats sometimes resulted and, in less fortunate mixes, fac-

Ch. Ali Khyber, whelped 1941. Winner of 10 Bests in Show and the Top Producer of the pre-1948 era, sire of 35 champions. Owner, Leah McConaha.

```
                                                            (Afghanistan)
                                        Ch. Sirdar of Ghazni
                                                            (Afghanistan)
                        Ch. Badshah of Ainsdart
                                                            Taj Mahip of Kaf
                                        Ku Mari of Kaf
                                                            Sonee
        Ch. Rudiki of Prides Hill
                                                            Westmill Omar
                                        Ch. Kundah of Prides Hill
                                                            Asra of Ghazni
                        Ch. Shireen of Prides Hill
                                                            Ch. Badshah of Ainsdart
                                        Lakshmi of Prides Hill
                                                            Zahera of Prides Hill
Ch. Ali Khyber
                                                            Khan Babar
                                        Ardmore Anthony
                                                            Dakkas Delight
                        Nerone of Pommel Rock
                                                            Baber Khan
                                        Shiela Beg
                                                            Dakkas Delight
        Pommel Rock Kashan
                                                            Ardmore Anthony
                                        Garrymhor Yenghiz-Khan
                                                            Ch. Garrymhor Souriya
                        Hamara of Pommel Rock
                                                            Kulli-Khan
                                        Zinanna of Ghanistan
                                                            Natasha of Kuranda
```

tors for slow growth and quick dropping combined to produce very poor coated specimens indeed. But the possibilities for Afghan show coats had been greatly advanced, and Khyber became one of the most successful American sires ever recorded, with 35 champions to his credit. Ali Khyber's lovely litter sister, Ch. Maharanee Kohibaba CD, was purchased, campaigned, and obedience trained by Marion Florsheim.

In 1944 the Rudiki-Pommel Rock Kashan breeding was repeated, producing Ch. Khanhasset's Kanda. Without seeing the dog, Charles Costabile purchased Ch. Kanda as a suitable mate for his famous bitch Ch. Rudika of Blakeen. The merger of Kanda and Dika formed the Kandika names seen on many modern pedigrees. Kanda astonished Texas and the nearby Southern states by winning six Best in Shows and numerous Hound groups when he arrived at the Costabile home. In consequence Kanda became the first Afghan Hound to win the valued Quaker Oats award as the top winning dog of all breeds in the Southern states during 1946.

Back at Khanhasset young Ali Khyber was put to Ch. Shibergam of Dunrobin (Ch. Westmill Humayun of Catawba ex Hamara of Pommel Rock), a further intensification of the European heavy-coated lines. In truth, much of this coat increase was in thickness and rate of growth on body and legs. Pasterns often remained completely bare, in the ballet dancer pattern. Feet were sparsely covered in many instances, giving a long-bodied, top-heavy look at first glance.

From the Khyber ex Shibergam litter, Ch. Karach and Ch. Karan of Khanhasset were retained by Mrs. McConaha. The youngsters developed quickly and when barely into his prime Khyber was temporarily retired to give his offspring greater opportunities. Ch. Karach matured magnificently, gaining exhibition success that bordered on the phenomenal, appearing ready to batter down all records set to date. From Best of Breed at the 1946 Specialty, he also took the group at Interstate where the Specialty was held. Five months later the AHCA arranged to hold its first independent Specialty judged by Charles Wernsman. Again Karach took the honors. In the next six months Karach had been chosen Best in Show three times and had taken seven Hound groups. But Ch. Karach of Khanhasset's career was in the nature of an explosion, for less than a year after he had gained his title, when at barely two years of age, Karach was defeated by leptospirosis, immediately fatal. The fancy was stunned. Many belatedly wished they had used the young male for stud, but Karach sired exactly one litter out of Far Away Loo, which was never offered for sale, being retained by the breeder, Mrs. Marjorie Jagger (later Mrs. Lathrop). This one-of-its-kind litter was the basis of "Majara." Peculiarly enough, it was more than Karach's

Ch. Khanhasset's Kanda, dog, wh. 1944 by Ch. Rudiki of Prides Hill ex Pommel Rock Kashan, multiple Best in Show winner, owned by Charles Costabile.

Ch. Karan (bitch) and Ch. Karach (dog) of Khanhasset, littermates and both multiple BIS winners. Karan was dam of 6 champions. By Ch. Ali Khyber ex Ch. Shibergam of Dunrobin. Owned by Leah McConaha.

personal quality that brought Mrs. Lathrop to him; it was the fact that she owned Karach's dam's sister, Ch. Dunrobin Daiquiri, but had been unable to get any issue from her when she was bred to Ch. Ali Khyber and other studs. Thwarted in obtaining the desired Daiquiri-Ali Khyber pups, Mrs. Lathrop bred Far Away Loo to Khyber's son from a similar breeding. The first Majara litter became the sole existing link from "Karach" to the future.

Leah McConaha was persuaded to bring out her great Ali Khyber again, as well as Karach's look-alike sister, Ch. Karan of Khanhasset. The now aging Khyber took control of the Eastern rings and won three of his total BIS when brought out of retirement. But he grew tired and soon left the banner to his daughter Karan who was to be reckoned with regardless of sex. She followed her brother's old footsteps by winning the Independent Specialty in 1948 under judge Ernie Ferguson who commented on her magnificent head and type. During the year she won nine Hound groups and Best in Show at Albany.

In 1948, the Afghan Hound Club of America decided to hold two Specialties, a Fall Show in conjunction with the Interstate All-Breed Club in September, and the Independent Specialty to follow in the Spring. The Fall show was somewhat experimental and was not repeated after the first try. At the extra Fall Specialty, with Leah McConaha as judge, young Ch. Majara Mahabat, from the lone Karach-sired litter, took the ultimate honors, which he repeated at the following Independent Specialty under a split judging assignment. Due to a tie vote in the judges' selection, Mr. McConaha judged the class dogs and Best in Show while Mrs. Boger did class bitches and Best of Winners.

We have come upon 1948 too soon and must back up a bit. At the end of WWII fighting broke out anew in the Afghan camps over revision of the Standard. Breed complaints had an age-old sound. In one area critics complained of all the "weedy little Afghans in the rings that couldn't catch a rabbit much less a deer." Elsewhere the complaint was that winning Afghans were much too large and distressingly coarse in head. Poor temperament was singled out as some specimens were dangerously headstrong while others were impossibly shy. Songs of judges' color prejudice against brindles and dark colors were sung, with a second chorus against the great variety of coat types and textures permitted on winners. The words "Afghan type" were becoming meaningless, it was moaned. A new and more highly detailed standard was seen by many to be the solution for all these sundry ills in the breed. Others politely suggested that a modicum of common sense, a little less kennel blindness and more attention to the current standard by judges and breeders might do as much good as a re-written standard. Tempers were rising again.

One thoroughly disgruntled fancier began to promote an International Afghan Hound Council to set up one standard for the United States, Europe and parts of Asia. This thought rang well with those impatient with cautious American efforts at serious revisions, and representatives from other countries gave the plan some serious consideration. In February of 1946 the *Gazette* announced that the group was meeting in New York City to write a standard "to emphasize the 'mountain type' of Afghan, with long slender skull, body balance and running gear to be stressed. This type of Afghan carries coat well down over the legs and is more elegant in profile . . ."

This, of course, was wild oversimplification of the existing problems embodying the inherent conflict between the early Bell-Murray type with elegant profiles and long slender skulls as opposed to the balanced, sturdier, long-coated Ghazni types. The embryo International Group was immediately deadlocked in stubborn disagreement over what actually constituted the desired "mountain type." The International Afghan Hound Council stuck to its task for a few months, receiving a fair press and some highly unsympathetic rebukes from the AHCA correspondents in the *Gazette*. As the Council members continued to describe the mountain type in terms of their own most admired local types, the International concept came to a quick natural demise.

In 1946 the revised English Standard was adopted by the British Kennel Club and the Afghan Hound Association. This standard was not drastically different from its predecessor and the changeover was easily accomplished. Most of Europe adopted the British Standard shortly thereafter.

Simultaneously, but independently, in America the latest Standard Committee, with Mrs. Porter's ancient trial standard in hand and many suggestions to consider, drafted changes and additions. Requests, even pleadings, were sent to the membership for more opinions on what points needed clarification or addition. The committee was made up of thoughtful breeders of long years in Afghans and many more years in other breeds. Some of the guiding lights, in addition to Mrs. Porter, were Charles Wernsman of Arken, Muriel Boger of Doreborn, and Eve Miner of Laineux, working industriously to clarify and complete a new statement. The new standard was completed in 1947, but hashed over gently until the following Spring meeting where the final vote was taken and the revised Standard overwhelmingly accepted. On September 14, 1948, the Board of Directors of the American Kennel Club approved the current Standard.

5

The Rise of the American Afghan Hound (1949-1969)

"So in just a few short years, the transition is complete from a wild dog of prey racing across distant plains under the banner of savage hillmen. He has now become a prancing exhibitionist at the nation's greatest shows, flaunting his beauty before the judges and winning his share of glory." Braden Finch (*Kennel Review* ad, June, 1949).

1948 brought a revised standard and a noticeable transition into the era of modern Afghan Hounds. The long-revered names of Prides Hill, Oakvardon, Five Mile, Arken and Khanhasset were over the top and gradually sliding back on the pedigrees. Rudiki at 10 years old died in 1947 of a broken heart, it was said, at being unable to accompany his beloved Marion Florsheim to Europe. Ali Khyber was retired and his younger brother Kanda, in Texas, broke off his leash and darted across a street into the path of a car, sustaining a crushed shoulder that sent him out to stud pastures. Ch. Rana, long retired, made his final home in California with Margaret Hawkins, siring a few twilight litters at the age of 11. In the New Mexico sunshine, Amanullah lived out a full 17 years. Most of the pioneer importers and breeders had given up their hounds, passed on, or traded their exhibitor's passes for judging licenses.

Barberryhill Dolly saw her 15th birthday in the Grandeur Kennel of Sunny Shay. Two very fine bitches aged imperceptibly during the decade, continuing to challenge the youngsters on special occasions.

Int. Ch. Felt's Thief of Bagdad (Ch. Sinbad the Sailor ex Kara She-Ba), dog, multiple BIS winner, owned by Kay Finch.

Ch. Black Ryn of Donde (Zenophon of Elcoza ex Ch. Laineux Dolly Deluxe) bitch, owned by Betsy Prior.

In 1949, the nearly 10 year old Ch. Rudika of Blakeen was entered at Fort Worth, Texas, as a special treat for some of her human friends visiting from the East. A bitch of permanent and undimmed beauty, Charles Costabile's Dika won Best in Show before many misty-eyed spectators. Ch. Maharanee Kohibaba, sister of Ali Khyber, spent her Fall years with Amelia White in Santa Fe, teaching the youngsters a lesson by topping a New Mexico show the same year. But these proud ladies were well-preserved remnants of a fast fading era.

In 1948 registrations had settled back from the record high of 1946 into a period of quiescence, not to surge again until 1956. But the breed held its position, hovering around the 45th spot in total registration, rising and falling with dogs in general. As previously stressed, the Afghan Hound was decidedly an "exhibitor's breed" with an inordinately large number of entries in competition primarily in the coastal areas of California and New England. Point requirements were at minimums elsewhere. The New York area point schedule for 1948 required an entry of five dogs for three points, 10 dogs for four, and 15 hounds (dogs or bitches) for the maximum five points. California requirements in 1949 were eight males for three points, 10 for four points, and 13 dogs for five. Competition was keen across the continent, but by the early 1950s, the balance of heavy entries leaned from the East to the fast-growing West.

In 1947 the West Coast Afghan Hound Club had been formed with Mel Strann as President and Betsy Prior as Secretary. Membership leaped from 14 to 40 within the year. New impetus came to the West with the influx of the Priors and other fanciers from the East. The Club fostered organized enthusiasm for the hounds, advancing their popularity with breathtakingly brilliant bazaar wrappings and silken pillows surrounding tribes of exotic multi-hued hounds elegantly draped along show benches, catching the eye of many fanciers-to-be. June of 1948 found the young West Coast club sponsoring the Harbor Cities Kennel Club entry to the tune of 62 Afghan exhibits, easily winning first place for their striking bench decor.

By 1949, the American Kennel Club requested that the name be changed to the Afghan Hound Club of California.

The Afghans which won the most in the Golden State in 1948 were two group-winning bitches. Previous to the arrival of the Priors with their gorgeous coated black and tan Ch. Black Ryn of Donde, a lovely black-masked red bitch named Ch. Buzineh Tabidan of Jurahn had been holding the males in their places. Soon, ignoring the "boys," the two contrastingly colored bitches fought it out until touched by the challenge of young Felt's Thief of Bagdad, owned

Ch. Karli Ben Ghazi (Ch. Five Mile Punjab Ben Ghazi ex Trina Kush of Hazarat), red dog, Best in Show winner and sire of 14 champions, owned by Ruth Tongren.

Ch. Yusseff, C.D. right above (Ch. Tufan of Ainsdart ex Ch. Shabra), sire of 10 champions, and his daughter, Ch. Zannette of Elcoza, multiple Best in Show winner, owned by Mrs. Lauer Froelich.

by a comparative newcomer to the breed, one Katherine Finch, well known in Yorkshire Terrier circles and as a ceramicist of note.

Not quite all the motion was from East to West, however. At the Los Angeles Kennel Club's 1948 show, a young lady held her pet hound by a length of clothesline rope as she embarrassedly glanced at the shimmering drape-coated Afghans on fancy leads led by highly-assured owners. Unable to escape from the benched showgrounds, she reluctantly entered the show ring with Punk and was both grateful and surprised to receive a blue ribbon. Soon the anxious steward pushed the pair back into the ring for Winners. That hound, not in the least embarrassed or flustered, "fit and strong without too many ruffles," was chosen Best of Winners for a five pointer under the noted judge, Dr. Wm. Ivens, Jr. The dog, later formally known as Ch. Five Miles Punjab Ben Ghazi, and his owner, Ruth Tongren, soon moved to the East Coast to found the famous Ben Ghazi Afghans. Punk became noted as a sire of champions including the famous Best in Show stud, twice winner of the Parent Club Specialty, Ch. Karli Ben Ghazi.

From 1948 onward, fanciers became breeders at the drop of a blue ribbon. Numerous names flash and go in the rings. Much as we would like to make mention of all these fine hounds, pay homage to their industrious owners and proud breeders, it would take several large volumes. Concentration on the development of the top winners and most prolific producers of champions is of the greatest value to the largest number of readers. Most well-bred Afghans of modern times are related to these great foundation sires.

"Elcoza," a kennel of great interest, owned by Mrs. Lauer Froelich, was born of unexpected wartime developments. Attracted to the breed, Mrs. Froelich had arranged to purchase a bitch from the English kennel of Dr. Betsy Porter on a forthcoming trip to Europe, but, the year was 1939 and with bomb scares above Britain, Mrs. Froelich thought twice and turned West to California and New Mexico instead. When visiting pioneer breeder, Margaret Nison, Mrs. Froelich was quickly attracted to young Yusseff, a nearly white son of Ch. Tufan of Ainsdart ex Ch. Shabra, and took the handsome male back to Pennsylvania with her. On their arrival in the East, she discovered that Dr. Porter, unaware of the interim travels and frightened for the safety of her beloved hounds, had already shipped, not only a bitch, Rani, but also her litter brother, Sardar Khan el Kabul, to America via the "Somaria." Fortunately, the hounds arrived safely, but the ocean liner was sunk on the return trip.

Mrs. Froelich was more than a little surprised to find that the exquisite Rani el Kabul and her large raw-boned brother were brindles, very heavily coated with high black masks. The coloration was unfamiliar to her and a great contrast to the solid pale cream Yusseff. The imported pair were of strong Sirdar of Ghazni breeding, with the brindle coming from their exceedingly impressive full-coated grandsire, Ch. Westmill Tamasar. Automatically finding herself "in Afghans," Mrs. Froelich adopted the affix of the family ranch, "Elcoza."

Yusseff and Sardar became champions in 1941. The charming brindle bitch, Rani, was mated to Yusseff, producing five champions including Ch. Zannette of Elcoza, who came into prominence as winner of the first Parent Club match on the fabulous Florsheim estate. Zannette joined the select roster of Best in Show bitches twice in 1946 and was topping the hound groups well into 1948. Said Mrs. Froelich, "Zannette was not the very best Afghan ever bred, but she was seldom denied placings for she came into the ring with a 'come hither look' and no judge could leave her unnoticed." This outgoing charm and spirit was a legacy from the born showman, Tufan of Ainsdart.

Mrs. Froelich, with Zannette and Yusseff, moved "Elcoza" to Indiana, establishing the first Afghan kennel in that sector of America. Ch. Sardar Khan el Kabul remained in Pennsylvania with Elcoza's former kennel manager, Mr. Gruel, joining the ranks of great sires in the breed through his famous breeding with Flo Flo of Ghazni, resulting in nine champions, several being very handsome brindles.

In the quiet Indiana years, Ch. Yusseff added C.D. to his name and, with his 10 champion offspring, became a valuable sire for other breeders as well as for Elcoza. Between campaigns, the sprightly Zannette was bred to Ch. Rudiki of Prides Hill, and also to his son, Ch. Ali Khyber, becoming the dam of four champions and other Elcoza offspring whose names pepper modern pedigrees.

Majara hounds invaded the breed through the lone litter sired by Ch. Karach of Khanhasset. The pedigree of Ch. Majara Mihrab tied into that of Ali Khyber, illustrating the relatively uncomplicated blending of Shaw McKean's imports with the later imported influences of the Pommel Rock hounds, plus a pinch of salt from Elcoza. Basic intensification of long muzzles, and great coat improvement met with marked success.

The fortunate Karach ex Far Away Loo litter produced Champions Majara: Mota Raja, Mahmoud, NurMahal, Mustapha, Mihri, and Mahabat. The last three perpetuated the growing tradition of producing BIS offspring. Pups from these hounds furnished im-

Ch. Majara Mahabat (Ch. Karach of Khanhasset ex Far Away Loo), multiple BIS winner and sire of 14 champions, owned by Marjorie A. Lathrop.

petus for other Eastern kennels. Mahabat's daughter, Ch. Lala Rookh of Estioc, owned by Patricia Leary, became the third bitch in history to top the Parent Club Specialty in 1956. In 1948 and again in 1949 Ch. Majara Mahabat, known affectionately as "Junior Bug," won the ultimate Specialty honors. It is said that when Mrs. Lathrop overheard that Mahabat's entry in the 1950 Specialty was frightening off the other Specials, she unselfishly withdrew his entry to encourage the participation of other champions. Best of Breed was taken by the imported Ch. Turkuman Nissim's Laurel, but the 14 months bitch Ch. Majara Mirza went BOS, and a black-and-tan Mahabat daughter, barely out of the puppy class, claimed the Winners Bitch trophy.

Majara followed a careful pattern of breeding by putting the black-and-tan Karach daughter, Ch. Majara Mihri, to Zombie of Dunrobin (litter brother of Ch. Shibergam of Dunrobin). The experiment paid off richly, giving rise to the remarkable Ch. Majara Mirza, only Afghan bitch to ever win the coveted Quaker Oats Award (Eastern division). During 1951, in the almost unbelievable short span of 10 months, Mirza took on the best all-breed competition the country had to offer, winning three BIS, one American-Bred BIS, and many hound groups. History proves her to be the last of the great show-winning bitches until the sex hoodoo was broken in 1964 by Ch. Pandora of Stormhill. Mirza, bred to her famous kennelmate, Ch. Majara Mihrab, produced four American champions and a bitch

Ch. Majara Mihrab (Ch. Majara Mahabat ex Zaritza of Elcoza), multiple BIS winner and sire of 15 champions, bred and owned by Marjorie A. Lathrop.

Ch. Majara Menelek (Ch. Majara Mahabat ex Ch. Karan of Khanhasset), BIS winner and sire of 15 champions, owned by Marjorie A. Lathrop.

Ch. Majara Mirza (Zombie of Dunrobin ex Ch. Majara Mihri), bitch, multiple BIS winner, owned by Marjorie A. Lathrop.

Ch. Hassen-Ben of Moornistan (Ch. Zaamarakuri of Ghazni ex Ch. Maymum of Moornistan), multiple BIS winner and sire of 24 champions, bred and oiwned by Dr. William Moore III.

sent to Spain that not only became a Spanish champion but the first bitch of any breed to win a Spanish All-Breed BIS.

Majara Mihrab, a fine show dog, was an even better stud, producing 17 champions by just seven bitches. In 1953 his name was added to the roster of breed winners at the Specialty. He also earned three all-breed BIS's and 18 group firsts. His pups, Chs. Moornistan Shazenan, Shahriar, and Maymun, by the imported bitch, Djadji vom Falkenwalde, and owned by Dr. William Moore, established a famous strain leading to the spectacular Ch. Hassen Ben of Moornistan.

In 1953 Mahabat was mated with his famous aunt, Ch. Karan of Khanhasset, to sire the fantastically coated, black-masked red Ch. Majara Menelek ("Minky"). From such a background, Minky's prepotence was a foregone conclusion and he took his place as a producer with 15 champions from six dams to lead Majara into the 1960s. The closely bred Majara hounds bore marked similarity in type, usually black-masked red, with some notable black-and-tans. Photos illustrate the profuse coating and fine carriage with other type marks of the kennel.

Development of the most successful Western kennel, "Crown Crest," is considerably more complicated. The story unfolds late in 1947 with Braden Finch's affectionate silver anniversary gift to his wife, Katherine, a "silver-blue" Afghan Hound named Felt's Thief of Bagdad. While not the first Afghan Hound at Crown Crest, the Thief, better known as "Thumper," was the beginning of the "great ones" and a continuing subtle influence on succeeding generations. "Thumper," a product of Western breeding, contained rare pedigree effects of the Peters' Afghanistan imports, Tazi of Beg Tute and Saki of Paghman, intermixed with McKean's Prides Hill hounds. The Thief's grandsire, Ch. Sahib of Prides Hill, was a handsome brindle litter brother of the great Rudiki owned by Dr. Frank Porter Miller, famous race horse owner and all-breed dog judge. A trace of the practically extinct Kushan breeding of Ch. Barberryhill Phillip to Samson's English import, Jalalabad Kara, is also involved. This pedigree, while not overwhelming in either size or coat, excels in graceful dignified elegance, refinement and Eastern head type, in a wide array of the most fascinating tints and shadings to be found. Thumper's dam, Kara-She-Ba, was described as being pure white with a jet black nose and eyes. The grand Thumper is fondly recalled for his unforgettable, but unmatchable, shade of muted blue-gray.

The Thief of Bagdad was bred by Joe Felt who dearly loved exotic elegances of color and character. He also preserved rare traces of the precious Indian import, Fatima, in her breeding to Ch. Tufan of

Ch. Felt's Allah Baba (Int. Ch. Felt's Thief of Bagdad ex Felt's Fatima), Ch. Taejon of Crown Crest (Ch. Elcoza's Ponder ex Ch. Winomana of Rreks), Int. Ch. Jublee Julian of Crown Crest (Ch. Felt's Thief of Bagdad ex Ch. Five Mile's Banu of Rebel Hill), owned by Kay Finch.

Ainsdart, through Felt's Fatima, who, when bred to Thumper produced a white-gold hound of unusual brilliance and majesty, Ch. Felt's Allah Baba. Both Thumper and Allah Baba enjoyed sparkling maturity under the guidance of Kay Finch, but were piloted by professional handlers Elsworth Gamble or Athos Nilson in the early days of their careers. Kay's breath nearly stopped on a wild afternoon when Thumper slipped his lead in group competition, dancing gaily around the ring while his handler frantically attempted to retrieve him. Despite the fact that he won the group, Kay vowed afterward to handle her own dogs. She developed an amazing rapport with both clay and fleshly Afghans which magically responded to each flick of her talented finger muscles.

Unfortunately for the preservation of these rare imported influences, the Felt dogs were rarely used for stud. Thumper sired seven champions with his daughters becoming especially influential on future pedigrees. Of Allah Baba's four champion offspring, Arnold Hartman's fine Ch. Rajah of Namtrah, a big red dog which produced delicately shaded brindles, is probably the best known son.

Late in 1948 the Thief of Bagdad took Crown Crest into the Best in Show rings at Pasadena, portending a future to come. Thief was the first Afghan in California since the reign of Oakvardon to stand alone before the top award marker.

Crown Crest hounds gained by the breeding of Thumper to Big Carmelita, sister of Ch. Little Carmelita, owned by Dr. Frank Porter Miller and sired by Ch. Sahib of Prides Hill ex Fatima's Queen of Sheba. Of the produced litter, Ch. Egypt's Echo and Ch. Egypt's Eudora, both of Crown Crest, play stellar roles in subsequent history. Eudora, a dark red brindle bitch, produced well for both Crown Crest and for her longtime owner John Buchanan. Echo, iridescent silver-blue like her father, lived out her days at Crown Crest. Kay and Braden Finch were impressed by Echo's very special quality and, in 1951, set off across country to find a similarly special stud for her.

On May 12, 1950, in Decatur, Illinois, Mrs. Leo Conroy attended the birth of a litter of silvers with black trims with fascinating possibilities. While on tour of the East, at the suggestion of Cissy Froelich, who had bred the sire of the litter, Kay and Braden paused to look at the yearlings. The couple from California had a fair idea of what they were looking for and were instantly struck by one regal silver-white, black-masked male pup with a remarkable flair and bearing. After striking a most remarkable bargain, young Taejon became Taejon of Crown Crest and was transported to the West Coast by his new owners.

Taejon, far better known as the great "Johnnie," hit California

Ch. Taejon of Crown Crest, dog (sitting up), owned by Kay Finch, multiple BIS winner and sire of 30 champions, and Ch. Crown Crest Taejblu Minx (Ch. Taejon of Crown Crest ex Ch. Egypt's Echo of Crown Crest), bitch, owned by Braden Finch.

```
                                                     Ch. Sirdar of Ghazni
                                    Ch. Tufan of Ainsdart
                                                     Ku Mari of Kaf
                     Ch. Yusseff, C.D.
                                                     Ch. Badshah of Ainsdart
                                    Shabra
                                                     Zahera of Prides Hill
       Ch. Elcoza's Ponder
                                                     Ch. Ali Khyber
                                    Ali Zhyber of Elcoza
                                                     Ch. Zannette of Elcoza
                     Kenya of Westgham
                                                     Ch. Yusseff, C.D.
                                    Laineux Coming Event
                                                     Natasha of Allsworth
Ch. Taejon of Crown Crest
                                                     Ch. Badshah of Ainsdart
                                    Ch. Rudiki of Prides Hill
                                                     Ch. Shireen of Prides Hill
                     Ch. Mo-Qua-Hee's Remus
                                                     Lakhsman of Enriallic
                                    Mo-Qua-Hee's Fantasy
                                                     Sitana of Prides Hill
       Ch. Winomana of Rreks
                                                     Ch. Tufan of Ainsdart
                                    Ch. Yusseff, C.D.
                                                     Shabra
                     Zuleika of Elcoza
                                                     Rama el Kabul
                                    Rani el Kabul
                                                     Mem Sahib el Kabul
```

102

with shock impact. He won the breed under Dr. Frank Porter Miller and went on to BIS at Riverside Kennel Club when barely 17 months old. By his second birthday he topped groups with regularity, developing his famous long, bright-silver silken coat trademark, matched only by his sparkling air of superiority. While not a particularly large Afghan, he "looked big," seeming to tower over his competitors. "Johnnie" ruled the Western rings for the next four years, three spent without a defeat in the breed. When he retired in 1955 to make way for younger Crown Crest hounds, he had shattered all previous Afghan show records, standing high with 19 all-breed BIS and four Specialty wins, including the 1954 AHCA Specialty judged by Chris Shuttleworth. As the judges' choice for Best Hound at the prestigious Westminster show in 1954 and 1955, a gorgeous head study of him appeared in *Life* magazine. Always a great favorite with the gallery, Taejon and Kay Finch were voted as one of the ten best Dog-Handler Teams of the past 25 years by the New York World Telegram. There were ringside critics who preferred to see breed specimens with greater "reserve and aloofness" in the rings, but the flamboyant Taejon was never short on dignity. He had that indefinable something, made up in part by his glamorous, shimmering coat, his striking gait, coloration, and unshakable inner confidence, and bolstered greatly by his owner-handler. Taejon of Crown Crest was a show dog of the first order, responsible for a decided upsurge in the breed's popularity and a heavy demand for the silver Afghan with the flashing black trim. In pedigree, Johnnie was the result of various combinations of Ch. Yusseff with different bitches. He was used as stud for the "Thief" daughters, Egypt's Eudora and Egypt's Echo. The multi-hued Echo litter ran from black to

Ch. Stormhill Silver Dream (Ch. Taejon of Crown Crest ex Ch. Khanorissa of Aldachar), sire of 11 champions, owned by Virginia Withington.

Ch. Desert Chieftain of Mikai, C.D. (Ch. Taejon of Crown Crest ex Kismi Khan of Crown Crest), Best in Show winner, and sire of 11 champions, with owner Virginia Mika.

103

the white of Ch. Taejanne of Crown Crest, foundation bitch for Hobart Stephenson's Patrician Afghans. Braden Finch claimed Ch. Crown Crest Taejblu Minx as his own personal pet, enjoying her coloration and character which was so like the blues behind her. The black-masked silver daughter, Ch. Crown Crest TaeJoan, marked like her sire, carried on the Crown Crest breeding program.

Johnnie produced thirty champions from the many bitches put to him. His best known sons of the era, famous for similar dark masks, silken silver coats, and free striding gaits, were Ch. Desert Chieftain of Mikai, owned by Virginia Mika, and Ch. Stormhill Silver Dream, foundation stud for Bill and Virginia Withington. Johnnie furnished valuable studs for other breeders, but at Crown Crest his daughters carried on for him.

In 1954 Kay Finch imported the German, Belgian and Dutch Ch. Ophaal from the Von de Orange Menage Kennels of Eta Pauptit, famous for show winning and racing Afghans and Salukis. The V.D.O.M. kennel adhered to a strict breeding program, with the greatly admired Sirdar of Ghazni as model. The only foreigner at V.D.O.M. was the silver-colored Chota, imported directly from the East, but who resembled the Sirdar type and did not disturb the established balance. With a firm picture of a close-coupled, working mountain hound in mind, Eta Pauptit bred for great structural strength and prominence of brisket with strong, upright head carriage in a highly maneuverable frame. Her hounds exhibited length of stride and shoulder angulation rarely found to such a marked degree in America. While there was very little emphasis on coat at V.D.O.M., most of the males came by excellent long, thick fur as a natural heritage from Sirdar.

In spite of being a BIS winner, Ophaal's fame was not to come from show records but, as with so many of the notable imports, as a remarkable prepotent stud. As the private stud of Crown Crest, unavailable to the public, Ophaal produced 27 champions from just five litters, a remarkable record. Bred to Ch. Crown Crest TaeJoan twice, 14 champions resulted from the now famous "gem" and "K" litters. By the late 1950s the produce of these two litters filled a section of Who's Who in Afghans, as litter brothers, Zardonx, Rubi and Topaz, all appear simultaneously in the lists of the top ten Afghans for 1957 and 1958. A member of the "gem" litter, named for Zodiac jewels, Zardonx made his name as winner and sire at Crown Crest. Rubi, when owned by Ruth Tongren, combined well with Ben Ghazi daughters. Topaz, heartbroken at the death of his beloved owner Al Hewitt in a plane crash, found solace and a permanent home as the stud of Gordon Miller's "High Life" hounds in Northern California.

Am., Can. and Mex. Ch. Crown Crest Zardonx (Ch. Ophaal of Crown Crest ex Ch. Crown Crest Tae-Joan), multiple BIS winner and sire of 15 champions, owned by Kay Finch.

Am., Ger., Belg. and Dutch Ch. Ophaal of Crown Crest (Int. Ch. Nereus van de Oranje Manege ex Pythia van de Oranje Manege), Best in Show winner and sire of 27 champions, owned by Kay Finch.

By 1958 Ch. Crown Crest Kabul of the "K" litter owned by Mary Stephenson, who had been seriously injured in an automobile accident during the year, was added to the list of the Top Ten. Sentiment clouded the eyes of many who watched Kabby stride to BIS at Beverly-Riviera, courageously handled by Mary who had finally overcome multiple leg injuries that had confined her to a wheelchair for many months.

As Charles Costabile watched Zardonx win the 1957 AHCA Specialty in New York, he was immediately convinced that mating

Ch. Crown Crest Mr. Universe (Ch. Ophaal of Crown Crest ex Ch. Hope), winner of 28 Bests in Show and sire of 31 champions, bred and owned by C. Costabile and Kay Finch.

his lovely Taejon-daughter, Ch. Hope, to Ophaal would produce exceptional quality. After lengthy discussion with Kay Finch, who was highly appreciative of Hope's many virtues, but preferred not to have her red imported dog at public stud, a co-breeding arrangement was worked out. As part of the contract, Ch. Hope went to Crown Crest. The Ophaal-sired litter was born in June of that year with a lopsided whelping of nine females and one male. Five of the bitches became titled, but the lone male, elected by Kay as t*he* bearer of greatness almost from birth, outdistanced them all, under the joint co-ownership of Finch and Costabile. This black masked golden male, Ch. Crown Crest Mr. Universe, appropriately named due to his arrival into the world with the Miss Universe pageant in progress on television, was familiarly known to all as "Mr. U."

By 1959 the meteoric rise of Mr. U marked him as the Afghan Hound to be reckoned with, and he went on to amass a record-breaking score of 28 all-breed Bests in Show, 96 Hound Group firsts, four independent Specialties, and top awards in Canada. He was handled throughout by Mrs. Finch, and the team of Kay and Mr. U clicked as had the teaming with Taejon in years past, bringing the Gaines Award for Best Owner/Handler in 1960.

The Florida circuit was enlived in 1961 by competition between the two fabulous breeder-owner-handler personalities, Kay with Mr.

U and Sunny Shay with Ch. Shirkhan of Grandeur. By the final day of the circuit, each pair had taken six Bests of Breed and three Hound Group firsts. Kay recalls Percy Roberts doing the breed judging in a large ring containing two bright patches of sunlight. As Mrs. Finch "happened" to stop Mr. U where the sun would best spotlight his proud bearing and glimmering gold coat she looked around for Sunny, and there she was—with the magnificent Shirkhan posed directly in the other sunlit spot. They shared a good laugh over it. On that day the younger Mr. U won out, culminating the day for Afghanites by winning the BIS.

With 31 American champions to his stud credit, Mr. U became the top ranking stud at Crown Crest until his death in 1968. Always an inspired showman, with glistening silken tawny coat, and firm outstriding front quarters, Mr. U was definitely reminiscent of his grandsire, Taejon, thereby giving many observers a tighter concept of "Crown Crest type" than was actually the case. Over two decades, from the late '40s through the '60s, via Thief, Taejon, Ophaal and his sons, Crown Crest was responsible for over 100 Afghan Hound champions, most of which took their pedestals as foundations or improvers of stock for owners throughout this country and in England.

In America, and to a lesser degree in Britain, the pedigree impact of Crown Crest cannot be overstated, although it became generally enmeshed with local or other acquired lines in a few short generations. Among the myriad Crown Crest spin-offs, one of the purest was Leo Goodman's Belden Kennel, based pretty exclusively on the matings of his Ch. C.C. Vegas Ghamblr of Belden (Ch. Crown Crest Khanazad ex Ch. Crown Crest Safari Sand-Star) to his Ch. Crown Crest Sancy (Ch. Crown Crest Dhi-Mond ex Ch. Hope) plus the later incorporation of Ghamblr's own dam, Sand-Star. Primarily, from the five different matings to the lovely Sancy, Ghamblr has sired 23 champions.

"Dahnwood" (Forrest Hansen and Don McElvain) noticeably intensified existing Crown Crest influences in the Northwest with their winning studs, Ch. Crown Crest Mr. California (Ch. Crown Crest Mr. Universe ex Ch. Crown Crest Eve Queen) and Ch. Crown Crest Zardani (Ch. Crown Crest Zardonx ex Mikai Tai Temple Doll). Zardani is probably best known as the sire of the highly impressive Ch. Dahnwood Gabriel that, in 1968, topped the National Specialty and won the Quaker Oats Award as Top Hound in the United States under the ownership of Judy and Herman Fellton in Georgia.

Various combinations of Crown Crest with other lines will become evident as this chapter continues, it being a rare modern pedigree that does not contain some of these threads.

107

Ch. Shirkhan of Grandeur, multiple BIS winner (including Westminster 1957) and sire of 43 champions, owned by Sunny Shay and Barbara Caminez.

```
                                                         Burma Kush el Myia
                                         Nehru of Ku
                                                         Nidja of Chaman
                        Ch. Taj Akbaruu of Grandeur
                                                         Chad of Prides Hill
                                         Doreborn's Karya
                                                         Amita of Prides Hill
        Ch. Blue Boy of Grandeur
                                                         Ch. Rudiki of Prides Hill
                                         Ch. Ali Khyber
                                                         Pommel Rock Kashan
                        Ch. Khanhasset Ginger of Grandeur
                                                         Shaitan Bedar
                                         Far Away Loo
                                                         Cleopatra
Ch. Shirkhan of Grandeur
                                                         Amanullah
                                         Ch. Umberto
                                                         Shiela Beg
                        Ch. Oakvardon Charon
                                                         Ch. Garrymhor Kishtwar
                                         Sita of Oakvardon
                                                         Morgiana of Kandahar
        Mahdi of Grandeur
                                                         Westmill Razuran
                                         Oakvardon Banneju
                                                         Ch. Westmill Natanz
                        Adera
                                                         Ch. Fatima's Son Tufan Khan
                                         Oakvardon Dera
                                                         Ch. Barberryhill Dolly
```

Ch. Shirkhan of Grandeur, born in August 1954, became one of this country's most famous and beloved hounds. Holder of the record number of BIS's for an Afghan between the times of Taejon and Mr. Universe, Shirkhan gave the breed one of its most unforgettable thrills when he was signaled by judge Bea Godsol to the supreme award at the world-famous Westminster show at Madison Square Garden in 1957. This magnificent pewter-gray dog became the third Afghan in history to take the Quaker Oats award, winning the Eastern division in both 1958 and 1959. As late as 1963, marked with a graying muzzle but with a youthful step, the nine year old Shirkhan forsook retirement to again top the breed at Westminster. Owned by the colorful Sunny Shay, Shirkhan was a product of Grandeur breedings, a name long established in Afghan Hounds.

In 1947 Sunny Shay and Sol Malkin jointly imported the handsome black Ch. Turkuman Nissim's Laurel from Juliette de Bairacli-Levy in England, a transaction that put Grandeur in the limelight. The exotic black hound, with a marvelously effortless gait, won Best in Show at Cincinnati in 1950, handled by Jerry Rigden. As a valuable imported stud force, he produced from various bitches many champions with notable fine hound type and interesting colors, but does not appear on the written pedigree of the great Shirkhan. Never one to follow fad or fashion in the breed, Grandeur

Ch. Blue Boy of Grandeur (Ch. Taj Akburuu of Grandeur ex Ch. Khanhasset Ginger of Grandeur), sire of Ch. Shirkhan of Grandeur, owned by Sunny Shay.

109

Ch. Tamerlane II (Ch. Oakvardon Charon ex Ch. Riverside Tuck of Pocono), dog, multiple BIS winner, owned by Mrs. George Skinner.

successfully preserved, enhanced and united some of the exotic hound assets of the very earliest American imports. Grandeur prided itself on a remarkable array of hound colors from Turkuman Black through Shirkhan Gray to the palest creams and bi-colors.

Shirkhan's pedigree illustrates a fascinating conservation of nearly extinct imports, seen on few other contemporary pedigrees. Behind his dam, Mahdi, is the great Ch. Umberto, preserved through Dr. Iven's handsome black-masked light-red Ch. Oakvardon Charon who also sired Dr. Iven's own Ch. Tamerlane II. The immigrant names of Ch. Garrymhor Kishtwar as well as Westmill Razuran and Ch. Westmill Natanz are seen as is offspring from the Tufan and Fatima merger; all in addition to the Prides Hill basics and Khanhasset influences, in a remarkable blending-pot of Afghan history. A very popular stud dog, famed for his gait, character and chiseled muzzle, Shirkhan was used in various outcrosses, spreading his genes effectively across the nation. The then unequalled total of 43 champions was sired by Shirkhan from the various bitches put to him.

In January of 1958, Sunny flew to California with Shirkhan for the Northern California Afghan Hound Specialty, held in conjunction with the Golden Gate Kennel Club benched all-breed show. Shirkhan gained another BOB, a Group first, and the opportunity to sire two California litters of marked future pedigree importance.

110

Hobart (Bud) Stephenson, Jr. took advantage of the visit to breed his exquisite Ch. Crown Crest Taejhanne (Tae-Joan's litter sister) to Shirkham, to obtain the well-known "blue" stud, Ch. Patrician Sherwood.

During Sunny's stay, Lois Boardman was able to mate Genii al Paraa (granddaughter of both Ch. Rana of Chaman of Royal Irish and Ch. Felt's Allah Baba) directly to Shirkhan. This breeding became the cornerstone of "Akaba" and its fantastic rise to eminence through the immediate production of the magnificent and sound-moving smoky brindle, Ch. Akaba's Top Brass, plus his lovely black-and-tan brindle-pointed sister, Ch. Akaba's Know It All. The famed Brassy became the proud sire of 25 champions. In 1962, Lois took him back to the AHCA Specialty, where he topped the huge breed entry on Sunday, and further distinguished himself by winning the BOB and Hound Group at Westminster the following day.

In 1961, Lois Boardman decided to intensify her strain by sending Akaba's Gigi in White back to be bred to Shirkhan. Gigi was a striking daughter of the very handsome all-cream Abez (littermate to Ch. Hope and Ch. Stormhill Silver Dream). An exceptionally fine, but never exhibited (due to superficial injury) young male named Akaba's Royal Blue emerged from the breeding. As a strong

Ch. Akaba's Top Brass (Ch. Shirkhan of Grandeur ex Genii al Peraa), brindle dog, multiple BIS winner and sire of 26 champions, bred and owned by Lois Boardman.

Two veterans. On the left, Ch. Akaba's Royal Flush (Akaba's Royal Blue ex Ch. Akaba's Brass Bangle), at about 8½ years old. Sire of 28 champions. On the right, Ch. Akaba's Sterling Silver (Akaba's Royal Blue ex Ch. Akaba's Know It All), at about 10½ years old. Sire of 12 champions. Both bred and owned by Lois Boardman. Silver was co-owned by Donna Bandy.
—*Fox & Cook PhoDOGraphy.*

believer in "inbreeding," and one of the breed's most successful exponents of it, Lois continued to further Akaba through the close interweaving of the members of the two Shirkhan-sired litters. In such breedings Akaba was soon specializing in the more exotic areas of the color spectrum, particularly the "blues" brindles, and creams. Akaba's Royal Blue (the only non-champion stud in the Top 50 Studs: he has 14 champions to date) was bred to Ch. Akaba's Know It All ("Smarty"). Out of this litter came Champions Akaba's Blue Devil and Akaba's Sterling Silver, both destined for stardom in the breed, but being of such dissimilar external appearance they sprouted quite disparate groups of partisan fanciers. As owner of "Devil", and co-owner with Donna Bandy of "Sterling Silver", Lois Boardman took both dogs to New York in 1967, and astonished her competition by showing Silver to BOB at the AHCA Specialty, and switching over to win BOB and Group 1 at Westminster with Devil. This left a trail of arguments behind as to which was the better dog. Silver was a tall, leggy, angular sort with a fantastic springy gait and carrying a close-lying cream-and-gray brindle coat. Devil was more "exotic," being fierce and wild in eye and expression, highly angulated, a mysterious dark gray blue color, and rather short in stature. Devil was nearly asphyxiated in an unfortuate accident with

112

a hot dryer over his crate, but somehow survived to later make a Specialty comeback. The ageless Sterling Silver was able to win good-sized shows at the age of 8 years. Both are well-remembered for their individual arresting appearances, as well as for their "get". Not too much later, the handsome brindle Ch. Akaba's Royal Flush (Akaba's Royal Blue ex Ch. Akaba's Brass Bangle) took his place as an important Akaba stud.

Fire was a tragedy for the Boardmans. Not long after they had laboriously trucked all dogs and possessions from California to Illinois, their home and kennels were gutted by fire. Some very fine Afghan Hounds and a lifetime of memorabilia were lost. A few studs and brood bitches were fortunately saved, and once the tragic interval had softened with time, Lois was again producing quality Afghan Hounds.

During the lull in Akaba a fairly pure derivative, "Coastwind" (Michael Dunham and Richard Souza), rose to prominence. Their record-breaking Best in Show and Specialty winner, Ch. Coastwind Gazebo, had been sired by an unexhibited littermate to Devil and Silver. The beautiful Ch. Coastwind Serendipity, litter sister to Gazebo, also at Coastwind, was bred to Akaba's Geronimo Blue, one of the males lost in the tragic fire. When Donna Bandy was forced to give up her Afghan Hounds, Ch. Akaba's Sterling Silver moved to Coastwind intensifying the "Akaba" influences.

The foregoing kennels tended to blend Shirkhan-blood with what in California is called "pre-Dutch influences". But mixtures heavy with Ophaal in combination with Shirkhan were also found to be successful. At Sahadi, in 1959, Joan Brearley united Shirkhan and her beautiful red Ophaal-daughter, Ch. Crown Crest Khalifah, to produce several noted champions and the upstanding, elegant black Ch. Sahadi Shikari, owned by Dr. E. F. Winter of Wisconsin. Dr. Winter unhesitatingly shipped his fine hound from East to West to the areas of the largest competition. "Sheik" became a noted multiple Specialty winner and formidable Best in Show contender. From the same litter, Ch. Sahadi Sessu, as will be seen later, left strong influences as a stud.

In the early 1960s a remarkable bitch came to the fore, after more than a decade of male domination in the top show awards, in the body of the stately brindle Shirkhan-daughter, Ch. Pandora of Stormhill. "Pan", bred and handled by loving owner, Virginia Withington, was from a litter sired by Shirkhan ex Ch. Stormhill San Dhal (homebred daughter of Ch. Stormhill Silver Dream). While Pan was eagerly battering down the Best in Show jinx for her

113

Ch. Crown Crest Khalifah (Ch. Ophaal of Crown Crest ex Ch. Crown Crest Tae-Joan), foundation bitch of Sahadi Kennels, dam of 10 champions, owned by Joan Brearley.

Ch. Sahadi Shikari (Ch. Shirkhan of Grandeur ex Ch. Crown Crest Khalifah), black dog, multiple Best in Show winner, bred by Joan Brearley, owned by Dr. and Mrs. E. F. Winter.

Ch. Pandora of Stormhill (Ch. Shirkhan of Grandeur ex Ch. Stormhill San Dhal), gray, gold and mahogany brindle bitch, multiple BIS winner and dam of 12 champions, bred and owned by Virginia Withington (Frei).

sex through vigorous campaigning, "Gini" Withington was keeping a watchful eye for a suitable mate for this exceptional bitch. Gini had a clear picture in mind of a quality male that generally resembled Pan, specifically possessing the same type of free-flowing gait, with a pedigree that included a good measure of the Shirkhan-combined-with-Dutch blood. Once seen, the handsome brindle Ch. Holly Hill Black Magic (sired by Ch. Sahadi Sessu) was selected to sire Pan's first litter. At the age of five, Pan stepped from her exalted rank as all-time top-winning Afghan Hound bitch (to that date) into the whelping box. The chosen combination proved so successful that it was later repeated. The net results included a number of well-known Stormhill champions plus International Champion Panameric of Stormhill, a top winner and producer in Scandinavia.

To enlarge Stormhill's breeding base but still retaining Pan as the focal point, for her third and last litter "Gini" settled upon the proven producer of quality, Ch. Mecca Tajma Khan of Tajmir. "Snoopy", as this male was affectionately called, carried 'Tajmir' from his dam, Ch. Tajmir's Desert Dream, a bitch bred by Pat Sinden Wallis out of solid post-Ophaal Crown Crest background. "Snoopy's" sire, Ch. Infashia of Grandeur, was responsible for Mary and Jim Nesbitt's "Mecca" Kennels; a name that was fast gaining distinction in the breed until Mary Nesbitt's tragic death via an automobile accident in 1971.

Ch. Mecca Tajma Khan of Tajmir (Ch. Infashia of Grandeur ex Ch. Tajmir's Desert Dream), black with white on chest, sire of 23 champions. Bred by James Nesbitt and Pat Wallis, and owned by James Nesbitt.

From the Snoopy-Pandora breeding, Ch. Pandora Sheik of Stormhill took his place as show winner and stud, together with "Panjet" and "Panther" from the previous Black Magic breedings. Out of deference to his sire "Snoopy" and Charles Schultz' fabulous gang of "Peanuts" characters, Pandora's Sheik is far better known as "Linus." Pandora daughters from the three breedings continued to produce well within the maternal breeding framework that had been established. With her twelve champion offspring (11 American), Pandora became the most outstanding BIS Afghan Hound bitch to achieve such remarkable success at both the upper show levels and in the whelping box, becoming one of the top producing Afghan Hound bitches of all time. After her third litter, a series of small strokes turned the highly vigorous Pan into a semi-invalid, but with great strength of spirit she lived out her years relaxing under her favorite tree at Stormhill.

Those that claim brindles and "dark dogs" are discriminated against in the show rings—and that song has been sung off tune since Badshah arrived in America—must explain why so many dark dogs are currently among the top winners in the nation. The percentages of light to dark winners shifted steadily through the 1960s. In Northern California, campaigned sparingly, never leaving the state but never ducking the toughest competition, the proud grey-brindle Ch. Javelin of Camri made his presence known at the BIS and Specialty level. Javelin would seem to be another of those rare lucky accidents of fate, being from two non-champion parents. His sire was a quality unexhibited son of Taejon (Jonte of Stri-Mar), and his dam, Karma's Jamil Khanum, was daughter of Ch. Rajah of Arken. Rarely used at stud, mostly due to his definite preference for only a few specific bitches, Javelin, nevertheless, proved remarkably prepotent in transmitting his magnificent headpiece, powerful driving rear quarters, and arrogant "type" of the old Badshah flavor. Bought as a family pet, Javelin—with his haughty bearing—was instrumental in making a first-rate handler out of his owner, Betty Richards. Traces of Javelin, especially through his breedings to the black-and-tan Top Brass daughter, Akaba's Brass'N Soot of Camri, C.D., spice many a fine Afghan Hound pedigree.

A spectacularly successful kennel built on a strength from one truly prepotent bitch is that of "Holly Hill" in Ohio. The story begins in Pennsylvania where Dr. William Moore III put his imported Djadji vom Falkenwalde to Ch. Majara Mihrab to form "Moornistan." From the resulting litter, Dr. Moore chose to mate his beautiful Ch. Maymun of Moornistan to Ch. Zaamarakuri of Ghanzi—a male that respresented a pure early American line through Ch. Zaadulla of Arthea and Winonie of Ghazni (Taejon's litter sister). An outstanding type with lovely heads, and practically unparalleled coat profusion, emerged from the blend, providing

Ch. Javelin of Camri (Jonte of Stri-Mar ex Karma's Jamil Khanum), gray brindle dog, multiple BIS winner and sire of 18 champions, owned by Betty and John Richards.

117

Ch. Samaris of Moornistan, the top producing dam of Afghan champions (17), owned by Sue and Ned Kauffman. Her littermate Ch. Hassan-Ben of Moornistan (pictured on p. 99) was sire of 24 champions.

```
                                                          Ch. Agha-Kush
                                      Ch. Rama Bhajan of Arthea
                                                          Ch. Zudiki of Arthea
                        Ch. Zaadulla of Arthea
                                                          Ch. Rudiki of Prides Hil
                                      Ch. Arthea Bathsheba of Five Mile
                                                          Ch. Zudiki of Arthea
      Ch. Zaamarakuri of Ghazni
                                                          Ch. Yusseff, C.D.
                                      Ch. Elcoza's Ponder
                                                          Kenya of Westgham
                        Winonie of Ghazni
                                                          Ch. Mo-Qua-Hee's Remus
                                      Ch. Winomana of Rreks
Ch. Samaris of Moornistan                                 Zuleika of Elcoza
Ch. Hassan-Ben of Moornistan
                                                          Ch. Karach of Khanhasset
                                      Ch. Majara Mahabat
                                                          Far Away Loo
                        Ch. Majara Mihrab
                                                          Ch. Rudiki of Prides Hill
                                      Zaritza of Elcoza
                                                          Ch. Zannette of Elcoza
      Ch. Maymun of Moornistan
                                                          Samindarwar's Cronos
                                      Azar v. Onkel Tom's Hutte
                                                          Rhani v. Weissen Hirsh
                        Djadji v. Falkenwalde
                                                          Emir v. Jugenheim
                                      Baroness v. Schonen Rhein
                                                          Aruna v. Falkenstein
```

"Moornistan" with the famed Ch. Hassan-Ben of Moornistan. His litter sister, Samaris of Moornistan, went to Holly Hill where her prepotence and exceptional qualities were wisely nurtured by Ned and Sue Kauffman.

Born in 1957, and quickly achieving her title, "Sam" made her brood presence known in her first litter sired by Ch. Dureigh's Golden Harvest. Two of the litter, Holly Hill King Lear and Holly Hill Vanity Fair, were called up from the 9 to 12 month Puppy Classes at the 1960 AHCA Specialty by judge Robert Boger to win both Winners Dog and Winners Bitch awards. This was just a sample of what Sam had to offer the breed. Whether outcrossed or linebred, under the Kauffmans' guidance, Sam proved to be a path to the shining lights. When put to Ch. Moonshyn of Moornistan, she produced the BIS Specialty winner, Ch. Holly Hill Draco. With Ch. Khabiri of Grandeur out popped the fantastically famous red Ch. Holly Hill Desert Wind, later owned by Mrs. Cheever Porter and piloted to such great show laurels by Jane Kamp Forsythe. As the dam of 17 champions, Sam is the top producing Afghan Hound bitch of all time. Sam provided additional fame for Holly Hill by producing the foundation stock for many other breeders, one of the most notable being "Ammon Hall." BIS Ch. Ammon Hall Nomad is the product of Ch. Holly Hill Desert Wind ex Ch. Holly Hill Lorna Doone. Samaris' daughter, Holly Hill Indus (sired by "Moon-

Ch. Bacha Khiva of Kubera (Ch. Hassan-Ben of Moornistan ex Ch. Majara Munshi), dog, owned by Erman M. Moore.

119

shine"), continued this trail of maternal dominance by almost equalling her dam's production record. Indus produced 16 champions. Through the decade of the 1960s, "Holly Hill" became a name in lights, adding considerable pedigree influence to the melting pot until Mr. and Mrs. Kauffman fully retired from active breeding of Afghan Hounds to become highly respected judges.

An area continually noted for its spawn of fine Afghan Hounds, Ohio is also home to Dewey and Reigh Abrams (Du-reigh), whose tenacious hold on the virtues of such dogs as "Rudiki", long after fad and fashion had passed the once-famed stud, have preserved much of current value to the breed. The very "typy" black-and-tan Specialty-winning bitch, Ch. Eljac's Dragon Lady of Dureigh, invariably received marked commendation from breeder-judges. Through "Dragon Lady" and the elegant Dureigh Champions Dark Victory, Randy of Hillbanks, Golden Harvest, and Swan Song, a sizeable pinch of "Dureigh" adds quality and "type" to many a show pedigree.

Quantity was never particularly evident in Afghan Hounds in the

Ch. Holly Hill Black Magic (Ch. Sahadi Sessu ex Ch. Samaris of Moornistan), brindle dog, sire of 22 champions. Bred by Sue A. Kauffman, and owned by Sharon R. Watson.

120

Ch. Dureigh's Golden Harvest (Ch. Dureigh's Dark Victory ex Ch. Dureigh's Dawn), sire of 15 champions, bred and owned by Dewey and Reigh Abrams.

Southern States, but quality could usually be found in a few individual dogs that were quite capable of holding their own in any competition. The revered names of "Longlesson" and "Mandith" are based in Georgia. In Tennessee, Ch. Pamir Storm Ho quietly amassed an enviable number of all-breed BIS wins. Owned by Miss Mary E. James, this flowing-coated hound was California bred by Ruth and Joe Emmert, sired by Ch. Stormhill Silver Dream ex Ch. Patrician's Victoria. "Pamir" as a kennel name was later transferred to Mr. and Mrs. Don Jensen, who continued the strain through a program of close line-breeding, leading to the striking winner, Ch. Pamir Ho Chester.

Once the home of "Kandahar", New Mexico had its modern counterpart in the Joh-Cyn kennels of John and Cynthia Guzevitch. From Sweden they imported a spectacular breeding pair of International Champions that were to have profound pedigree effect in America. The male, Tanjores Domino, was a handsome and very unusual-appearing dog, sporting a rare blue-and-cream coloring, marked in what is now called—in his honor—the "Domino pattern" (better known as "grizzle" in Salukis). Imported with "Domino" and bred to him was the glorious black-and-tan bitch, Taj Mahal Kenya. These hounds were not greatly dissimilar in background, from the Dutch V.D.O.M. Afghan Hounds. They excelled in angulation,

121

Ch. Artemus of Province (Ch. Zeno of Province ex Ch. Salima of Province), red dog, Best in Show winner and sire of 20 champions. Bred by Eugene Jantos, owned by Jane Jantos.

length of neck and elegant character, as did their offspring. Due to business pressures, within a few short years Afghan Hound breeding came to a close at Joh-Cyn, and Mrs. Guzevitch confined her Afghan Hound activity to painting, sculpturing and judging. Nevertheless, the Joh-Cyn dogs have found their way into a number of notable modern pedigrees, and the current craze for "Dominoes" may well increase this effect in the near future.

Brandt and Dorthy Houtsma, in California, put their beloved black-and-tan Ch. Sandhihi Dominja Joh-Cyn to her kennel mate, Ch. San-Dhi's Hatim Tai of San-Dhihi, C.D. (a son of Ch. Crown Crest Kabul). This planned mating produced the most "glamorous" Afghan Hound to grace the middle and late 1960s in the form of the popular "Baba" (Ch. Sandhihi Joh-Cyn Taija Baba). While being handled to multiple Bests in Show and Specialty wins by Brandt, Baba acted as press agent for the breed, especially in the Group and BIS lineups. He was too "pretty" to be believed, lovely head and eye, regal carriage, invariably immaculately groomed with shimmering pale gold coat accented by a dark mask, and an eye-catching flowing gait. Baba was a gentleman, totally attuned to Brandt's every move. Wherever he was shown, the requests for "one just like him" piled up. But Baba was never at public stud, for his

122

owners were having too much fun campaigning him to trouble themselves with visiting bitches or litters. Destiny decreed that there were never to be any males "just like Baba", for his only legacy to the breed came in the form of a unique daughter, lone survivor of his only litter.

But what a daughter she turned out to be! In 1967, Baba was mated to Dr. Gerda Kennedy's Ch. Shangrila Pharahna Cleopara (sired by Ch. Swedveikas Joh-Cyn—making this a linebreeding on the Joh-Cyn imports). The single survivor of the litter was Ch. Shangrila's Pharahna Phaedra ("Phaedra"), top-winning bitch since the days of Pandora, owner-handled to the dazzling heights of 11 Bests in Show.

Under the hand of Dr. Kennedy, "Shangrila" became an active kennel of considerable size, combining the basic stock of Joh-Cyn, Akaba and Scheherezade into a recognizable strain that filtered across the country.

Lt. Col. Wallace H. Pede brought the English winners, Ch. Bletchingley Ragman of Scheherezade, and son Ch. Alibaba of Scheherezade, C.D., together with some fine English bitches, to the American show scene in 1962, providing new pedigree blood. "Ragman" was a rather sedate black-masked red, while "Ali" was a very flashily marked black-and-tan. Scheherezade breeding has remained unusually pure and closely linebred on the basic imported stock, characterized by strong-jawed "English" heads, long necks, and exceptionally well-angulated quarters, fore and rear. Via the public

Ch. Alibaba of Scheherezade (Ch. Bletchingley Ragman of Scheherezade ex Tasha of Zabul) British import, dog owned and bred by Lt. Col. W. Pedé.

Littermates, Ch. Patrician's Victoria (Ch. Rajah of Namtrah ex Ch. Crown Crest Taejhanne), cream and blue brindle bitch, and Ch. Patrician's Myles, light red dog, owned by Ruth and Joe Emmert.

Ch. Zaamarkuri of Ghazni (Ch. Zaadulla of Arthea ex Winonie of Ghazni), dog, owned by Mrs. Mary K. Blecker.

use of his studs and sales of puppies, this bloodline has seeped through the United States. "Wally," a retired Air Force Lieutenant Colonel, has become one of the few Afghan Hound breeder-judges to adjudicate in England, Australia, Finland and the United States.

The Canadian kennel of Mary Matchett should be mentioned in the roster of notable American pedigree influences, for through the years some of the "El Myia" hounds have found their way into American pedigrees. The hounds of "El Myia" were originally imported from the "Chaman" line of Molly Sharpe in England. The Kophi kennels of Greta and Myles Phillips has also produced dogs whose influence is being felt in American pedigrees.

The American Afghan Hound eventually found his way north to the state of Alaska, where several members of the breed have won BIS awards, acclimatizing themselves well. Mrs. Nosky's Ch. Khy's Sheik and later Marge Webber's Ch. High Life Bibbi have taken the awards. These two dogs were good friends, as were their owners, with one living in Anchorage and the other in Fairbanks. When Khy's Sheik broke loose from a handler's car and roamed an Alaskan forest, refusing to come to strange human beings, Marge Webber put Hi Bibbi into the car and raced for the area where the other Afghan was last seen. At the site, she let her Afghan loose, mindful of the chance she was taking, but the dog found his friend and, once in sight of someone he knew, the panicky lost dog allowed himself to be retrieved by Marge and soon was heading on to Anchorage where his owner awaited him.

Ch. Ninth Turn Argus (Ben Ghazi's The Silver Shadow ex Ninth Turn Black Market), black dog, Best in Show winner, bred by Susan H. Hamlin, owned by Frank A. and Diane La Greca.

Ch. Pamir Storm Ho (Ch. Stormhill Silver Dream ex Ch. Patrician's Victoria), sire of 10 champions, bred by Ruth and Joe Emmert, owned by Miss Mary E. James.

Ch. Pamir Ho Chester (Ch. Pamir Storm Ho ex Ch. Kabul's Carol of Patrician), black mask silver dog, multiple BIS winner, bred and owned by Donald A. and Georjean N. Jensen.

Ch. Ammon Hall Nomad (Ch. Holly Hill Desert Wind ex Ch. Holly Hill Lorna Doone), black mask red dog, multiple BIS winner and sire of 15 champions. Bred by Jay Ammon and Sue Kauffman, and owned by J. Playfair and M. P. Gray.

Ch. Eljac's Dragon Lady of Dureigh (Ch. Dureigh's Dark Victory ex Ch. Dureigh's Fai of Hillbanks), bred and owned by Dewey and Reigh Abrams.

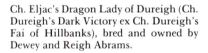

Ch. Patrician's Sherwood (Ch. Shirkhan of Grandeur ex Ch. Crown Crest Tae-jhanne), blue dog, sire of 12 champions, bred and owned by Hobart (Bud) G. Stephenson, Jr.

126

In this chapter we have attempted a roster of breeders that were responsible for an overwhelming percentage of Afghan Hound champions in the expanding 1950s and '60s, either directly through the use of their stud dogs, or by breeding stock they supplied to others. Limits of space prevent our mentioning many other worthy dogs, including some that were, or are, among our personal favorites. We are distressingly aware of promoting that rather faulty impression that these Afghan Hounds were "kennel dogs". Do not be misled. Kennel names did not necessarily a kennel make. Through these decades, well into the late 1960s, the top winning and producing hounds were—more often than not—beloved house pets, proudly handled in the rings by their owners. Only the very large kennels, such as Grandeur and Crown Crest, averaged more than a couple of litters per year, and even at Crown Crest, the dog Mrs. Finch was actively campaigning took its place as the "indoor dog", spending many hours by her side and sleeping in her bedroom. The usual successful fancier adopted a kennel name out of pride of identification. He (or she) bred an occasional litter, keeping the promising pups within a crowded household situation until "show homes" could be found for the extras. Bitches were placed under "breeders' terms", requiring the return of some puppies that would carry the home kennel name before being sold. Stud owners eagerly accepted "stud fee puppies" in lieu of at least some of the monetary fee, placing their brand on them before selling, and proudly following their "kennel name" in the AKC *Gazette*. The fact that this type of activity would lead to an inverse pyramid of puppies was not yet evident. As a delightful Sunday afternoon hobby, the breeders hoped only to have their hands on another "good one", as worthy as the one just retired to the hearthside. They had little hope of breaking even financially, readily accepting the challenge and camaraderie as the biggest part of the profits.

As should be quite evident to the reader by now, the tendency to use professional handlers was very low. A special pride came from personally winning above the Breed level with an Afghan Hound. Some of the very best handlers—all owner-handlers—in the dog game arose from the ranks of Afghan Hound enthusiasts. Pervasive awareness that the sensitive Afghan Hound should, and does, disport himself most proudly in collaboration with his loved ones was accepted. An inspiring breed memory was furnished by young Jennifer Sheldon who, when only 11 years old, successfully led her muchloved black Ch. Khabiri of Grandeur to BIS at Lackawanna Kennel Club in 1962. Edith Tichenor of "Dea Zenga" regularly finished champions, carrying them into the group ring while in her teens.

The tendency for novices, as well as veterans, to handle their own Afghan Hounds promoted a close-knit "family" atmosphere around the rings.

The volcano loudly erupted in the middle 1960s, but few were aware of the extent of its disturbance. Seasoned exhibitors stood glued to the Afghan Hound rings, chatting with old friends, idly wondering where all the new dogs and strange people were coming from. They were vaguely aware that an upsurge in all-breed registrations had hit, reflected in fewer parking spots, greater show bedlam, and the demise of the sadly outgrown benched show (except for such stalwarts as Westminster, Golden Gate, and Santa Barbara).

Gradually the realization came that the once "rare" Afghan Hound had quietly become commonplace at shows in almost every state of the Union. The fine dogs of Illeana Miller kept the breed in prominent view at the Group and BIS level in Puerto Rico, as did those of Dr. Rudi Maffei in Hawaii. Additionally, Dr. Maffei became a special friend to the breed through his keeping a voluntary fatherly eye over many Afghan Hounds that were stationed in Hawaii's unavoidable quarantine kennels. Despite his busy medical doctor's schedule, Rudi has become an invaluable dog-link, for Afghan Hound fanciers, between America and those ports for which Hawaii has become a stop-over.

Registrations for 1949 to 1969 (see P. 132) portray the startling growth of the breed, most of which erupted at the Show level. The breed was definitely garnering more than its share of Group and BIS trophies, and fanciers from other breeds were more than anxious to get onto that type of bandwagon. Puppy demand for show stock—in person, by mail order, or through professional handler emissaries—jumped sky-high. Entries ballooned at Specialties, passing 100, and then the 200 mark, until selection of two judges became a necessity for many local breed clubs as well as for the Afghan Hound Club of America.

From short hours, to full days, a blurring parade of show-Afghans gaited by. Sometimes, circus-like, fanciers were forced to try to watch two rings being judged at the same time. Open Classes, and Special Classes, turned into the most grueling endurance tests for dogs and handlers alike. Jumps in major point requirements followed the fantastic increase in entries, especially in California—the bellwether State. The inland States were soon affected, reflecting some honest upsurge of the breed locally, but far more the result of circuits. Bands of Afghan Hounds in need of majors piled up in regions where smaller entries made up a major. This ploy caused the points to become inflated from one end of the country to the other, as handlers traveled further and further in hopes of finishing dogs.

Ch. Shahmir's Sampson (Crown Crest Zorro ex Ch. Holly Hill Vanity Fair), black mask red dog, multiple BIS winner, bred by Carol Murphy, owned by Galen Outhier (handler).

Ch. Shangrila Pharahna Phaedra (Ch. Sandhihi Joh-Cyn Taija Baba ex Ch. Shangrila Pharahna Cleopatra), black and tan bitch, multiple BIS winner, bred and owned by Dr. Gerda Maria Kennedy.

Ch. Kismet's Red Baron (Ch. Sirocco of Camri ex Ch. Kismet's Little Egypt), black mask red dog, Best in Show winner, bred and owned by John and Shirley Handley.

Two disturbing changes in the complexion of the breed had become screamingly evident by 1969. First, a high percentage of the seasoned breeder-owner-exhibitors mentioned in this Chapter had retired from active exhibition. They drastically curtailed, or closed, their breeding programs in favor of becoming licensed AKC judges. That is as it should be, but, in result, much of the roster of remaining, or incoming, exhibitors and breeders was made up of comparative newcomers. These fanciers too often lacked hard-won perspective, pursuing a naive expectation for quick champions—to be automatically followed by a litter of same—in vain assumption that their show stock, from pedigrees rich in Champions, would automatically produce nothing less.

Second, the use of professional handlers in the fast-increasing show tempo rose dramatically. The Afghan Hound most emphatically became the professional handler's darling. Rather than relying on the relaxed apprenticeship gained by learning to show one's own dog, bolstered by the glow of minor point wins, and learning by one's own mistakes, many novices, and the not so successful, relinquished the in-ring schooling technique, in favor of professional know-how. This is not to be construed as disapproval of professional handlers, but to point out that in the past history of the breed the breeder/owners worked themselves up the hard way to become professionals in their own right.

The happy concept of the Afghan Hound as a combined pet and showdog began to fade as a result of the new emphasis on the superficials, particularly involving coat. Well-meaning owners allowed their dogs to become handler-guided hothouse flowers with every hair protected, living in padded crates, and exercised by means of the Jog-A-Dog.

Those that knew, and loved, the independent, even stubborn, nature of the rugged Afghan Hound with its insistent penchant for emotional bonds only towards its chosen people, saw, in the widening acceptance of a lifeless statuary type of long-furred perfection, a terrifying, but unstoppable, result of the Show World frenzy.

Ch. Caravan's Blue Passion (Ch. Akaba's Blue Banner ex Akaba's Moonlight Sonata), light silver blue bitch, Best in Show winner. Bred by Elizabeth and Vincent Leap, owned by Glorvina R. Schwartz.

Ch. Ambrosia Bon-Nanza (Ch. Holly Hill Sultan ex Ch. Holly Hill Bon Voyage), black masked red dog, Best in Show winner. Bred by Dann O. Maly, owned by Phil and Andrea Peck.

Ch. Benvikki's A-Bit of Harmony (Ch. Harmony's Bandit ex Kuh-I-Baba), black mask apricot dog, multiple BIS winner. Bred by Benson P. Lee, owned by Vicki Parker Lee.

ANNUAL AKC
REGISTRATION OF AFGHAN HOUNDS

Year	Regis-tration	Year	Regis-tration	Year	Regis-tration
1926	4	1947	444	1968	3,408
1927	1	1948	417	1969	4,605
1928	5	1949	465	1970	6,127
1929	0	1950	377	1971	8,049
1930	1	1951	472	1972	9,023
1931	0	1952	449	1973	10,549
1932	1	1953	424	1974	10,918
1933	6	1954	386	1975	10,412
1934	27	1955	469	1976	10,045
1935	21	1956	524	1977	9,416
1936	82	1957	636	1978	7,878
1937	80	1958	794	1979	6,833
1938	125	1959	691	1980	6,259
1939	148	1960	668	1981	5,421
1940	135	1961	831	1982	4,540
1941	217	1962	889	1983	4,106
1942	218	1963	1,092	1984	3,374
1943	138	1964	1,242	1985	2,915
1944	134	1965	1,820	1986	2,398
1945	310	1966	1,922		
1946	526	1967	2,660		

6

The Explosive American Afghan Hound Scene (1970 into the 80's)

"Those who entered the breed in the late '50s and early '60s did so at a very critical and, in a way, opportune time. . . . We were still able to establish ourselves and get a little foothold before the onslaught. And these times made fighters out of us all."—Mike Dunham, *Afghan Hound Review.*

THE registration picture of the 1970s bore the outline of an extruding volcano, swelling and remodeling upwards, to a liquid and unstable dome, to gradually deflate when the force was spent. The upward magna momentum of the late '60s caused a then record-breaking 6,127 registrations in 1970—bubbling higher each year to a temporary apex of 10,918 in 1974. To put that figure in time perspective, in that one year more Afghan Hounds were registered than in the full 16-year period from 1949 to 1964. Each of the four years, 1973-74-75-76, erupted over the 10,000 mark. Thereafter the slant was downward, lava turning to dry ash, returning to 6,259 registrations in 1980; a remarkable symmetry to the decade's bell-curve. The drop continued and by the end of 1986 was down to 2,398 registrations.

The era was also characterized by the raising, and the razing, of

Gods—human and canine. The pervasive national aura, fired by Madison Avenue techniques, was that incredible odds, if not Mother Nature herself, could be overcome—if only the right food supplement was added, the right authority consulted, or the right photograph published. A decade of glory for the few, delusion and disappointment for the many. Only the stalwart, and the incredibly lucky, rode jauntily through the '70s.

With the astronomical rise in registrations came not one shred of evidence that the Afghan Hound had gained a more respectable niche as the family pet. The loud and insistent demand was for Show Winners—or promises thereof. Tragically many pups lived not much longer than it took to register the litter as seasoned breeders, fully aware of the lack of pet homes, admitted to quietly euthanizing all pups outside the perimeter of show stock.

The verbal blame for the overflow of Afghan Hounds crowding into Humane Societies, running the streets, or becoming objects of "new home desperately needed" ads in the local papers, was on the so-called backyard breeder, or puppy mill. But, as many notable fanciers had begun with a family pet that had come to double as a show dog in more relaxed days, a lot of backyards had become kennels. The derisive epithets came to refer to almost anyone guilty of producing a litter—other than the speaker and the speaker's best friends. Those ghastly puppy mills that bred specifically for the pet trade, played a small part in the deluge, but far less than show-fanciers preferred to believe. While the Afghan Hound bitches were pleasantly prolific, the puppies turned out to be ugly, troublesome and low in demand. Even the mass-raised nonentities boasted royal lineage, and were peddled as show prospects to the unwary.

Before entering the drama of the '70s, some perspective is in order. As a fairly rare breed in the '60s, the show Afghan Hound glittered in isolated geographic sites of traditional density. Across the United States widely separated proud breeder/owners felt a strong sense of kinship with each other. The ties, if not person-to-person, were through club newsletters, magazines and Specialty Shows. The socially accepted culture pattern was that, after the proud making of a new champion, a breeding would follow to provide a new dog to exhibit. The expectation, somewhat naive as it turned out, was that the ensuing litter (if properly thought out) would supply stock as good, if not better, than the best of its parents. Underlying this was the assumption that any overflow pups not retained by the breeder would be eagerly welcomed by envious also-ran exhibitors, those looking for the perfect addition to their own line, and by fanciers from other breeds growing jealous of the Afghan Hound's impressive lead in Hound Group wins.

Ch. Mecca's Falstaff (Ch. Mecca's Blue Silks Karu ex Mecca's Turnadot of Abashagh), self-masked cream dog, a top producing sire of 50 champions. Bred by J. Nesbitt and P. McMahon, and owned by Barbara Guidebeck.

```
                              Ch. Infashia of Grandeur
                  Ch. Mecca Tajma Khan of Tajmir
                              Ch. Tajmir's Desert Dream
          Ch. Mecca's Blue Silks Karu
                              Ch. Dureigh's Golden Harvest
                  Kahlua Karu
                              Jalabad Ariana Karakum

CH. MECCA'S FALSTAFF
                              Ch. Infashia of Grandeur
                  Mecca's Shoe Shine Boy
                              Ch. Tajmir's Desert Dream
          Mecca's Turandot of Abashagh
                              Ch. Ali Baba of Scheherezade
                  Amira Fatima of Abashagh
                              Beniharr's Autumn Heather
```

135

The fairy tale seemed real—for a while. Rapid proliferation of well-bred pups brought a swinging upsurge in the number of new champions and euphoric owners (and breeders). Few noticed the built-in Catch-22, in that any number advantage concerning the AKC point requirements gained in one year would dissolve later out of its own weight.

A chart of the rise in California requirements for a three point major, at five year intervals, contrasted with the totals in new champions and registrations nationwide, is revealing:

| California 3-point Major | | | National | |
Year	Dogs	Bitches	New Champions	Registrations
1955	7	6	40	469
1960	14	14	56	668
1965	18	17	91	1,820
1970	35	29	102	6,127
1975	41	37	125	10,412
1980	34	30	119	6,259
1984	22	27	173	3,374

To explain the picture in terms of California (the bellwether state): as point requirements jumped upwards, the immediate solution became the taking, or sending, of dogs to those adjacent States where point requirements were less stiff. Thus the tremendous California Open Classes (where most of the dogs had some points, but might not live long enough to make it to the magic 15) could be circumvented. The ploy took quality Afghan Hounds into the boondocks where majors were cheaper and Group competition supposedly a bit less formidable. The tactic worked—until the bill came due. To the AKC an increase in entries is an increase; with each following year those outlying States, with barely a half-dozen actual Afghan Hound residents, were allotted greatly inflated major requirements. Undaunted, exhibitors merely traveled further and further inland. The byproduct of the scheme was the whetting of local appetites for one, or more, of the beautifully manicured Afghan showdogs. Such purchases increased the tempo of local competition and provided an occasional local new champion as early interest on the unpaid balance of numbers to come. As a result the breed continued to flow, like molten lava, across all the show grooves of the United States. In the interests of camaraderie, confusion and pride, local Afghan Hound Clubs proliferated as fast as Match Chairmen could be found, with an eye to giving prestigious Specialties just as soon as possible. In spinoff, with the growing pressure of locally-owned regally bred Afghan Hounds, the reputation—and reality—of the breed as luxuriantly beautiful continued to rise to tighten in the overall high breed quality, and its professional appearance, nationwide.

In numbers of dogs exhibited, the outpouring of Afghan Hounds at

Ch. Khayam's Ares (Ch. Ammon Hall Nomad ex Ch. Khayam's Kism of
Scheherezade), black and tan dog, multiple BIS winner and sire of 19
champions. Bred by Dr. Doyle and Betty Rogers, and owned by Walter
Greene and Carl Sanders.

Ch. Cani's Summer Breeze (Ch. Genesis Caelus of Jaffna ex Cani Foxy
Lady), black and blue brindle bitch, BIS winner, bred by Ardie Libke, owned
by H. Nave and L. Guerrero.   —*Missy Yuhl.*

Ch. Sandina Starstream (Ch. Coastwind Gazebo ex Ch. Akaba's Blue Bonnet of Sandina), black masked red brindle dog, multiple BIS winner, bred by Glorvina R. Schwartz, owned by Sandina Kennels.

Ch. Sandina Sparkling Champagne (Ch. Dynasty's Wild Goose Chase ex Ch. Caravan's Blue Passion), blue cream brindle dog, multiple BIS winner. Bred by Sandina Kennels, and owned by Viki Highfield.

Ch. Sandina Spellbound (Ch. Zafara Brother Love ex Ch. Caravan's Blue Passion), dark blue dog, multiple BIS winner and sire of 14 champions. Bred and owned by Sandina Kennels. Handler—Glorvina Schwartz.

the show-level moved the breed solidly into the Big Four, from coast to coast. The other three, all from the Working Group—German Shepherd, Doberman Pinscher and Great Dane—respectively ranked 2nd, 6th and 16th in registration, compared to the Afghan Hound's 28th position (1974), proving the Asiatic breed to have an inordinate penchant for exhibition as its reason for existence in America.

The innocent belief that all one needed to have a champion was a well-pedigreed healthy dog, and money to pay the entry fees, mimicked the recurrent chain letter game. Benefits accrued to the instigator, whose name was on top of the list, at the expense of the latecomers. There was little, if any, intentional chicanery—just a mathematical inevitability. A figure that puts the title-hunt rigor into perspective is that, with a 1964 registration of 1,242 Afghan Hounds just 85 new champions were listed that year. With over ten thousand (10,918) registered in 1974, 89 made the title that year. The phrase "already pointed" became utterly meaningless in its commonality and as a false indicator of prosperity.

With this backdrop in place, the drama of the '70s among the upper echelon contenders can begin.

After a lightning year of raking in breed, Group and BIS wins, including the top spot at the Afghan Hound Club of America (AHCA) National 1969 Specialty, Ch. Coastwind Gazebo (Ezra) entered the '70s as flag-bearer, catapulting Coastwind Kennels into national prominence. Under the hand of Marvin Cates, Ezra took charge of the western half of the U.S., drawing abreast of and then passing (in numerical wins) the slightly older Ch. Ammon Hall Nomad, then being campaigned mainly in the eastern half of the country. After a dizzying round of shows Ezra was retired in 1970, while still a young dog. He is probably most fondly remembered by those that saw him at the Channel Cities Show in 1975, brought out of retirement at 10 years of age, as a respectful courtesy to Kay Finch. She could not deny the still strong-moving proud stallion, giving him his 100th BOB win to thunderous approval from the ringside.

The incomparable Shirkhan of Grandeur died in April of 1970 at 16 years old. As a gene reservoir he had become an incredible tree trunk from which many healthy branches had budded off in the '60s. Admiring fanciers continued to flock to the Shirkhan-derived pedigree shadows, setting their own dog-roots into genetic proximity.

Heavy with Shirkhan-genes (through Akaba) Coastwind, in Northern California expanded along its own vision. While Ezra was making national friends on the campaign trail with Marvin, the local reputation of Coastwind became attached to a pair of much admired bitches, handled by breeder, Richard Souza. Champions Coastwind Serendipity (Ezra's sister) and the Ezra daughter, Ch. Coastwind

140

Ch. Zebec Sakr Splendora (Ch. Zebec Achates ex Ch. Kassan's The Primadonna), black and tan bitch, BIS winner. Bred by Cathy Slay and June E. Boone. Owned by James Barnhart, Walter Greene and Carl Sanders. Handler, Carl Sanders.—*Sosa*.

Ch. Kabik's Free Style (Ch. Kabik's The Challenger ex Ch. Kabik's Ban-Detta of Zuran), multi-BIS winning bitch. Bred and owned by Chris and Marguerite Terrell and Gail Savage. Handler, Chris Terrell.

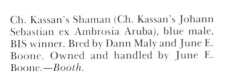

Ch. Kassan's Shaman (Ch. Kassan's Johann Sebastian ex Ambrosia Aruba), blue male, BIS winner. Bred by Dann Maly and June E. Boone. Owned and handled by June E. Boone.—*Booth*.

Ouija, advanced the kennel plan. When the former's son, Ch. Coastwind Nepenthe, was put to Ouija in 1970 she produced the breed's most influential sire, the brindle Ch. Coastwind Abraxas.

As a new pedigree symbol Coastwind sent highly charged tendrils across the United States and overseas. Ch. Coastwind Holyman distinguished himself and the home kennel not only as a show-winner, but as a stud force for David Roche and those Australian breeders who partook of his genes. Ch. Coastwind Obsidian gained admiration and left sperm in his flying trip to Germany, blending well with local lines. When not a stud dog he was the live-in pet of Waldo Kolbo, who lived just a short jump from Coastwind Kennels.

Notable at the turn of the decade was the Dynasty Kennel of Fred Alderman in Illinois, built on a combination of Crown Crest and Akaba. While not of explosive note, a steady array of worthy champions seeped from his line, as will be seen as the chapter progresses. These dogs played their part in the intense collection of Shirkhan genes, in combination with those bitches from various other lines, that brought so much of the country into the woven plaid of Coastwind/Akaba/Dynasty/Grandeur threads.

Bursting onto the scene with the brilliance of a spotlight in 1970 was the radiant presence of Glorvina Schwartz and the Sandina Kennel. Partaking heavily of the Shirkhan-based mix previously described, Sandina arose from building upon two fine bitches. These were Ch. Caravan's Blue Passion and Ch. Akaba's Blue Bonnet of Sandina (Bonnie), the latter a BIS bitch under Glorvina's hand. Bonnie bred to Ezra (Ch. Coastwind Gazebo) produced a fiery stallion type like his sire (but striped brindle) in Ch. Sandina Starstream. Capturing 12 all-breed BIS's in 1975, he became the undisputed flag-bearer for the breed in eastern United States and Canada. Proving this dog not to be a lucky breeding accident, he was retired before hitting the prime of life, at four years of age. This made way for the next Sandina star—Ch. Sandina Sparkling Champagne, from the litter of Passion bred to Ch. Dynasty's Wild Goose Chase. As a pale dilute-brindle, well named for color and connotation of the best, this dog moved into the place vacated by Starstream to become the top-winning Afghan Hound in the country for 1977—always owner-handled. Glorvina carried the goblet of Champagne without spilling a drop, until coming up with what she felt was an even better vintage brew. By breeding Passion to appropriately named Ch. Zafara's Brother Love, she emerged standing next to the BIS placard with Ch. Sandina Spellbound, a romantically colored dark blue, with some-what less showmanship than his predecessors, but more old time breed character. In what had become a characteristic "strike while the iron is hot" campaign strategy, Spellbound was all-breed BIS 28 times in two years of being shown before retirement at the age of four. The combined picture of the sedately aristocratic Glorvina with her immaculately groomed and beautifully conditioned hounds, sailing around the ring or standing for all to admire, made the combination one of the special ambassadors for the breed throughout the '70s. But as Brother Love was not whelped until 1974, we are moving through the decade much too fast.

Holding the Women's Lib flag aloft was the impudent black and tan Ch. Shangrila's Phaedra, winning her laurels at numerous all-breed shows and Best of Breed at the 1970 AHCA National Specialty under Herman Fellton. In breaking records she shattered those of the earlier Ch. Pandora of Stormhill. But Phaedra found it difficult to combine a career and motherhood; she served more as advance guard for Shangrila than purveyor of it. Gerda Kennedy's most notable pedigree effect, by virtue of champion get and widespread utilization by other breeders, stems from the super-elegant black and silver Ch. Shangrila Pharoah Gandharra. Shown sparingly, Gandharra, sired in 1967 by the fine producer Ch. Sasha of Scheherezade ex the lovely Ch. Akaba's Royal Gold, developed his reputation first from pictures and then by word of mouth. The range of important pedigree strands that he sent spinning into the '70s is evident by his get. The champion get carry such kennel names as: Alarickhan, Cabazon, Jaffna, Jenfield, Marvalka, Stormhill and Xanadu.

Less well known, but useful as a gene bearer, was Ch. Shangrila Pharoah Bhima. Particularly notable was his son, a remarkable dog with lasting quality, Ch. Shiloh Addis Abeba Superstar, who took at least one good-sized BIS award for each of five years, 1974 through 1978.

Texas, big in reputation for so many things, came into its own as a sizeable center of Afghan Hound breeding in the '70s and from a wide array of pedigree bases. Dr. Doyle Roger's repeated nick of Ch. Ammon Hall Nomad combined with Ch. Khayam's Kism of Scheherezade produced a remarkable array of fine champions. The most famous of these champions were brothers, Ch. Khayam's Apollo and Ares. Both black and tan with superficial similarities, they were as different under the coat as was their personal stories.

Ch. Khayam's Apollo rose to shining prominence as a just-finished young champion that Gini Withington carried to BOB at the '71 AHCA National Specialty. Living up to his rich promise this dog, as half of a remarkable duo-combination with handler Gene Blake, became the Afghan Hound to rule the rings, especially east of the Rockies, for the next three years. Bred to a variety of bitches, from an interesting assortment of backgrounds, his dominant qualities passed through his get. As an older dog still able to win a few, he retired to the

Ch. Bakali Cymbeline of Zuvenda, 6 weeks in whelp (Ch. Mecca's Falstaff ex Adrienne of Shirkden), black and tan bitch, bred by Geraldine Cumberland, owned by Karen B. Usry (Martin) and Geraldine Cumberland.

Ch. Abiszet Syncopare Sun Godess (Ch. Khayam's Apollo ex Barbary Coast Cameo Cove), black masked red bitch, bred by Patrice J. Tuttle, owned by Peter C. and Brigitte Kaiser.   —*Cook.*

144

loving home of Betsey and Allen Tully where he continued his stud career.

Through the quirks of circumstance the brother Ares did not come into serious competition until 1974 having moved through four different homes before safely landing into the appreciative fold of Walter Greene and Carl Sanders. Under Carl's leadership Ch. Khayam's Ares became one of the most solidly accepted dogs in the history of the breed as reflected by his record of 21 Bests at Afghan Hound Specialties. As a dog that continued to "grow better—not older" he won a large BIS All Breed at the remarkable age of nearly 11 years, and then repeated at 12 years old. He won Best in Specialty at the AHCA in New York City and topped the breed the following day at Westminster in 1976. While a late-comer, after his brother, in standing at stud he was used very sparingly but produced some fine champions in combination with several different lines. Seemingly ageless, proud and powerful, shown without stylistic tricks, Ares demonstrated the lasting qualities of a fine Afghan Hound.

The state of Illinois was a noted center of Afghan Hound production from the '40s onward. This continued into the '70s, but through the strange vagaries of fate many of its best known names had packed it in by the end of the decade or moved to other states. Pat Sinden Wallis Stephenson's Tajmir Kennel began in Illinois but moved wherever she did. Her three-kennel named Ch. Ammon Hall Ter-Caj of Tajmir topped the AHCA Specialty in 1972 under Bea Godsol. Basically of Holly Hill blood, he carried the tradition begun by Ned and Sue Kauffman, who had retired to Florida to become highly respected multi-Group judges. Holly Hill shreds remained in Ohio as part of Jay Ammon's Ammon Hall until Jay also retired from active breeding and went into judging. These are some of the many venerable kennel names of the '60s that now have moved to the back of the pedigrees.

The name of Tajmir remained in Illinois through the Nesbitt's famous Ch. Mecca Tajma Khan of Tajmir (Snoopy to his many friends). With the tragic death of Mary Nesbitt in an auto accident, Mecca dissolved. Posthumously the name continued to flare brightly through the unforgettable Snoopy grandson, Ch. Mecca's Falstaff, with the Guidebecks in Georgia. Falstaff, or "Hap" as he was far better known, has become one of the most venerated dogs, and studs, in the history of the breed. Seemingly a case of the right dog at the right time, found by the right person (chosen as a 4-months-old pup) Hap became a dog for all seasons. His list of champion get proves him to have been incorporated into an incredibly wide variety of pedigree backgrounds with huge success. The number of really experienced breeders the country over who put their most cherished bitches to him

145

is a remarkable tribute to the dog. It is not easy to put the finger on the precise quality of Hap that caught so many diverse breeders' eyes. Certainly it was not his show record, not any heavy advertising, and not his color—unmasked cream (at that time considered a detriment to winning). Perhaps Barbara caught the reason in asserting "his serene belief that we existed solely to wait on him was unshattered, and there was no ignoring him." The Guidebecks were not alone in being captured by his compelling demeanor and beauty. As a very cherished ancestor Hap lives on in bits and pieces, in all colors, and both sexes.

As the '70s emerged, the Afghan Hound Club of America felt the swell of overpopulation problems and mutterings over traditional acceptance of the day before Westminster as the only conceivable time for the National Specialty. From February 1947 the New York City date and site had been accepted, partly due to reflected glory from the prestigious Westminster Kennel Club Show falling on the then numerically small Afghan Hound breed. But by 1970, the breed had become its own spotlight.

The breed explosion brought a chasm between Specialty and Westminster entries. As the Madison Square Garden tour de force evolved into a jousting of champions fighting for Group level TV exposure, most of the class animals, and many of the champions shown at the Specialty were not even entered at the all-breed show. As the horrendous inconvenience and expense of New York City in February brought howls from the exhibitors, the sanctity of the tradition came into question at the AHCA Board of Directors level. It was not to be easily set aside.

By 1970, the Board accepted the necessity of hiring two judges, in fear that the entry would pass the limits set by the AKC for one judge to pass on in a day (175). That year Eunice Clark presided over 76 bitches. Herman Fellton did 91 class dogs plus intersex, including 4 veterans, 33 specials and one brood bitch bringing the total entry to 205 and proving out the Board's wisdom. Entries continued to rise. In 1971, Wally Pede had 110 dogs; Gini Withington checked 106 bitches, 3 veterans, 38 specials and one brood bitch for a total of 148 animals. The near-crisis came in '73 with James Prior's duty of 125 dogs well under the limit; but Bea Godsol's 123 class bitches plus intersex brought her to the wire—174.

With no hope that numbers would diminish, the question continually plagued the AHCA Board. Many suggestions were proposed, but none received a majority approval. Some consideration was given to eliminating the puppy classes. The catalogs indicated that the majority of entered puppies were locally owned. Exhibitors out of driving range, forced to ship dogs by air, mainly brought ready-to-

146

Ch. Zafara Brother Love (Ch. Coastwind Abraxas ex Ch. Jubilan's Second Spring), dog, Best in Show winner. Owned, bred and handled by Bob and Bobbi Keller.   —*Ludwig.*

Ch. Genesis Caelus of Jaffna (Coastwind the Hermit ex Jaffna's Royal Velvet of Akaba), dog, BIS winner and sire of 19 champions. Bred by Jo Ann Stover and owned by H. Nave and L. Guerrero.   *Ludwig.*

147

win adults. Sentiment for retaining youngsters as an integral part of the breed picture prevailed.

As an experiment, the AHCA tradition was bent in 1975 by the approval of two National Specialties, one in New York City in February and a second one held in Arcadia, California, sponsored by the AHCA California members. In February, Rodrigo Quevado, Jr., up from Mexico, judged dogs; Dr. William Waskow managed bitches and intersex—with a total of 170 entrants—awarding the medium-sized, high impact Ch. Rajah's El Cid, of the Brunings, the Best of Breed. California-based AHCA members, led by Mary Rogers, went all out to make "their" National a roaring success. With supreme optimism no limit was set and three judges were hired. The Kauffmans, Ned and Sue, split 226 class animals. Alys Carlsen did intersex, including 25 specials, awarding a sentimentally-favored Best of Breed to the seven year old Ch. Panjhet of Stormhill. Panjhet was brought out of retirement fit and fresh and most lovingly handled by Sandy Withington (now Frei).

The show was considered by Westerners as a real victory over the stranglehold they saw Easterners having over the National event. But three judges had not been needed. The entry indicated that, while Californians were willing to ship themselves and their dogs cross country in droves, few Easterners were willing to do the same. Of the 275 dogs entered only 15 came from the East Coast, Mid-West and Texas.

Just one Specialty was held in 1974 and that back at the Statler-Hilton in New York City, but the hiring of three judges was maintained. A dog entry of 135 was judged by E. M. Gilbert, Jr. In an exceptionally exciting event Karen Usry's typy black and tan bitch, Bakali Cymbeline of Zuvenda (a Falstaff daughter) went Winners Bitch over an entry of 113 under Thelma Brown, and on to BOB over 44 specials under Jay Ammon—to become the second Afghan Hound and the first bitch, to take the National from the classes. In 1952 Karli Ben Ghazi had taken the breed from the classes at the AHCA National Specialty and had repeated the win as a champion in 1955.

An avalanche of Afghan Hounds continued to bring the AHCA aggravation. The monster of over-production with its scaly skin of false, or impossible, promises fostering massive ethical neglects, had grown to fire-breathing proportions. With the best of intentions the AHCA Board opted for the role of St. George, but soon found it could reach no more of the nodding horror than its sweeping tail.

In beautiful idealism the Parent Club Board devised a Code of Ethics to be signed by all members and serve as a collective good example for the rest of the country to follow. The Code detailed approved and disapproved major practices in the breeding, selling and advertising of Afghan Hounds. Moved wholesale into it was the AHCA "Biological Defects Committee Recommendations." To achieve strength the document was made mandatory with signature required to insure continued membership. The Code stated that "Violations of the Code by any member would be subject to disciplinary action by the Board of Directors."

The dragon slowly began to open its eyes and stoke its lung fires. Smugly assured that they had accomplished a much needed job, the Board turned towards more tangible assists for non-AHCA members. A 32 page booklet, *Introduction To The Afghan Hound*, was designed, made rich in illustrations and offered to regional clubs, as well as individuals, for a nominal fee. The Introduction booklet was warmly embraced by the members and friends; the mandatory Code of Ethics ripped the AHCA into opposing camps.

In taking dead aim at the most obvious source of Afghan Hound puppies, the Code was specific, and binding, in demanding "Bitches should be bred no earlier than 24 months of age, no more than two out of three seasons, and shall be made to produce no more than three litters in a lifetime." Up to that point, despite the fact that a tremendous number of registered pups were directly, or indirectly, the result of breedings made by members of the AHCA, to a person they saw the root-problem as the other person. Once the fingers began to jab, the drowsing dragon moved into a wakeful state.

Afghanites, being raging individualists, bristled at mandatory restrictions or controls—for themselves. Fanciers connected with pedigree-valued bitches that had previously produced more than three litters in their lifetimes, fanned resentment embers. The Board was soon to learn that what had seemed to be overall Club agreement had been, in fact, the sleepy signature of a preoccupied monster. The actual preferring of charges by some long-standing AHCA members against another for breach of the "bitch clause" set the fires to raging ferociously.

The Board's dilemma was classical; "Damned if they did and damned if they didn't." A sizeable faction of the Club considered the clause right and reasonable for the problems of the day and demanded the charges be considered. Just as large a group had reservations about the wisdom of a ban, stating you can't legislate ethics, demanded the Code be revoked. With good logic they asked—"Why the restriction just on bitches—when one stud dog can sire infinitely more pups in one lifetime?" Unsuspected personal antagonisms surfaced, along with name calling, bringing on the hottest crisis the Board was to face in the '70s.

One breeder-defendant, hauled up on the charges, in a surprise argument put the case to rest, and the Board in an untenable position.

Two Great Ladies, Sunny Shay and Mrs. Reigh Berry Abram. Ch. Boy Blu of Grandeur (Dominator of Grandeur ex Phadra of Grandeur), blue dog, bred by Sunny Shay, owned by Sunny Shay and Roger Rechler. —*Vicky Cook Photography.*

Ch. Blu Shah of Grandeur (Ch. Boy Blu of Grandeur ex Rubicon Rhea Silvia), slate dog, multiple BIS winner. Bred by Priscilla Senior, owned by Roger Rechler. —*Wm. P. Gilbert.*

In defense he pointed out that the AHCA Constitution plainly stated: "The objects of the club should be (a) to encourage and promote the breeding of pure-bred Afghan Hounds. . .". The Code clauses that discouraged breeding came into conflict with the over-riding governing document.

Finding themselves hoisted on their own petard, so to speak, the Board rescinded the Code in 1976—in a mixture of embarrassment, resentment and relief. To weld the fragmented Club towards a smoother common purpose, the Board's first act was to officially delete the offending words from the Constitution, and substitute the phrase, "to preserve and protect the breeding of Afghan Hounds . . .".

Next a wary and less idealistic Board set out to develop Guidelines with the same general aim as the Code, but under voluntary compliance. Broken Club segments were brought to some semblance of unity by the design, and acceptance, of a brochure entitled "*Recommended Practices*." The introduction spelled out its attitudes and aims:

> "Whether an owner, exhibitor, or breeder, the Afghan Hound enthusiast is often confronted with decisions and courses of action which can impact the continued improvement and preservation of the Afghan Hound breed, and the well-being of his, or her, individual dogs. All too often, because of inexperience or lack of forethought, the decisions made and the courses of action pursued are unfortunate ones, with lasting detrimental effects.
>
> With these voluntary guidelines, which represent a distillation of the personal codes of conduct and concerns of its members, the AHCA is setting forth acceptable practices and a number of precautions; and is directing them to any and all involved with our breed with the intent that the pitfalls be avoided and the pleasures enhanced."

The Guidelines passed in February 1978. The document left no one ecstatic, but gave no grounds for suit against the AHCA or its members. As a model for ethical-minded breeders to hold, and for novice owners to take as a warning, it served a much needed purpose. During the brouhaha, but unnoticed until the 1977 statistics were in, the downturn in the Afghan Hound puppy deluge had begun to accelerate.

The scenario for show success became a two-fold game in the '70s. One was tried and true genetic superiority. Success begat success. Would-be breeders of winners flocked to already distinguished and fashionable names. These names, in turn, gained even greater prominence through ballyhooed names of their titled get. As in previous decades the percentage of new champions with titled sires held at over 90%. The titled dogs with champion dams ebbs and rolls, but averages over 50%.

Secondly, but of importance in the welter of exhibits, was the managing and packaging of the dogs. One useful ploy was the careful placing of littermates into widely separated States, preventing their competing with each other, and giving each owner the assumption that they had, if not first pick, at least second. As added insurance some sales contracts required the utilization of professional handlers.

The laws of supply and demand twisted out of whack, in that the demand was only for winners and caused show dog prices to spiral into the ridiculous. The game is predicated on the fact that for every winner there has to be a large number of losers, regardless of the pedigrees and promises involved. Buyers of the latter felt understandably cheated. In disappointment they labeled their unhappy experiences the result of greed, but in truth the evidence is far stronger for expectations on all sides outrunning reality. Concerning the exchange of money, where exorbitant prices were asked and received, much greater sums were expended on advertising and travel to keep the product in full public view.

The conscientious occasional breeder who wanted no part of the heavy maneuvers was caught in the middle. Surrounded by meglaomanic and one-up-manship, one confided, "If I don't ask inflated prices for my most promising pups, buyers assume there must be something wrong with them—and go elsewhere."

When promises failed, and/or special problems arose, as happens rather commonly in this imperfect world, the question of proper restitution loomed large. Despite the sentimental portrayal of the dogs as our companions, legally they are bought and sold like any other piece of chattel, and subject to the same non-sentimental civil contractural laws. This came as a severe shock to many unwary buyers and naive sellers. It was the dogs, themselves, that bore the brunt of the suffering.

While our sympathies lie with the masses of Afghan Hound dogdom, too often the object of more problems than pride, as with any history, the heroic storyline follows those particular dogs, and owners, who kept their heads above the hungry waves.

For much of the breed's exhibition history, Washington and Oregon were considered the source of cheap points for the Californians. This had the stimulating effect of sharpening the quality of the local dogs; by the '70s a number of Northwest breeders had developed stock that could hold its own anywhere in the country. In Washington, Al and Ingrid Stewart put their Ch. Dynasty's Bon Bon of Wildenau to Coastwind the Hermit in 1973. The mating produced the spectacular oystershell-brindle Ch. Wildenau's Bonvivant (Vanti). He was personally piloted by Ingrid to the head of a number of Hound

Groups and on to become a multiple BIS winner in 1975 and '76. Catching the eye of breeders wherever he was shown, Vanti earned the opportunity to prove his stud capabilities. He became an admirable producer not only for the Stewarts, but for several other West Coast breeders, including Californians. The worm had turned, indeed.

As the bellwether state, it was California that first mirrored not only a downturn in entries and registrations, but also the passing of the Afghan Hound as a sort of automatic contender for the top Group placing that gave a shot at the supreme BIS spot. From the mid-70s on few Afghan Hounds were to make it through the gauntlet. The Withingtons' Ch. Pandora's Sheik of Stormhill was one of the lucky. Late in the decade the California-based Ch. Genesis Caelus of Jaffna managed a breakthrough to carry breed laurels to the peak twice in 1978. He also finished No. 1 for the number of Afghan Hounds defeated that year. The outgoing and personable Caelus, owned by Hank Nave and Lou Guerrero, was yet another Hermit son from a breeding with Jaffna's Royal Velvet of Akaba. Another high impact-in-motion dog, Caelus passed on the proud talent for topping all challengers to his charming daughter, Ch. Cani's Summer Breeze, who distinguished herself as the decade moved into the '80s—but again that puts us ahead of the story.

Hermit became one of the very few non-champion stud dogs of real note in the breed. As anti-social as his name, he was not even a passable showman, but when bred to stable and outgoing bitches, his other sterling qualities flooded through, and handsome showdogs with great pizzazz resulted.

A lovely Hermit daughter, the Specialty winning Ch. Jubilan's Second Spring, was bred to Abraxas in 1974, resulting in the dazzling and most exotic white Ch. Zafara's Brother Love (Moby). A multiple All-Breed and Specialty winning dog, Moby had the distinction of being on the list of top winners in the breed at the same time as his son, Ch. Sandina Spellbound. Owned by Bob and Bobbi Keller in California, Moby helped to prove the long cries of color prejudice against pale-faced Afghan Hounds to be a thing of the far past. The Afghan Hound had become a truly rainbow breed.

In 1975, one of the remaining black masked reds, Ch. Lipizzan's Big Red Machine, strode to BOB at the AHCA Specialty under Mrs. James Edward Clark. Living in the Midwest with the Howard Rubacks, the vitality of this dog was aptly utilized by professional handler Ralph Murphy, a former successful breeder of Afghan Hounds. Ralph well understood the breed character.

The AHCA Specialty of '76 brought out an intersex judge with a long tradition of Afghan Hounds behind her. Betsy Prior firmly summoned the handsomely mature 7-year-old Ch. Khayam's Ares to

BOB. That marked the first occasion for two littermates to have won the National, with brother Apollo having won the same award five years previously.

In 1977, the AHCA again moved to two shows a year. The Felltons took turns in handing out top awards that year. Judy did the honors in New York, awarding BOB to Dr. Burger's handsome bitch, Ch. Shangrila Pharahana Kunasata. Herman found, and pulled out, the venerable Ch. Coastwind Abraxas at the September National in Dallas, Texas. If a vote had been taken for a new permanent site for the National at that time, it undoubtedly would have gone to Texas, if only for the easy atmosphere and marvelous entertainment at the after-show dinner. The Texans gave shows at which the dog is brought as an excuse to attend, rather than the prime reason for entering.

Nevertheless, a singleton AHCA Specialty was held in New York City in '78. Doing intersex, Gini Withington happily awarded BOB to the domino male, a combined show and lure coursing winner, Ch. Zuvenda Renegade of Esfahan, F.Ch. He proves conclusively that the two attributes are in no way mutually exclusive. This show in New York City was held for reasons of expediency, not renewed support for the site. The death knell tolled irrevocably in 1979. In celebrating the wake of the site, Mary Stephenson's choice of Ch. Kaftan Korrigan for BOB—jointly owned by the two Carols, Esterkin and Reisman, representing a blending of East and West—led the festivities. The New York Statler-Hilton in February was abandoned. A new plan based on a continuous round of revolving regional sites, to be hosted by the local AHCA members, under the auspices of the AHCA, was put into permanent action. While a less autocratic concept, the complexities and logistics of each succeeding show, was to make each event somewhat experimental, yet exciting for all that participated, with a sharing of responsibility over a broader base.

October of '79 found the Specialty in Louisville, Kentucky. In the green grass country, Sandy Schwartz singled out for the top honor the stately black and tan Ch. Jamica's Rani Fafner. Much admired by breeder judges from adolescence onward, the dog had been taken over by Mrs. Cheever Porter to make a respectable all-breed showing from '76 through '78 on the charts. At Mrs. Porter's death, he returned to his former owners. Showing with verve the nearly seven-year-old did his owner Janet Carr proud, capping the end of the '70s.

Moving back somewhat, it was in June 1978, at the Southport Kennel Club show that Sunny Shay died—as she had lived—proudly handling her beloved Afghan Hound in the ring. Never far from the game, whether selling, advising, or showing, Sunny outlived disasters and monumental successes including the fire that gutted her kennel and took the life of many of her dogs. Acquiescing to an offer of sanctuary, Sunny moved to Roger Rechler's home on Long Island. The remaining dogs became jointly owned, more or less, between Sunny and Roger as continuation of Grandeur. Little did either realize that the stage was being set for Roger to inherit and carry the legendary name into the '80s due to circumstances beyond either's control.

With great joy Sunny had recently come up with a new dog that she showed with special pride, despite—or maybe partly because of—his bare pasterned cuffs and appearance—an appearance that could only be termed old time, from the wild expression, flying topknot to doughnut ringed tail. Sunny triumphantly brought Boy Blu of Grandeur to a quick championship under breeder judges who appreciated the moderate physical type and who were happy to give the nod to the cake—minus excess layers of frosting. The dog appeared to be off and running as the latest Grandeur breed symbol. But, as Sunny would have been the first to declare, the Fates were not to be over-ridden. On the sad day, acting just as Sunny would have wanted, her friend Mike Canalizo—once recovered from having seen Sunny fall—moved in to take the handlerless dog and carried him to the top of the Hound Group. Not only did Sunny's death dramatically change the destiny of Roger Rechler, but its effects were similarly profound on Mike who went on to become handler/manager for Grandeur under Rechler's ownership. He was particularly well suited for this position after long years of friendship with Sunny and as an admiring student under her casual tutelage.

Winners Dog on the day of Sunny's demise was a stud-fee puppy sired by Boy Blu, chosen by Sunny and given the name of Blu Shah of Grandeur. Mike continued to exhibit the taupe-colored Blu Boy for a while, as something he and Roger felt Sunny would have wanted, but there was a sort of ghostly quality that attached itself to the dog in his personification of the timelessness of Sunny. With something of relief, Mike switched to the younger Blu Shah as a more comfortable, and equally good, vehicle with which to carry on the Grandeur name and fame. Having some outcross blood through his dam (Priscilla Senior's Rubicon Rhea Silvia) Blu Shah nevertheless shrieked of Shirkhan-type tradition in color and outline. Blu Shah firmly moved Grandeur as an entity into the '80s to become the longest active kennel name in the breed's American history. Moving to the top of the charts in 1981, Blu Shah was well-received by all-rounders and specialists alike.

The abrupt death of Sunny sent shivers through many segments of the fancy, producing a jolting sense of their own mortality to those who had known her for years. The idea that Sunny, like any other mortal, would not live forever, was somehow logical to the mind but inconceivable to the spirit. Her own idiosyncratic existence had provided an exotic touchstone for rudderless days due to her own certainty of just what she and the breed were all about. In many a mind her death marked the end of an era. Ironically this happened at a time when the breed was beginning to show some quiet return to a greater stability of which she would have certainly approved. In an era that had come to behave like an untamed stallion with the bit in its teeth, racing headlong downhill, with most riders clinging for dear life—in the arrogant illusion that they were still in charge—Sunny knew the difference between just holding on for the ride and actually regaining hold of the reins. This peculiar clarity of view lent others a sense of reassurance by her very existence, even if at times it was severely tinged with irritation at her persistent individuality.

But life moved on relentlessly, and into the '80s. New dog names, including that of Blu Shah, became the topics of contemporary conversation. The 1980 National Specialty was the first of the revolving AHCA Specialties. Prior to that the Southern California, Dallas and Louisville Specialties were considered floating Specialties, as each of these shows was the second Specialty that year with a National still held in February in New York City.

In July of '80 it was the Northern California AHCA members' (under the chairmanship of Ang and Joanne Montesano) turn to host the first revolving AHCA Specialty which was held in Palo Alto. Intersex judge Jay Ammon, relocated on the West Coast, pointed to a black-masked, creamy colored Falstaff son with exceptionally handsome and classic outline, named Camri's Bentley, as BOB. Bred by John and Betty Richards, Bentley was just one more in a long line of Specialty winners with the Camri name, all dogs that were never broadly campaigned, and which were quietly put out to pasture when one of the next generation became of an age for Betty to show. Considered a pinnacle achievement, Bentley went BOB from the classes and was retired as of his National Specialty win.

In moving to Oklahoma City, the 1981 AHCA National was in the hands of Bud and Pauline Ledbetter and the local AHCA members. Judge Carol Esterkin decided upon the young Ch. Zuvenda Razcym for the breed. Proving that blood will tell, it is well worth noting that both of the parents of this sterling dog, Ch. Zuvenda Renegade of Esfahan and Ch. Bakali Cymbeline of Zuvenda, took the breed wins at the National in 1978 and 1974 respectively.

In 1981 the Parent Club Specialty, chaired by Archy Clot, increased its aims by having a full day public educational symposium preceding the January judging date in West Palm Beach, Florida.

Well attended and enjoyed, this activity was added to the tradition of the National when feasible.

Acknowledging a reduction in entries, only two judges were hired for Florida. Sue Kauffman adjudicated bitches. Betty Stites did dogs and intersex, putting to the supreme honor the powerful moving dark brindle, Ch. Province Applause Resolution. Owned by the Jantos, and shown by Gene, the dog was the result of a co-breeding combining the sound qualities of the Province line with Ch. Alharin Applause, both heavily flowing back to the older Moornistan line. Ned Kauffman acted as Symposium Chairman with his usual flair and excellence.

As the 80's dawned, a meteoric dog appeared in the West that, with increasing brightness, streaked to the front of the breed parade, creating flashings that were soon to shine nationwide. The ebony and cream lustre of Ch. Kabik's the Challenger (Pepsi), under the respectful hands of breeder/owner Chris Terrell, sent this remarkable animal shooting not only into the top winning Afghan Hound of all time, but on to top winning dog All-Breeds 1982, Quaker Oats Hound Group winner, Kennel Review top winning Hound of all time, and into retirement after winning BIS at Westminster in 1983. Westminster BIS judge Derek Rayne stated, "Truly he has the look of eagles and on this night he could have outrun the desert wind. He was in perfect bloom and by the way that he showed he knew that he owned the Garden!"

The Terrells, based in Washington State, had quietly been breeding generations of fine champions, while constantly striving to move closer to their ideal through different combinations of Grandeur-based lines. Pepsi was the happy result of putting the lovely Falstaff daughter, Ch. Kabik's Mindy, to their Abraxas son, Ch. Kabik's Standing Ovation. This merger tied together the direct get of two somewhat different Top Producers—Falstaff and Abraxas—with stunning results. Including Pepsi, his close relatives, and the backup generations still at Kabik, this kennel was catapulted into a position of undeniable prominence in the early '80s.

Pepsi came out of retirement to win the 1983 AHCA National Specialty and the Tournament of Champions. To enter the Tournament each dog has to have won an all-breed Best-in-Show or an independent parent club National Specialty in the previous year. On March 30, 1984 at Chicago, Illinois, Pepsi went BIS at the Tournament of Champions and was declared the Show Dog of the Year.

The 47th National Specialty was held July 28 and 29, 1983, on the campus of the University of California, Santa Barbara, California. This marked the beginning of the second time around in the AHCAs cross-country Specialty concept. The AHCA had now provided everyone in the Afghan Hound fancy an opportunity to attend a National. The weather, light sea breeze off the Pacific Ocean, blue skies and green grass provided the ideal setting for the gorgeously groomed entry of 336 Afghan Hounds which made up the 449 entries—not counting the Lure Coursing entries. Ed Gilbert and Carol Esterkin co-chaired the Specialty—the many workers both from the AHCA and the fancy made it a success. The day before the Specialty the AHCA hosted a "hands on" Sighthound Symposium which was conceived and perfectly executed by Conni Miller. Rachel Page Elliot of *The New Dog Steps—Illustrated Gait at a Glance* fame showed her incomparable 16mm slow motion film on dog gait. Her commentary, along with her stop action projector, provided the attendees with the opportunity to benefit from years of experience in one sitting.

The second day started early with Sweepstakes. The 104 entries were judged by Betty Richards. This was followed by Ned Kauffman Jr. ruling on 116 dogs. Betty Mae Regan judged the great Ben Zari's Dusty Dawn, UD, LCM in Utility, followed by judge Jim Thomson doing Novice and Open obedience. That evening under the lights, the ASFA Lure Course was judged by Joan Aaron and Joyce Taddeo. The third day started with Miss Pamela Irene Brink judging Junior Showmanship, placing Jennifer Perrigo Best Junior Handler. This was followed by Judy Fellton judging 143 bitches—followed by 18 Veterans on Parade. Forty-two specials, WD and WB were judged by Ned Kauffman Jr., who awarded Pepsi BOB. Pepsi had come out of retirement just to be shown at the National. The three days of tight schedules—symposium, show, dinners, meeting and camaraderie— didn't end that evening. Most exhibitors stayed on for both the Lompoc and Santa Barbara K.C. shows. One of the retired Afghan Hound breeder (Kaihorn) judges, Midge Horn, puts together the AKC/Parent Club slide/tape education programs. The AHCA Board requested Midge to make the first showing of the Afghan Hound program to the general membership at the 1983 annual meeting. This program should benefit the fancy by providing breeders, exhibitors and judges with an excellent opportunity to study the breed standard.

Leading the bitch side of the parade into the '80s, also with her full story yet to be written, was the Caelus daughter previously mentioned, Ch. Cani Summer Breeze (Windy). As one more of the select group of bitches to become multiple BIS winners, her great femininity shown even more brightly at the regional breed specialty level where she lays claim to more than a dozen wins.

The dog with the most spectacular record of regional specialty wins, at this time, is the Texas-based Ch. Jonathon L. Seagull

158

Ch. Yucatan Knight Vision (Ch. Sephira Amra-Shah of Taj Mahal ex Ms. Cee Jay of Yucatan), black and tan bitch, BIS winner. Bred by Robert and Carol Penta, owned by Kevin and Barbara Cassidy, Robert and Carol Penta. Handler, Barbara Cassidy. —*TNT*.

Ch. Genesis BT Express (Ch. Camri's Black and Tan Rebelion ex Ch. Genesis Jazz Solo), black and tan dog, BIS winner. Bred by Lou Guerrero and Hank Nave. Owned by Clay Jennings, Lou Guerrero and Hank Nave. Handler, Lou Guerrero. —*Missy Yuhl*.

159

Jedashi with over 27 to his credit. The dark blue dog, better known as, of all things, Gorilla, remains a threat to all comers under the caring hands of Israel Garcia and Don Davidson, and a joy to those thrilled by him. Their Casa Real kennel name is moving into the winners circle.

There are now, and always have been, impressive dogs in the breed that, for reasons known only to themselves, disport themselves with maximum impact only in the presence of fellow Afghan Hounds. There was a day when this condition was ascribed to unpopular color, but that condition is surely past. These dogs are not well-reflected on lists that give high weight to All-Breed BIS wins, but they stand out like treasured cameos at the Specialties. Fortunately, they are not overlooked by perceptive breeders, and thereby send their harmony of breed-type into the cauldron genepool of the breed.

September 4 and 5, 1984, saw the 48th National Specialty in Denver, under the guidance of Helen Haas and Nancy Crader, with an entry of 262 Afghan Hounds. Judges Robert Stein and Archy Clot shared the conformation judging. BOB was Ch. Cani Summer Breeze, owned by Ardie Libke, Hank Nave and Lou Guerrero. High scoring dog in obedience, under judge Helen F. Phillips, was Natasha Dawn, owned by Rafael Fontela, with a score of 190. September 6 was the day for the Lure Field Trial judged by Gary Roush and Emmet Roche. Best in Field was won by Alfie's Ebony and Ivory, F.Ch., owned by John and Connie Sullivan. Not only is the Specialty truly National, but the triple threat aspects of the Afghan Hounds are now demonstrated also.

During the period from 1979 through 1984 the following kennel names have stood out among the roster of champions: *Abashagh* (Claudia Cochrane); *Addis Ababa* (Joan Backus); *Ambrosia* (Dann Maly); *Applaus* (Sandra Motz); *Arbol Loco* (Carlos A. Rubiano); *Bonanza* (Margaret Pugh); *Camri* (Betty Richards); *Caravan* (Vincent & Elizabeth Leap); *Cavu* (Betsy Hufnagel); *Chanhu* (Nora Dodson); *Charikar* (Dick & Georgiana Guthrie); *Chubel* (Belle Anna Burr); *Coastwind* (Mike Dunham & Richard Souza); *Cypress* (Jia Miller); *Dacasha* (Cathy Lursen); *Dayspring* (David Sorey); *Dureigh* (Dewey & Reigh Abram); *Dynasty* (Fred Alderman); *Elmo* (Peter Belmont); *Fox Run* (Virginia Colin Stee's); *Genesis* (Lou Guerrero & Hank Nave); *Heatherwood* (Stan & Barbara Brindle); *Jeherans* (Ken & Dorothy Juby); *Jorogz* (John Rogers Morton); *Jubilan* (Judith Bloom); *Kabik* (Chris & Marguerite Terrell); *Kalepas* (Loraine & Ted Sapelak); *Karzaks* (Tim & Mary Taylor); *Kassan* (June E. Boone); *Mafreeka* (Dr. Rudi Maffei); *Mahali* (Lynne Schanzle); *Persia* (Ron & Rose Mary Bridges); *Picascio* (John Lo Cascio); *Sanallah* (Al & Sandra Weinraub); *Sandina* (Glorvina Schwartz); *Scarabet* (Karen

Ch. Anrobs Gone With The Wind (Ch. Zebec Paragon of Anrob ex Ch. Jiratchmir's Whirlwind), black dog, BIS winner. Bred by Judy Umeck and Theresa Greene. Owned by Robert and Angela DiNicola. Handler, Robert DiNicola.—*Ashbey*.

Ch. Kassan's Nina Nerina (Ch. Scharlau O-Havoc ex Ch. Ambrosia Bon-Dir), black mask red bitch. Bred, owned and handled by June E. Boone.—*Ritter*.

Ch. Cypress Silent Echo (Ch. Sharif's Sky's The Limit ex Ch. Karamoor's Colony of Cypress), black mask red dog, BIS winner. Bred by Jia M. and Jack D. Miller and Pat Kimberly. Owned by Jia Miller and Pat Kimberly. Handler, Jia Miller.—*Graham*.

Carter); *Scharlau* (Don & Ellen Petryca); *Shikari* (Mary Lou Benjamin); *Stormhill* (Dave & Sandy Withington Frei); *Summerwind* (Bruce & Rosemary Sutton); *Tagenes* (Eugene Ridnour); *Tallaway* (Charlotte Clevenger); *Thaon* (Jay Hafford & Tom Morehouse); *Tifarah* (Richard & Janis Reital); *Timu-Ka* (Dr. Phillip & Dolores Haims); *Tully* (Betsey & Allen Tully); *Wildenau* (Al & Ingrid Stewart); *Willowmoor* (Gene & June Vaccaro); *Xanadu* (Roger & Johanna B. Tanner); *Zafara* (Bob & Bobbi Keller); *Zebec* (Walter Greene & Carl Sanders); *Zuvenda* (Kevin & Karen Martin).

While continuing to breed champions remains the essential name of this game, novice, or over-eager exhibitors would do well to bear in mind that the notable number of show wins, even of seeming Cinderella dogs, represent not only quality animals, but a considerable outlay of time, money and determined efforts. Untraveled and unadvertised dogs, although locally well-respected, remain all but invisible in the welter of nationwide shrieking broadcasts. The full page cannon blast continues to drown out the modest whisper, regardless of content. Like all hobbies this one can—and often does—get out of hand. Many a fancier has climbed onto the tail-chasing game of trying to better a record already set by one of his own dogs—for fear someone else will usurp the momentary pre-eminence. Admittedly, the well-advertised hounds get the most frequent calls for stud services, and often to better quality bitches, and their puppies are most in demand. But in a surprisingly short time once-famed names fall off the ends of the pedigrees with records remembered only by those who go to break them.

In these days where the opportunities for natural challenge and real purpose for the hunting hounds of Afghanistan are very few, the least we can do is deliberately supplant that void with respectful understanding and affectionate attention, free of concern for the blue ribbons they do, or do not, win for us.

7

Conformation and
Official Breed Standard

Unless rough standards are available from the land of any breed's major development, and such is definitely not the case with Afghan Hounds, establishing a detailed breed standard can be a perplexing task. In Afghanistan, the hounds developed through a process of natural selection within isolated tribes, creating various geographic types. With a broad range, the gaze hound physical type was preserved for the elementary reason that any pup who strayed too far from this functional build forfeited his natural ability to overwhelm fleet game, thereby destroying his value as a hunter.

The newspaper article from Kabul, by Gulbaz, describing the three *tazi* coat types, is as near to an Afghanistan standard as has been found. Dated August 1962, it could scarcely be applied to past generations without caution, but its brief comments are provocative and compatible with Western concepts of correct breed type: "The animals should have a long, pointed muzzle, a prominent protuberance over the dome of the head, and the distance between the two pelvic bones should be at least four fingers placed side by side. Crooked legs, a short muzzle, and narrowness of the 'Kargas' (rhyming with 'bus'), meaning the diaphragm or breastbones, are disqualifications. Large breastbones are an asset on the grounds that the animal has large lungs and therefore a great 'wind.' 'Tazis' are neither docked nor are their ears cut." (The last sentence differentiates the "Tazi" from the "Siahbundy" or Afghan Sheepdog, which do have ears cut and tails docked.)

Lacking basis for a cohesive breed standard from Afghanistan, early descriptions were logically based on notable Eastern specimens that impressed canine authorities of the day. In England, the outstanding Zardin was given the banner of leadership. The Afghan Hound type in America was derived from British stock and a written standard based on a British document.

In this book we are mainly concerned with the current American Standard but have included reference to some obsolete standards for the historical insight they provide. Dates show the divergence in concepts between English and American documents in the 1930s and the 1940s and despite undeniable British influences on the current American Standard, the document stands very well by itself, not as an imitative copy, but as a well-thought out description of a majestic, unique and useful breed of dog.

The basic purpose of the breed standard is twofold. The foremost duty is the *delineation of the breed's characteristics* in such a clear fashion that a reader who knows next to nothing about dogs could stroll into his first show and pick out a representative of the breed. Such breed characteristics include structural outline, range of size, coat type, coloration, head shape, ear and tail formation, and expression. The other duty of the breed standard is to set up criteria for the recognition of superior specimens within the breed. Breed-judging consists ideally of comparing several highly similar individuals against a Standard of perfection, but, in actuality, the dogs are compared against each other, and against the judge's image of other noteworthy specimens. Ruling factors here are not angles and inches so much as elements of "type" (the hallmark of the breed) plus the total balanced appearance and working efficiency of the dog's standing and moving parts. There is certain to be honest disagreement in the manner in which different knowledgeable human beings value these factors, and in Afghan Hounds the dog's structure is virtually hidden by a long coat. For this reason we have included, not only an expanded Standard section, complete with the authors' interpretations, but also a small dose of anatomy to help the thoughtful fancier better understand the underlying form involved.

In reading the following discussion of the Standard, it would be well to hold firmly in mind the sage advice written by the President as of 1964 of the Afghan Hound Club of America, Donald A. Smith: ". . . in studying the standard and in evaluating dogs, always try to get back to the complete entity. Study the standard in detail—not for the sake of details nor in order to talk about your dog's virtues and my dog's faults—but to fix in your mind a clear and complete picture of how a truly good Afghan is put together . . . how he should look, stand, move and act."

164

OFFICIAL AKC STANDARD
FOR AFGHAN HOUNDS

The current Afghan Hound Standard was drafted by the Afghan Hound Club of America and adopted by the American Kennel Club on September 14, 1948:

General Appearance—The Afghan Hound is an aristocrat, his whole appearance is one of dignity and aloofness with no trace of plainness or coarseness. He has a straight front, proudly carried head, eyes gazing into the distance as if in memory of ages past. The striking characteristics of the breed—exotic, or "eastern," expression, long silky topknot, peculiar coat pattern, very prominent hip bones, large feet, and the impression of a somewhat exaggerated bend in stifle due to profuse trouserings—stand out clearly, giving the Afghan Hound the appearance of what he is, a king of dogs, that has held true to tradition throughout the ages.

AUTHORS' COMMENTS—The primary purpose of breed identification has been covered here. Included are the notable attributes that place the Afghan Hound apart, from even the closely related Saluki. Topknot, exotic expression, hip bones, cowboy chaps, and his king of dogs demeanor contribute little to hunting efficiency, but they are priceless in preserving the uniqueness of the breed. About the only explanation that is missing is the term "straight front" which refers to the dog's appearance from the straight-on view.

Head—The head is of good length showing much refinement, the skull evenly balanced with the foreface. There is a slight prominence of the nasal bone structure causing a slightly Roman appearance, the center line running up over the foreface with little or no stop, falling away in front of the eyes so there is an absolutely clear outlook with no interference; the underjaw showing great strength, the jaws long and punishing; the mouth level, meaning that the teeth from the upper jaw and lower jaw match evenly, neither overshot nor undershot. This is a difficult mouth to breed. A scissors bite is even more punishing and can be more easily bred into a dog than a level mouth, and a dog having a scissors bite, where the lower teeth slip inside and rest against the teeth of the upper jaw, should not be penalized. The occipital bone is very prominent. The head is surmounted by a topknot of long silky hair.

165

Ears—The ears are long, set approximately on level with outer corners of the eyes, the leather of the ear reaching nearly to the end of the dog's nose, and covered with long silky hair.

Eyes—The eyes are almond shaped (almost triangular), never full or bulgy, and are dark in color.

Nose—Nose is of good size, black in color.

Faults—Coarseness; snipiness; overshot or undershot; eyes round or bulgy or light in color; exaggerated Roman nose; head not surmounted by a topknot.

AUTHORS' COMMENTS—The head of the Afghan Hound is unabashed in its show of bone, veins and character. It is of the utmost importance in matters of beauty and utility and should never be softened with pads of fat, loose skin, or evidence of grossness. In head type, the Afghan, in a league with the other sight hounds, is *dolicocephalic* (head considerably longer than broad, as differing from the *brachycephalic* or shortheaded breeds). This long bony muzzle fronted by powerful jaws and large teeth is the prime maiming tool of the gazehound for grasping or slashing at victims or opponents. While some Afghan Hounds rip for the jugular veins, others "hamstring" victims by severing heel tendons and a few have been known to spring like great cats onto the back of their victim crunching the backbones. The usual disposal method with hares, rabbits, and vermin is to grasp them by the spine and shake them until the vertebrae snaps.

The Afghan's nasal bone should be as long as possible ending in large black nostrils, capable of full and rich intake of air (so necessary for hunting endurance) set into a heavy black nose leather. (Note: "nose" means the leather, not the whole muzzle. Dark masks are attractive but nowhere specified in the standard.)

Looking down from above the impression is that the long nasal bone serves as a well defined ridgebeam from which the sides of the muzzles drop abruptly. For the touch of Roman nose, the nasal bone has a slight rise to it. The flat or concave muzzle ("dished") is incorrect as is any gross exaggeration of the Roman convexity. The mildly arched nasal bone is forced to meet the frontal bone at a slight downslope causing a noticeable incurve just in front of the eyes—that should never be confused with a true stop (an abrupt rise and fill-in of the frontal bone in a stair-step effect). The very important frontal bone should form a well-defined upstanding triangle, based at the eyes, rising in a domed apex, to a ridgy saggital crest that leads to the very pointed occiput. The sides of the skull should drop away from the frontal bone and "crest" fairly steeply. Any dip, depression, or lack of distinct formation of this frontal

166

The structure of this head is very desirable. Note the excellent chiseling of a long nasal bone, the presence of a frontal triangle above the eyes, and a smooth zygomatic arch from eye to ear. These characteristics form the proper slant-back skull and small, deep-set almond eyes. Both this drawing and the one on the opposite page were made expressly for this book by Lois Gossner.

triangle is a fault, distorting the total head shape as well as the ears and eye type.

Lips ("flews") should be tight and not hang below the mouth line.

The request for a skull "evenly balanced with the foreface" refers, in part, to the fact that the midpoint of head length, from occiput to nostrils, falls between the eyes. Aside from any illusion provided by topknots, the head, upon examination, should illustrate such total balance, with muzzle and skull parts joining smoothly. Rounded and broad backskulls or disproportionately short, narrow or thin ("snipey") muzzles seriously disrupt the aristocratic head line.

The widest part of the skull necessarily falls at the broad point of the zygomatic arch where it passes the point of lower jaw attachment. This arched bone runs back from the base of the eye, protecting the eyeball within its hollow, to the ear opening, and is analogous to the human cheekbone. For the sake of refinement, the Afghan Hound head should have as smooth, low-curved and inconspicuous a zygomatic arch as is possible.

Topknots, receding at the temples until the broadest point of the zygomatic arch is revealed, create illusionary coarsening effects. Profuse topknots, hanging well over the eyes, blur easy perception of correct skull and eye form. Some judges mistakenly believe that what doesn't show can't matter much, but the lack of classically shaped heads and eyes is a matter for serious breed concern.

Faults of round, large or bulging eyes result from incorrect head shapes. The eyeball must lie in a deep oblique plane along the zygomatic arch to form an almond shaped aperture, necessitating definite "fall-away" of the nose from the nasal ridge in front of the eyes and a well-defined frontal triangle.

Eye expression depends on a variety of factors: size, shape, and placing of eye frame as well as the dog's mental attitude. Color of eye and fur surrounding it must be considered. The natural occurrence of dark eye-pencilling with slanted outer-eye lines (so commonly found on masked hounds) or orange dashes over the brow of black-and-tan hounds give "Oriental" aspects. Dark eyes tend to recede and appear deep, being preferred in Afghans as in most breeds. The light eye with its yellowish iris is aesthetically undesirable, often giving its wearer a startled look. Unfortunately, the really deep dark, hard eye of Shaw McKean's time has become a very scarce item today.

Proper Afghan expression, not easily described in words, varies with the specimen somewhat, but must be in keeping with the Oriental character of the breed. It might be a look of complete inscrutability. Some handsome hounds have a piercing, warlike stare that freezes the advances of strangers—while others have a gentlewise gaze in character with the timeless passive wisdom of the Orient. The addition of Mandarin chin whiskers certainly contributes to the Eastern aspect. Pleading, trusting, puzzled, surprised or vacant expressions are foreign to the King of Dogs.

Being far sighted, the Afghan Hound tends to pull back his head and "look down his nose" at close objects, contributing to the highly desired, arrogant air.

168

This drawing illustrates a head with excessive stop, rounded skull, circular eyes, coarse bone, and insufficient muzzle length.

The outer ear occurs at the rear point of the zygomatic arch, with the leather curving above it, tying ear placement into the important zygomatic arch effects. The ears should be set as low and far back as possible to create the leanest head effects. In this day of overwhelming topknots, however, the length of ear and its fringes do more for the flat ear effect than the actual set. The Standard's request for ear leathers that reach nearly to the end of the nose would seem to be stretching the word "nearly," for any ear leather that falls much below the beginning of the lip line on an adult dog is of good average length. The silky hair fringes that line the ear leathers can grow to fantastic lengths and, with luck and meticulous protection, fall well down onto the mature dog's shoulders.

The importance of large, powerful teeth and a tight, punishing bite could hardly be overemphasized on a gazehound. Both the level bite and the scissors bite are efficient weapons for slashing, tearing, biting or gripping. The scissors has one advantage in that the incisors grind down more slowly with age, not being in constant working contact as in the level bite. The undershot bite (lower teeth projecting beyond uppers as in the Bulldog) may be useful for gripping but not for much else. The overshot bite (teeth of upper jaw closing well ahead of the lowers) is entirely too loose for effective holding power. A good bite calls for a well-fitted lower jaw as well as upper. Any sign of shallow, narrow, or poorly fitted underjaws is seriously detrimental to a game dog.

Neck—The neck is of good length, strong and arched, running in a curve to the shoulders which are long and sloping and well laid back.

Faults—Neck too short or too thick; an ewe neck, a goose neck; a neck lacking in substance.

AUTHORS' COMMENTS—The demand for a long-strong-powerful arched neck is common to all gazehounds for not only does it add great nobility to the structure, it is essential for any animal that is expected to reach out, from a full gallop, to grasp or bite his prey. Necks that are short appear thick and unattractive and, while such necks do not lack power, they lack length of reach for picking up the skittering hare and are dangerously ineffective in keeping the dog's vulnerable body away from the teeth and claw of adversary.

An anatomical rule of thumb calls for neck-length, from occiput to neck junction—to equal head length from occiput to end of nose. In a breed so prone to changing outline illusions, adolescent necks submerged in profuse standoff coat appear much shorter than they actually measure. More noble length mysteriously appears as a longer and closer-lying adult coat develops. In correct patterning the long hair on the sides of the neck thins out along with a natural short-haired saddle down the backline.

Fully as serious as the too-short neck is one that is too long and narrow. A poverty of musculature along the top, or the sides, results in the "goose neck" or one "lacking in substance." Dynamically, this seriously weakens concerted strong action of head and neck with body and shoulders. The tube-like goose neck produces a stove-pipe effect, and is sometimes misguidedly accepted in the name of

170

elegance. Closely related to it is the "ewe neck," natural on some breeds of sheep but forming a faulty upright right-angled junction on dogs. The ewe neck is concave on the upper surface. A powerful neck of proper length and substance is far more than a matter of aesthetics. The requested arched neck stems from a curved nape made of powerful muscles radiating down from the base of the skull, gradually widening towards the withers to form a gentle "curve" which, when properly formed, runs smoothly "to the shoulders." These are muscles of constant conjunctive importance, not only for grasping prey, but through chain-reaction connections with every movement of the central body and forelegs. Shoulders will be further detailed under "legs."

> *Body—The backline appearing practically level from the shoulders to the loin. Strong and powerful loin and slightly arched, falling away towards the stern, with the hip bones very pronounced; well ribbed and tucked up in flanks. The height at the shoulders equals the distance from the chest to the buttocks; the brisket well let down, and of medium width.*
>
> *Faults—Roach back, sway back, goose rump, slack loin, lack of prominence of hip bones; too much width of brisket causing interference with elbows.*

AUTHORS' COMMENTS—In 1929 Jean Manson wrote an article for the *American Kennel Gazette* describing the characteristic Afghan body type that bears repetition today. We quote: "Another thing 'outsiders' do not realize and this is the Afghan's enormous strength and power. This is due to their graceful outline and rather chiseled appearance and elegance. A hound which is well developed should possess hard muscle and a great deal of it should be in the hind quarters; the shoulders are not so well equipped, but should slope into the long, strong neck. Bones should be heavy and the feet as large as possible, all joints very flexible, and the greater the depth of brisket the better, with a neat tuck-up under the loin.

"The great thing in breeding is to keep this strength, muscle and bone without producing coarseness. Thick heavy shoulders, thick loins, and a wide chest, etc., give a general appearance of cumbersomeness. A hound of this variety might be heavy and strong, but his lack of agility would be far too great a handicap to him, apart from his unattractive appearance.

"On the other hand, weedy, light-boned hounds are not coveted, however pretty and graceful they may be. It has to be remembered that they are sporting dogs, not drawingroom pets. Their forefathers have done rough work, and it will be a thousand pities if we allow them to degenerate into ornaments."

171

To this sage description we might add that a good Afghan is lean at all times, but never scrawny. A rule of thumb says that just the tops of three dorsal vertebrae should stand above the backline as evidence of proper weight. There should never be deep valleys between ribs, but neither should they be filled smooth with fat layers.

The Standard words on topline requires careful attention in terms of both surface appearance, and underlying structure. Externally, in illusion, the standoff puppy-coat conceals, the shedding period misleads, and the smooth adult saddle accentuates the backline of Afghan Hounds beyond that of other breeds.

The intent of "practically level from the shoulders to the loin" in the Standard glides into "strong and powerful loin and slightly arched." The adverbs "practically" and "slightly" wisely acknowledge that even a level vertebral line has differing heights of muscle-anchoring spinous processes (and muscles) forming its dynamic surface outline. The processes are the longest, and the vertebrae buried the deepest, under the sector called withers—which, in fact, can rise and fall with changes in the dog's neck or back positions. At the withers the spines slant backwards (in opposition to foreleg muscle pull) and diminish in height down to a point that may appear as a dent in the backline. Under the dent is the anticlinal (11th) thoracic vertebrae, which, together with the 10th, makes up a pyramidal shaped sector that carries the condensed and intersecting major muscle groups connecting the working front and rear ends of the animal. Because muscle-ends taper at this point, a natural V may occur on otherwise firm-backed dogs. This dent must not be confused with a "swayback"—where the central body loosely drops down from the withers into a true vertebral sag manifest in the area of the 10th and 11th vertebrae.

Loin muscles run from the anticline, over the last thoracics, across the lumbars, and conclude on the pelvis. The spines under the loin musculature are, or should be, extremely broad—rather than tall—to hold a thick muscle cable running the full length. From its tapered end at the anticline, when strongly developed, this all important power-pack of musculature appears prominent and "slightly arched." Such a formation is decidedly different from the "roach"—an actual rising convex curve of underlying vertebrae. As a combined distance-trotter, and speedy galloper, both done with unparalleled agility, the Afghan Hound rightly needs a strong balanced level topline that neither flows uphill, nor down, in stance or trot.

The loins usher in the hip section. The hip bone, correctly called the pelvis, is a stationary bony formation through which the fused sacrum section of the vertebrae passes. The actual hip joint is in the lower half of the pelvis, joining the hind leg in a ball and socket

172

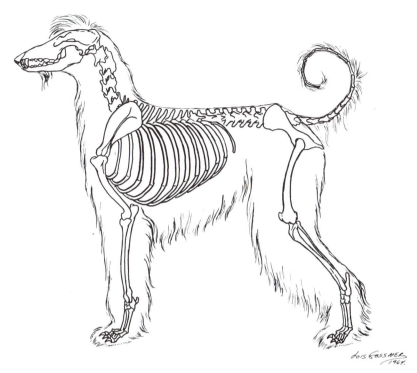

Afghan Hound skeleton, drawn from X-rays by Lois Gossner.

connection. The "seat bones" make up the rear ends of the pelvis. Those points, commonly called "hip bones" that project above the backline, are the upper prominences of the pelvis as it curves away from the sacrum. In the traditional rawboned Afghan Hound frame, these appear as bony knobs, typically large and well-developed, visually accentuated by the demarcation line of the fur pattern. These bone-tips should never be hidden by pads of fat. The entire pelvis should be quite broad with the seat bones well separated. Any narrowness of rear quarters through the loins or the pelvis is to be strongly discouraged. Contrary to circulated propaganda, the Afghan is no more double jointed nor structurally swivel hipped than other breeds.

The largest difference, aside from coating, between the Afghan and related gazehounds such as the Borzoi or the Greyhound, is in the full profile. The Borzoi outline has a grand curving flow to it. The Afghan backline is considerably more angular, from its abrupt high head carriage, through the level back, past the bony pelvic protrusions, to a rather stark rumpline and a tail that curves out and thrusts itself upward. A portion of this difference emanates from the shoulder area, where on the Afghan Hound, the spinion processes (spires that project above the vertebrae as muscle anchors) are shorter, placing the spinal column nearer the surface and contributing to the extreme high head carriage and level back of the breed.

Like the Borzoi, the Greyhound has the drawnout horizontal "S" curve of vertebrae from neck to line of tail, with a spinal curvature that tucks the pelvis into a steeper grade than is found on average breeds. It is interesting to note that Track Greyhounds, often less pronounced in "roach" are apt to have somewhat more definite hip bones and higher tail carriages than their more fashionably built show brothers.

In the eyes of some writers and judges, the Afghan Hound with his harsh rumpline is considered "goose rumped" as a breed, but the goose rump is listed as a fault—with reference to any pelvis that drops unduly sharply, creating a restrictive angle at the point of hind leg attachment. Such a narrowed angle cuts down the possible backward extension of the hind leg in action. The impression of the goose rump in Afghans when not actually present comes from the decisive incline from prominent pelvic tips to the seat bones, in the absence of a fat-softened croup drop. This is demonstrated by the overweight Afghan whose pelvic angle has not changed but, with invisible hip bones and rounded rump, suddenly appears to have gained a decidedly more horizontal pelvis than when in a leaner state.

The Afghan Hound, being less drawn-out in line than the Greyhound and built for maximum maneuverability is expected to fit the standard request for a square dog, a challenging feat to achieve in conjunction with maximum angulation of quarters. In complicated matters of proportions, owners may find it most informative to take actual measurements. Factors of angulation, body type and coating create some amazing constant and sometimes changeable proportion illusions. Judges see only how the hound looks to them and there is no point in arguing that the dog is pure square, when they say "too long." Seek the underlying reasons for the disproportionate appearance instead.

As with all gazehounds, the Afghan must have great depth of ribs ("well let down" brisket) and, at maturity, on a level with the dog's elbows. His body breadth is medium with the important rib cage, housing heart and lungs, never to form such a broad oval (barrelled) as to cause interference with elbows gliding back and forth in motion. Certainly the rib cage should not be narrow or flat ("slabsided"), fully as serious a fault as too much width. Ribs themselves should be broad and long, well carried back onto the dog's body, softly arching outward for maximum breathing capacity.

174

The breastbone (sternum or keel) deserves mention. The sternum, connecting the right and left sides of the ribs, begins as a prominent projection at the base of the throat and runs in a downcurve between the front legs to form the floor of the brisket. Examination of the forechest area indicates the actual breadth of the forequarters. The old reliable rule of thumb asks for about four fingers' width between front legs. A shallow or narrow sternum indicates skimpy front ribs, a "pinched" brisket, and lack of lung room.

Tail—Tail is set not too high on the body, having a ring or curve on the end; should never be curled over, or rest on the back, or be carried sideways, and should never be bushy.

AUTHORS' COMMENTS—Most of this is crystal clear except for the problem of the tail set. "Set not too high on the body" is open to diverse interpretation but hardly substantiates the popular concept that the Afghan's tail should be "set low but carried high," calling for a rather improbable spine, the tail being merely the outside extension of the spinal column. Factors to be considered are pelvic lengths and angle of inclination plus the nature of the tail itself. A pelvis that is unusually tilted towards the horizontal automatically produces a "high set" tail, while the "goose rump" rear cants the tail into a "low set" position. Greyhounds, with their spinal curve and tucked-under pelvis, come by a true low set (and low carried) tail quite naturally. Afghans should have neither low nor high set tails, but good middle-of-the-road caudal appendages indicating a functional 30° pelvis. The curl of the tail is of remarkable visual importance. Any tail that begins its tight curl near the body appears considerably higher-set and shorter than the tail that does not take much of a swing until past the midpoint. The tail with the tiny doughnut on the end looks far longer than the broad loose curl. The straight tail just looks terrible. In spite of great apparent variation in Afghan tail lengths, most of them, when stretched full length along the hind leg, finish about one to one and one-half inches above the hock tip in mature hounds somewhat shorter than the tails of other gazehounds. Tails vary in tensile strength, and the good Afghan tail has considerable "spring" to it. (Note: There is not one word in the Standard implying that any Afghan Hound must hold its tail high, either naturally or as aided by the handler, when the dog is standing in a show pose.)

Legs—Forelegs are straight and strong with great length between elbow and pastern; elbows well held in; forefeet large in both length and width; toes well arched; feet covered with long thick

*hair; fine in texture; pasterns long and straight; pads of feet un-
usually large and well down on the ground. Shoulders have
plenty of angulation so that the legs are set well underneath the
dog. Too much straightness of shoulder causes the dog to break
down in the pasterns, and this is a serious fault.*

*All four feet of the Afghan Hound are in line with the body, turn-
ing neither in nor out. The hind feet are broad and of good
length; the toes arched, and covered with long thick hair; hindquarters powerful and well muscled with great length between
hip and hock; hocks well let down; good angulation of both stifle
and hock; slightly bowed from hock to crotch.*

*Faults—Front or back feet thrown outward or inward; pads of
feet not thick enough; or feet too small; or any other evidence of
weakness in feet; weak or broken down pasterns; too straight in
stifle; too long in back.*

AUTHORS' COMMENTS—It may be helpful to see the front leg
in rough analogy with the human arm. Both have shoulders, upper
arms and the canine lower leg takes the place of the human fore-
arm. The joint at the base of these bones, so large and obvious in
puppies, is the wrist in man but the pastern joint in dogs. The
pastern length is made of bones analogous to the human hand. The

dog walks on the last three joints of these bones which, instead of
being free as human fingers, are doubled up to form arched toes. The
dew claw is a vestigial thumb.

For "great length of foreleg" the bones between elbow and pastern must be noticeable and measurably longer than those of
shoulder and upper arm. Forelegs should be well-boned ending in
very large feet. These long, broad feet with lengthy and high-arched
toes in a heavily furred webbing are strong characteristics of the agile
Afghan Hound. English canine anatomist, Dr. R. H. Smythe, says
that "The Afghan possesses non-skid brakes, lacking in the Greyhound. That is why Afghans travel much better than Greyhounds
over rough or slippery ground." Non-skid factors of thick rough
pads, and hairy, semi-retractile long arched toes enable the foot to
contract for braking action. Such feet are a requisite for the Afghan
and should never be overlooked by judges. No short toed "cat" feet,
please!!

It is the authors' opinion that the description of pasterns is the
most confusing one in the standard. "Long pastern" readily fits into
line with long leg bones and large feet. But "straight" is the puzzler.
"Straight" could well mean upright (vertical) as in some breeds, but
there are specific anatomical reasons to doubt this. According to
McDowell Lyons and other canine experts, the combination of well-

sloped shoulders, upper arms set well underneath the dog, long fore-legs and long pasterns—necessitates a somewhat sloping pastern to place the heel pad directly under the center of gravity where it belongs. In England the sloping pastern receives acknowledged preference in the breed.

We can only speculate that the term "straight pastern" might refer to the front view of the dog. The problems of crooked pasterns has been, and still is, thoroughly pertinent to the breed as a continuing serious fault. McDowell Lyons wrote about this in *Popular Dogs,* June, 1956: "Standing facing you, the dog's front pads should turn outward slightly . . . created by a slight rotation of the pastern joint, and not a bend of this joint . . . On the inward swing, this pad comes in line with the direction of motion and action is over the two center toes. Without this slight out-turn, the action is over one center toe and the outside smaller toe, which is not so efficient as the former." Although such compensatory action may preclude the absolute dead-straight front right through the toenails, it in no way excuses east-west feet that crook outward from the pastern joint, as such bent pasterns do anything but advance the cause of straight motion.

The broken-down pastern is quite different from the normal sloping pastern, being also found on the dog originally blessed with upright pasterns, there being more concussion on this type of un-yielding leg. The crooked pastern can also break down in record time. This pastern talk may be academic to those who think of Afghan legs as pillars of flying fur, but firmly muscled and flexible pasterns are absolutely essential in the production of the correct reach-and-spring Afghan gait. Broken down pasterns may be likened to human fallen arches in that most of the foot's strong flexing ability has been lost. Pitiful effects of slack pasterns are quite evident in gait, as symptoms of flopping pasterns (most noticeable on the back stroke) and poor step rebound appears.

As the pastern joint has a certain amount of lateral flexibility, twisted pasterns often indicate leg and trunk faults by compensating for lack of strong columnar leg support. Exhibitors know that some cases of out-turned feet respond to repositioning of the elbows rather than of the feet. The dog with the skimpy rib cage frequently turns his feet outward to form a broader base of balance. This effect is highly undesirable in the Afghan Hound. The barrel-chested hound, with elbows pushed to a stance broader than the point-of-shoulder (juncture of shoulder and upper arm) may tend to toe in-ward. Invariably, gait faults follow all such pastern deviations.

The width between the points-of-shoulder and between the elbows should be equal. The term "elbows well held in" does not call for narrow elbows, but for a minimum of open space between the upper arm and the brisket, thoroughly dependent on a correctly built rib cage of a gently spread "U" shape rather than of a narrowing "V" shape.

In addition, a well-developed and moderately prominent sternum (breastbone) is an important indicator of proper breadth and length of the front ribs. Insufficient character of these front ribs is generally accompanied by narrow bodies and a crossing-over action of the forelegs, seen far too often in the Afghan rings.

The Standard calls for front legs "well set underneath the dog" in a well-angulated shoulder blade-upper arm junction. In truth, much of this "set underneath" is illusion caused by the slide of coat off the back of the elbow and down the back of the legs. But it is more characteristic of the Afghan Hound, than other gazehounds, and adds to the compact appearance of the breed. A line dropped perpendicularly from the back edge of the shoulder blade should just touch the actual back edge of the elbow. Such a test does not prove either layback or layunder but indicates a proper proportion of the bone lengths. Dogs with more vertical upper arms usually have upright pasterns and small cat feet, together with a forward center of gravity which is not in keeping with the essence of the Afghan Hound.

Afghan Hound fronts: Left, poor, pinched chest and toed out; center, excellent front; right, poor, barrel chest and toed in.

Hind legs, down from the stationary pelvis, are comprised of the upper leg (thigh or femur) and a small kneecap, called in dogs the "stifle joint." Beneath this, the dog's lower leg corresponds to the human calf, called the "second thigh." The second thigh terminates in the "hock joint," roughly corresponding to the human ankle, with the uppermost point-of-the-hock analogous to the human heel. The full length of hock replaces the human instep, and again we see that the dog walks on his toes. Gazehounds differ from smaller dogs in the length of their long bones from hip to hock, producing a shorter hock area by contrast. The Standard states that the coat gives the illusion of a somewhat exaggerated bend of stifle; this is true, as the great length of hind leg bones actually reduces the apparent angle of the stifle-joint on uncoated gazehounds. A definite bend at both stifle and hock is absolutely necessary for proper folding and reaching of hind legs in proper hound stride, and the careful judge will not allow profuse coating to blind him to the importance of these angles.

Much that is said of pasterns is also pertinent to hocks in that strong hind leg flexion requires tight springy hocks. Slack or overlong hocks too often lean inward, producing cow hocks, with hind toes turned outward in compensation. Out-turned hocks are also evidence of weakness. In either case poor columnar transmission of drive power results, and the Afghan's typical "high style," driving rear quarter gait will be absent.

The impression of the hind legs being "bowed" slightly from hock to crotch when viewed from the rear, is due to a desirable broad mass of muscles on the upper and lower thighs in conjunction with a rather broad pelvic formation. The leg bones themselves should fall into a perfectly straight line.

Coat—Hindquarters, flanks, ribs, forequarters, and legs well covered with thick, silky hair, very fine in texture; ears and all four feet well feathered; from in front of the shoulders, and also backwards from the shoulders along the saddle from the flanks and ribs upwards, the hair is short and close forming a smooth back in mature hounds—this is a traditional characteristic of the Afghan Hound. The Afghan Hound should be shown in its natural state; the coat is not clipped or trimmed; the head is surmounted (in the full sense of the word) with a topknot of long silky hair—this also an outstanding characteristic of the Afghan Hound. Showing of short hair on cuffs on either front or back legs is permissible.

Faults—Lack of a short-haired saddle in mature dogs.

AUTHORS' COMMENTS—We treat the entire subject of coat

with trepidation, because of its wide scope of natural variation. The traditional coat pattern, described in the Standard is that of a mature coated hound. But in coat, as in so many facets of his make-up, the Afghan Hound insists on retaining tremendous individuality, with coat maturity (the development of a smooth-haired saddle) occurring anywhere from 10 months to 3 years of age—a remarkably wide span. For each hound that quietly passes from a puppy coat to the adult pattern shortly after its first birthday, there are other well-coated puppies which will show no true natural saddle until their second birthday. At the other extreme, too many well-patterned yearlings continue to drop coat and go quite bare. Adolescence in the Afghan can be both awkward and misleading. The modern deification of the champion with precocious coat maturity is sadly naive, for such indications are not necessarily signs of lasting quality for either the coat or for the dog that wears it.

A wild increase in the prevalence of the great, dripping-coated Afghan Hound of the last few decades has contributed to the breed's high standing in the show ring and with a mink-loving public. The modern American Afghan Hound's drape of coat is now more synonymous with lush beauty than with any original utilitarian purposes. In the Afghan Hound's native land, reasonable quantities of such fur had genuine value, furnishing insulation in the great extremes of desert and mountain temperatures in the arid country. It has been said that the topknots "keep the sun off the brain" and prevent sunstroke. While this may be open to scientific skepticism, certainly thick coating does give certain climatic advantages and more importantly buffers the hound's sides and feet from bruising jagged rocks and ridgy upland crags as Afghanistan is primarily stony and arid with seasonal, low sharp grasses as vegetation. Evidence from this country, however, indicate that the sheer quantity of the Afghan Hound's hair played a small part in native evaluation of the dogs. The following quote (*Zafar-nama*, op. cit., p. 25) from the 14th century A.D. states: "A year later Sharifu 'd-Din returned to this vicinity, which apparently had been subjugated from Timur's governor, and again mentioned three hounds, noting that once a year they were shorn as sheep, and the hair was used by the women in making felt of a high quality, which was prized in the markets of Herat."

Fanciers deploring excessive coat as "impractical in the Afghanistan mountains" have taken up the wrong cudgel. Afghan natives quickly turn any disadvantages of animal hair to their own ends. At shearing time of their sheep, the addition of a few pounds of hound hair has long been known to enhance their felts and wools. By the next freeze, a practical short mantle of fur has again sprouted from the dogs. Such seasonal clipping is an affront to most Western fanciers, but dog hair that has been combed and brushed (and occasionally cut) from our hounds has been woven, alone or in conjunction with other wool, into charming and durable garments for the owners that like to literally "wear their dogs".

Today a super abundance of coat seems to be blurring some of the hound's other sterling qualities and there is absolutely nothing in the Standard that implies "the more fur the better." Moreover, many of the great coats do not conform to the correct natural pattern and texture and are no longer particularly becoming to the kingly hunter, as they dilute the effect of the sturdy angular hound beneath them. There are several rather important details in the Standard's wording that are being neglected in the rush for great coat and young champions. In addition to the natural short haired saddle, the Standard clearly requests that the hound be shorthaired "from in front of the shoulders" which means on the sides of the neck. This should not be glossed over. Smooth neck sides greatly enhance the effect of lean elegance, as heavily furred necks automatically appear foreshortened. Also, super-coated hounds tend to carry the fault of the bushy tail.

Some of this apparent difficulty stems from the fact that once these hounds have passed their first birthday, they are judged by adult standards which are not always applicable. Consequently, impatient exhibitors strip a little fur here and there, attempting to pass off woolly-fuzz puppy coats as the mature item, despite the fact that with many dogs the draping coat, short-haired saddles and sleek neck-sides may not emerge for many more months. Ignorant judges who penalize quality youngsters garbed in obviously in-between coats without making inquiries as to the dog's age are as much to blame for the current confusion over coat in the breed as are the dishonest exhibitors. The Afghan Hound would benefit from something akin to a "teenager class" of the type seen in many European countries and Mexico where precociousness is not rewarded— but merely tolerated with a "wait and see if it holds" attitude. More understanding of and attention to coat tampering on the part of the judges and less subterfuge by exhibitors would bring about the same purpose. Where and when available, the Afghan Hound greatly benefits from the AKC 12-18 month class.

The Standard clearly states that bare pasterns and hocks in the form of "cuffs" is perfectly acceptable. In fact the "Turkish pants" can be quite attractive, as they lighten the look of a heavy leg with the break at the pastern. However, cuffed hounds demand large heavily-coated feet to avoid a top heavy tiny-footed appearance.

181

Coat texture is described as "thick, very fine and silky." Any coarseness of coating or lack of the silky effect dulls the coloration and brings about an unbecoming bushiness. The Standard makes no mention as to whether the fur should be flat or wavy, both types being common in Afghanistan.

The ethics of trimming Afghan Hounds cannot be ignored in this book. The emergence of the now common "great coat" with its frequent side effects of long-lasting and excessive facial hair and late developing or non-existent saddles in conjunction with hordes of impatient exhibitors unwilling to wait for the natural pattern of smooth hair to emerge on saddle, cheeks and elsewhere, has evoked widespread sly stripping, clipping, and plucking of the Afghan Hounds. Trimming is especially evident in geographic areas where competition is very keen and often Afghans are professionally groomed. Fully aware of this trend, the Afghan Hound Club of America has consistently reaffirmed its stand against all tampering of the natural coat pattern. The end result has been a double standard that is greatly confusing to the novice who reads the Standard prohibition on trimming, only to reach the show grounds and be told, not only by earnest fanciers, but also by many "helpful" judges, that his dog would look better if "cleaned up" on saddle, shoulders, neck and jaw line. Until the day when judges begin to penalize this flagrant infraction of the standard, decisions to trim or not to trim remain with the conscience of each exhibitor.

Height—Dogs, 27 inches, plus or minus one inch; bitches, 25 inches, plus or minus one inch.

Weight—Dogs, about 60 pounds; bitches, about 50 pounds.

AUTHORS' COMMENTS—As wide variation of height and weight constituted one of the greatest differences in the early Afghan imports, it was especially important that the Standard clearly specify an ideal range for both facets. Weight stipulations are not included in the European standards, giving American fanciers the edge on ascertaining proper substance for a good Afghan Hound. Tests prove that a lean, well-muscled, 27 inch male that makes the 60 pound weight is a fairly heavily boned gazehound, quite in line with breed descriptions dating back before 1900 in which the Afghan Hound was consistently described as similar to the Saluki but more sturdily built. As size advances or diminishes, an accompanying change in weight, at about 5 pounds to the inch, is justifiable. Proper attention to this height-weight ratio should ferret out the truly coarse or weedy Afghan Hound immediately.

The Afghan Hound is best known for his grand versatility. He must be large and powerful enough to pull down a stag gazelle, a cunning jackal, or his legendary foe, the snow leopard which is about 60 pounds of clawing dynamite. He must also be refined and light enough to stick on the heels of the illusive fox or the agile hare. While the best hare hound should not be expected to be the best leopard hunter, extremes of size in the breed should be strongly discouraged lest the dogs sacrifice their versatility and revert to the weirdly dissimilar Bell-Murray and Ghazni types once again. Any acceptance of giantism with its tendencies towards awkwardness, overly refined, skimpy or "weedy" individuals, must be considered as serious steps backwards in the continuation of the best of the breed.

The oversized hound looms as the greater menace as he "stands out" in classes by virtue of size and impresses many judges. It is to be hoped that judges and exhibitors will better familiarize themselves with the actual space encompassed in the ideal size range specified in the Standard in order to accurately gauge which specimens are or are not within its range. (Some judges have been known to make chalk marks at the 27 and 25 inch height on trouser legs, a commendable act.) Once the facts of the matter are established, the importance of the dog's size must be weighed against the appearance of the whole dog and the way he handles his body in action. In the Standard there is no ground for size disqualifications and exceptions to the prescribed range warrant judicial penalties as with any other infringement.

Color—All colors are permissible, but color or color combinations are pleasing; white markings, especially in the head, are undesirable.

AUTHORS' COMMENTS—The Afghan Hound is permitted a rainbow of colors. Partiality for specific coloration has brought many new fanciers into the breed, but the Standard is quite clear in its lack of prejudice. Only white comes in for discrimination, and rightly so, for true white in dogs is not a color, but the lack of it. Afghans that appear totally white are accepted on the grounds that such "whites" are actually very pale cream or gray animals. Signs of white markings, in the form of white feet or tail tips, are undesirable. White marks on the head, in the form of blazes, are most noticeable and specifically criticized in the standard. As the unattractive blazed and white-marked Afghan was accepted in show circles until the 1948 Standard revision, such "spotting" factors are deeply imbedded in the breed and bear careful weeding. (Note: Small white marks on the extremities at birth frequently fade away. See Chapter Seven.) Any evidence of poor pigmentation, be it white marks, less than jet black eye rims and nose leathers, or light eyes, are disapproved of in the Afghan Hound Standard.

183

Gait—When running free, the Afghan Hound moves at a gallop, showing great elasticity and spring in his smooth powerful stride. When on a loose lead, the Afghan can trot at a fast pace; stepping along, he has the appearance of placing the hind feet directly in the footprints of the front feet, both thrown straight ahead. Moving with head and tail high, the whole appearance of the Afghan Hound is one of great style and beauty.

AUTHORS' COMMENTS—Very little is actually written about gait in most breed standards, an aggravating fact to the novice who naively expects the intricacies of motion to be spelled-out in a few well-chosen words. It has recently become fashionable to deprecate standards for their lack of detailed descriptions of gait. In some instances, carping is justified; in others, it is not. The dedicated "dog people" who write breed Standards know that good gait in one breed is not too dissimilar from that in other breeds, except where extreme structures demand special effects as in the "rolling gait" accepted in some very heavy-bodied breeds. All breeds are aimed towards facile progress across terra firma. For the interested novice we recommend study of the well-illustrated texts on the subject in Rachel Page Elliott's *The New Dog Steps,* Howell Book House, to be used in conjunction with actual observation of moving dogs. The fascinated student will soon find himself espying gait differences in every street mongrel as well as in pure-breds. An interesting fact soon crystallizes: It is the "in-between dog," not highly angulated, medium sized, moderate in body width and depth, and slightly longer than high, that has the least gait difficulties regardless of lineage. When the middle-of-the-road is left in the interests of specialization, gait problems multiply. The abnormally short-legged, heavy-bodied, long-legged, short-backed, and massive-headed breeds upset canine frame ratios. Yet from such extreme types arises the super-utility that has given rise to breeds such as the squat badger-catching Dachshund or the gigantic Wolfhounds.

The spectacular action of the Afghan Hound derives from the rigorous hunting conditions of its homeland, enhanced by a flowing fur coat. Unfortunately, far more is known about the terrain and climate of Afghanistan than of the precise hunting modes of its dogs. Rarely has the hunting mode been detailed by reputable first-hand sources. In true irony the one in-person view of a hunt in Afghanistan, involving dogs, makes the hounds the prey rather than the predator. Peter King, in *Afghanistan: Cockpit in High Asia,* Taplinger Publishing Company, 1966, ©1966 by Peter King, describes the steppe hounds as follows (reprinted by permission): "By jeep and horse we followed a pack and by evening had managed to capture five, which satisfied the Governor. He wanted them as presents for his son's new bride, and, of the five, he selected three and set the rest free. They fled with terrific acceleration into the night to rejoin the pack who were mournfully sitting on a rocky crag a mile away, undoubtedly waiting to hear the dying screams of their mates as they were eaten alive by savage humans. I would have liked to have had one of these Tazis, as they are called in Afghanistan, but their export is forbidden and the perfection of the wild ones put me off the interbred, pampered show types one sees outside the country."

The paucity of information was demonstrated by the November 1965 issue of the *AHCA Afghanews*, which was devoted entirely to hunting. The best that could be gathered from Afghanistan was a couple of snapshots of small, sparse coated native hounds standing among rifle-toting men, all about to go on an Ibex hunt. The background, resembling the low end of an abandoned gravel pit with loose talus slopes and a few patches of scrub weeds, proved the most revealing aspect. The rest of the special issue carried observations by Jackson Sanford, one of the few who had utilized the breed extensively for hunting. Quotes from Sanford's notes, after using purebred Afghan Hounds to hunt hares, bobcats, and coyotes in the Southern United States during the 1940s, appear in this Chapter for their pertinency in Standard phrases.

Contrary to those who insist the Afghan Hound Standard is shy of practical gait instruction, it actually abounds in clues to dynamics— and to the differences between the all-purpose Afghan Hound and the Gentleman's galloping specialist, the Greyhound—to those who seek them. Corroboration is embedded in Sanford's words: ". . . the outstanding characteristic of the hunting Afghan . . . is his great versatility. I believe him to be matchless in his adaptability to varying conditions of terrain, and to the diverse characteristics of the indigenous game species."

The Standard does not minimize the importance of a flashing gallop, but does better delineate those features involved in the gait by which the breed happens to be judged in the show ring, and the one in which its most valued qualities are best evident. This has been well-called a reconnaissance trot—fit for distance seeking with the body held in high-bodied collection for instant changes of direction.

Combining the brain, equilibrium and muscles in an energy efficient state of constant readiness for abrupt adjustments the collected trot demands exquisite handling of the center of gravity to achieve a sort of weightlessness through balanced posture. This aim underlines much of the Standard.

"Proudly carried head, eyes gazing into the distance" is a specific clue to seeking. (The romantic "as if in memory of ages past" is a pretty piece of poetic license.) Additionally, there must be an "absolutely clear outlook with no interference."

With head and arched neck in proper position, naturally, the shoulders are able to settle into their most "laid back" position, giving a proper shaped upper arm freedom to angle under the dog. This places the center of gravity to the back of the shoulders, freeing the legs for quick and easy motions. An inner vitality manifest in "head and tail (held) high"—vibrantly indicates, in motion, alert and searching posture.

A quiet phrase, too often overlooked, but indispensable to a collected trot is "loose lead." The impressive high-style action that is natural to really superior Afghan Hounds can be adopted only when they are allowed free control of their faculties. Moving at a comfortable speed, on a loose lead, the quality Afghan Hound displays a taut-topline and a well-crested nape of neck. Such dogs appear exceptionally compact, square in fact. Once unstrung out of collection the same dog sacrifices its taut body-line, tries to throw its head forward, and literally becomes longer, and lower, in result. The handler-trick to counter this is to string up the dog, on lead, which endangers their balance and distorts the natural breed-typical outline from head to tail.

The correct reconnaisance trot is far from a forging at the end of the lead. That ploy puts the dog into an unnatural tautness, similar to a hauling pose, with the center of gravity thrown forward and added thrust developed by the rear quarter. To the misinformed this may give the impression of good gait but it is all wrong for this agile breed. Improper posture, and excessive speed results in an ill-timed scramble of legs. As a practical consideration the fast-forging gait would be disastrous over uneven, or slippery, terrain. In the show ring it prevents viewing fine specimens at their breed-typical best.

Jackson Sanford assures us that good "hunting Afghans (do not) lose footing, except under truly extraordinary circumstances; in too many cases such a misstep would be fatal." Yet, in modern rings it is not at all rare to see Afghan Hounds skidding and stumbling. Handlers blame the size of the ring, or type of footing, loathe to admit that, by tight leads and uncontrolled speed they, personally, hamper the dogs from coping with conditions that are sheer luxury compared with slick rocky slopes.

Leg motions have the underlying duty of transporting the body forward. This is accomplished, in large part, by the shoulder-upper arm or scapular-humero (S-H) joint and muscles that radiate from it. In motion this joint moves upwards, forwards and slightly inwards— along an arc preset by the shape of the ribs over which the scapula glides. Body muscles, such as the body-spanning long latissimus dorsi and the supporting pectoral group, attach to the underside of the S-H joint. They are played out with each upward and forward motion of the flexing joint and further stretched by the advance of the humerus while the leg is in the air. A forward muscular impulse is released by the lift of the hind legs, allowing the body to travel forward. Compounded by the momentum gained from the reaction to the feet pushing the ground, various gaits become available.

Inner structural faults as a cause of improper gait are not readily apparent to the naked eye, but effects are. Improper muscle resiliency (stretchability) at the S-H joint restricts action. When pectorals lack full suppleness, forelegs may become tied-in, reducing joint mobility of the humerus in the sagittal direction. This can promote a knees-up hackney action with excessive pastern-lift that allows the foreleg to remain off the ground long enough for the rear leg to take a non-interfering stride. This is quite different from the even-ended prance of an aware hound excitedly moving as if on strong spring-jointed legs. The latter dog often needs only to settle down to move with more expansive ground covering purpose.

The Author's Comment under Body explained how the back and loin contribute to the agile Afghan Hound action. Some Greyhounds trot in a collected style for short spurts, but rarely sustain it due to breed type differences. Sanford said: ". . . although the Greyhound is appreciably faster at top speed on a straight course, the Afghan . . . accelerates much faster, is much more agile, and above all, will always, when matched against any number of Greyhounds, be the first to spot game."

For weight-transfer combined with high-headedness, the Afghan Hound's hind legs should work, and place, more under the hipjoint than does the Greyhound. "Good angulation of both stifle and hock" refers to a flex-legged position that allows instant acceleration, forwards, upwards or sidewards. Exhibitors Please Note: The fad of placing the hindlegs well behind a line dropped from the rear projection of the pelvic girdle places these legs into extension—rather than flexion—forcing the animal to bring them back under itself before it can move forward, and costs the breed its precious balanced stance.

The "impression of a somewhat exaggerated bend in the stifle" is enhanced in motion by the swing and drape of flying coat. This makes actual flexion/extension of joints difficult for the eye to perceive accurately. To gain the maximum impression of angulation under the coat, overlong lengths of hind legs have become tolerated, bringing the problem of stiff sickle hocks into the breed. A sort of reachy-shuffle ensues. Pendulum action, from the hip, lacking joint flexion, and proper lift of hind feet can be observed by watching dogs move at a moderate trot. The balanced and correct dog will look all the more marvelous at such a speed.

A demand for "hind feet are broad and of good length" expands the theme. Dog hind feet will be the broadest, and longest, when placed under the dog in a four-square balanced stance. Due to contractions of muscles controlling hocks and toes the feet become smaller (move onto tiptoes) the further they are placed behind the hipjoint. Just one more of the myriad features that take place under the skin, but are subject to being enhanced, or diminished, as much by stance and coat quantity as by pure anatomy.

In its original intent the gait phrase, "the appearance of placing the hind feet directly in the footprints of the front feet, both thrown straight ahead," warned against deflecting leg joints sideways. Flying elbows, twisting hocks, and flipping pasterns have always plagued the breed. But the word "straight" must not be taken too literally, for, technically, legs must converge to a varying degree to allow the dog's paws to land directly under its center of gravity. Convergence derives from the slight inward swing of the S-H joint, radiating down the leg, increasing with the speed of the dog. If the S-H arc of motion is imperfect, deflections caused will resound down the leg, causing lateral tossing, knitting and purling, from joint to joint.

The degree of convergence of the forelegs should be matched by that of the rear. A four-square Afghan Hound does not narrow track in the front, and compensate by spraddling in the rear—or vice versa. Such tricycles compensate for lack of stability at the narrower end. The four-square Afghan Hound places "the hind feet directly in the foot prints of the front feet" rather than side-winding or landing well short of where the front feet appear to have just left. This spacing is reasonable for a moderate collected trot. Less reach is to be expected at the walk and jog-trot; trotting at a forced speed is asking for foot-fall timing problems.

The fragment—"The Afghan can trot at a fast pace"—demands a warning sign! It has become seriously derailed from its original connotation, that of contrast between the Afghan and those breeds prone to more hastily move right into their primary function of the gallop. Used to describe the long-distance endurance seeker, just as much as the chaser, the phrase was a properly understood part of the Standard decades before careening handlers began to turn the Show Ring into the Race Track—with fast-forging Afghans leading the race at the Hound Group level.

Traditionally, the word of choice for the rather unique, and certainly awe inspiring Afghan trot has been "floating"—suggesting well-jointed legs seemingly divorced from an aloof body yet serving as superb shock absorbers for it. As shock absorbers the breed-typical word for proper action is "springy" in tribute to powerful elastic flexing (in the sagittal plane) of the leg joints, resulting in broad ground-covering strides.

As a fine exponent of the double-suspension gallop, particularly when prey has been sighted, the Afghan Hound's traditional style differs slightly from other gazehounds, in showing a special springiness and tendency to intermittent gazelle-like high bounds for better viewing.

Standing, or in motion, the Afghan's inner specialties remain alertness, agility and a strong sense of independence. The most tragic thing that could happen to this magnificent breed would be to degenerate into a mindless race of handsome long-haired statues, perfection in photos, but ordinary in life. The wise motto of Jackson Sanford—"The breeder will best solve his problems who does not lose sight of the fact that his is a task of preservation than of improvement" is no less true of exhibitors and judges.

Temperament—Aloof and dignified, yet gay.
Faults—Sharpness or shyness.

AUTHORS' COMMENTS—To some, the combination of aloofness and gaiety is unreconcilable. The answer is that they do not necessarily occur simultaneously but both can be an integral and highly developed part of these clownish hounds. The mature Afghan, so devastatingly aloof to some strangers, is still irrepressibly exuberant with family and close friends. A breeder, once queried about the main difference, aside from coat, between her Salukis and Afghans, immediately replied, "The Afghan has a far more robust sense of humor." Here is the breed's charming "gaiety."

Sharpness (biting, snarling and fighting) or shyness (cringing and slinking) are to be penalized as manifestations of possibly neurotic personalities. The aloof Afghan may not make friendly overtures towards strangers, but neither should he panic or behave in a nasty manner. The King is above such behavior.

The top producer of Afghan Hound champions—Ch. Coastwind Abraxas (Ch. Coastwind Nepenthe ex Ch. Coastwind Ouija), brindle dog, sire of 66 champions. Bred and owned by Coastwind Kennels (Mike Dunham and Robert Souza).

```
                                          Ch. Shirkhan of Grandeur
                            Akaba's Royal Blue
                                          Akaba's Gigi In White
               Akaba's Geronimo Blue
                                          Branwen Sheen Kamri
                            Chandara Shinti-Yan
                                          Chandara Shiraz of Tranwell
          Ch. Coastwind Nepenthe
                                          Akaba's Royal Blue
                            Akaba's Allah Kazam
                                          Ch. Akaba's Know It All
               Ch. Coastwind Serendipity
                                          Shaadar's Roi D'Arghent Sijmon
                            Ch. Shaadar's Blajnhe of Karl
                                          Lakoya's Sijat Kashyan

CH. COASTWIND ABRAXAS
                                          Akaba's Royal Blue
                            Akaba's Allah Kazam
                                          Ch. Akaba's Know It All
               Ch. Coastwind Gazebo
                                          Shaadar's Roi D'Arghent Sijmon
                            Ch. Shaadar's Blajnhe of Karl
                                          Lakoya's Sijat Kashyan
          Ch. Coastwind Ouija
                                          Ch. Akaba's Top Brass
                            Akaba's Brass Blizzard
                                          Thais of La Paloma
               Akaba's Bubbling Over
                                          Ch. Crown Crest Mr. Universe
                            Bachas Dehezrie
                                          Zsa Zsa of Zaka
```

8

Breeding

"Let us grow careless in breeding and the Afghan will lose his tremendous differences and gently slide back to become like other dogs. We must guard against any tendency to lose top-knot; to coarsen head; to shorten legs; to raise hocks; to lose those picturesque hips; to raise too much coat or not enough; to lose that characteristic high head carriage with its accompanying high tail. To lose any of these characteristics would be disastrous and to lose many would be to lose our dog."

Dr. A. W. Combs,
A.H.C.A. Bulletin 1942

THIS chapter is divided basically into three topics for the convenience of the reader: picking a mate; selecting puppies; and color breeding. As a general dictum, it should be stressed that no breeding of Afghan Hounds should be done without the express intent to produce offspring that conform as closely to the Standard as possible and that will be delightful companions, sound in body and mind. There is not now, nor has there ever been, any large unfulfilled demand for pet Afghan Hounds, but there is a market for top quality show specimens. As a natural by-product of breeding for the "world beaters" there are more than enough second string pups to fill the "companions only" demand. The majority of non-show pets should never be used for breeding for the completely practical reason that there are just not enough suitable homes waiting to accommodate them.

191

Ch. Coastwind Gazebo (Akaba's Allah Kazam ex Ch. Shaader's Blajnhe), black mask red dog, multiple BIS winner and sire of 29 champions. At right, "Ezra" turning. Bred and owned by Coastwind Kennels.

Ch. Sasha of Scheherezade (Ch. Alibaba of Scheherezade, C.D. ex Benihaar Autumn Heather), black masked golden dog, sire of 25 champions. Bred by Bonita Visser and owned by Lt. Col. and Mrs. Wallace H. Pede.

Picking a Mate

The Afghan Hound is not the dog for everybody. Impulsive attraction to their picturesque appearance at shows or elsewhere brings cries of "I wish I owned one of these . . ." from the gallery, but this is no guarantee that the admirer is willing or able to make the personal sacrifice of time required to keep such a hound in his admired state of beauty. Few sights are less attractive than a neglected and matted Afghan Hound, a shamefaced prince in tatters and sores. Many casual admirers cannot cope with the breed's effusive and changeable temperament. Still, fortunately for the preservation of the breed, there are some people who are just right for Afghan Hounds, who on acquiring one, soon could not imagine life without these wonderful creatures which demand so much from their owners in the way of care but which give so much pleasure in return. The Afghan Hound is not an inanimate status symbol to be kept on a shelf, but a very lively bundle of flesh and fur.

Being deliberately negative at the thought of overbreeding and its consequences in puppy mills and dog pounds, we list the following points of when not to breed:

1. Never breed just so that "Scheherezade" can have one experience with motherhood before she is spayed.

2. Never breed with the mistaken idea that it will prevent further false pregnancies in a bitch so inclined. Spaying is the only permanent answer here.

3. Never breed expecting to make a profit on the litter. The Afghan Hound is not that kind of breed. Raising a healthy litter, with the costs of shots, food, advertisements, and expenses such as the stud fee, is expensive.

4. Never breed unless you are in a position to properly feed and house the pups indefinitely, as it may take some time to find suitable owners.

5. Never breed a sickly hound or one with doubtful mental stability. The breeding process improves neither a dog's health nor its mentality, and both problems could be hereditary.

6. Never breed a poor or sub-average specimen of the breed. In reality, it is often far cheaper to go out and buy a quality hound than to work up to one through inferior breeding stock.

In Afghan Hounds, as in all breeds, a number of serious hereditary defects occur with varying frequency. In the "native state", stringent demands of natural rearing culls the puny pup, the faltering adolescent and the mildly disabled adult. In our insulated world of domestic pets, sentimental owners and sympathetic veterinarians apply all the miracles of Love and Science to the saving and raising of the weak and the strong alike. Commendable as this reverence for canine life is, the hereditary aspects of preserving the weak and faulty—to become the basis of future generations—is frightening, especially to those who have seen how quickly serious genetic problems can take over a breed.

Entire books have been written which delve into the wide range of genetically-induced physical (and mental) problems; therefore, we make no attempt to cover them here. Fortunately, the American Kennel Club gives guidance by wisely setting disqualifications covering some of the most glaring troubles. Even the one-time breeder owes it to the breed, and himself, to study these precepts and apply them to any Afghan Hound considered for mating.

AKC "Rules Applying to Registrations and Dog Shows", Chapter 16, Sec. 9 states: "A dog which is blind, deaf, castrated, spayed, or which has been changed in appearance by artificial means except as specified in the standard for its breed, or a male which does not have two normal testicles normally located in the scrotum, may not compete at any show and will be disqualified."

Chapter 16, Sec. 9-A: "A dog that is lame at any show may not compete and shall not receive any award at that show."

Among the less obvious principles, let it be known that—per AKC "Guidelines for Dog Show Judges"—a judge must excuse from the ring any dog that attempts to bite, or that snarls and will not permit a judge to examine him.

It is in these specifically AKC-mentioned areas that "guarantees" are made with promises of refund or replacement should such defects develop on dogs purchased as "show stock". Of even greater importance is the absolute prevention of any dogs and bitches with signs of such defects, whether overt or clinical, from mating. They should be neutered to avoid "accidents". Should an accidental mating occur, a quick trip to the nearest veterinarian for an injection of a canine aborting hormone should prevent the mis-mating from developing into an unwanted litter.

Unfortunately, all of the above conditions can exist in Afghan Hounds, as in all breeds, without owners being really aware of it. Dogs do not complain verbally—in most instances, and have exceptional compensatory facilities. Judges frequently are presented with the embarrassment of such defects in the ring. Veterinarians find a number of dogs to be blind or deaf (partially or completely), or quite "lame" from degenerative joint diseases, to the complete surprise of the owners. Some fanciers don't even know the meaning of "two normal testicles". Entirely too many cases of serious defects are missed, and then passed on to the next generation, due to owner's ignorance, or unwillingness to look for the signs.

Ch. Akaba's Royal Flush (Akaba's Royal Blue ex Ch. Akaba's Brass Bangle), blue brindle dog, BIS winner and sire of 28 champions. Bred by Lois R. Boardman and owned by Lois R. Boardman and Mary Alice Kerrigan.

Ch. Khayam's Apollo (Ch. Ammon Hall Nomad ex Ch. Khayam's Kism of Scheherezade), black and tan dog, sire of 25 champions. Bred and owned by Dr. and Mrs. Doyle N. Rogers.

195

Routine physical examinations should be given old breeding stock by a veterinarian. Special investigations should be made for all problems mentioned.

Blindness, in Afghan Hounds, in the form of hereditary lens cataracts, has been reported in young dogs (1 to 5 years of age) with some frequency. Incipient signs of cataracts can be found on clinical examination, with dilation, long before any vision loss. Dogs with cataracts can make amazing adjustments to fading sight and may well live out their lives without owners sensing any problem. Judging from special mass clinical testing in the breed, the incidence of the problem is something near to 1%, but known cases have been seen from such a wide array of diverse backgrounds, including imported stock, that the genetic potential warrants ocular examinations of all breeding stock.

Somewhat the same condition exists with hip dysplasia, a hereditary disease of the hip joints. While less of a problem in Afghan Hounds than in most big dogs, enough documented cases have been seen in a wide variety of show lines to call for X-raying as suggested by the Orthopedic Foundation of America. Compensation can change a clinically serious case of dysplasia to one that is quite undetectible, except through X-ray. Breeds that have ignored the menace of hip dysplasia in its milder stages are now seriously enmeshed in its clutches, to the point of near hopelessness. Let it not happen to the Afghan Hound.

The AKC ban against dogs being "changed in appearance by artificial means" refers to a large body of repairable, but often hereditable defects such as entropic (inturned) eyelids, poor bites, large congenital hernias, and any other superficial change done for medical or cosmetic reasons. This prohibition now includes the pectineotomy, a cutting and tying off of the petineus muscle, to alleviate the degenerative process of hip dysplasia. It would also include cataract repairing, or the surgical improvement of faulty testicle placement. Obviously, many of the "changes" cannot be detected in the ring, or anywhere else, but only a foolish breeder falls for the "out of sight, out of mind" routine, as the gene structure remains as defective as ever. If the "sins of the father" are not visited upon his children, they still may turn up in the grandchildren or someplace else down the line. Conscientious and aware stud owners should not accept bitches that are in the least suspect in the above areas, and should demand proof of examination and clearance where it can be had.

The non-ending controversy over whether specific defects, at any given time, are due to environmental trauma or illness—as opposed to genetic pre-determination (or combination thereof)—provides rationalization fuel. It is far better to err in the direction of not breeding than to take chances. All living Afghan Hounds are entitled to all the love, care and respect they can muster—but many are the unwise roads to the next generation in a world where Humane Societies are hopelessly overburdened with surplus stock. And Afghan Hounds are no strangers to their confines.

A word of caution about breeding contracts. There are no standards for such agreements. To point up common pitfalls, the AHCA, in 1978, developed *Recommended Practices for the Owner, Exhibitor and Breeder of the Afghan Hound,* with copies publicly available on request. The General Recommendations of the Biological Defects Committee of the AHCA is an Appendix to this document. These are non-compulsory guidelines meant to alert the fancy to those vexing considerations for which there are no hard and fast rules, but which should be considered beforehand. Particularly troublesome are co-ownerships, forced breeding contracts and stud fee arrangements. Pups bought on breeding terms can become definite liabilities. Stud-owners range from those who believe a stud fee carries no obligation past the male dog covering the bitch, regardless of whether, or not, a litter ensues. The singleton pup may, or may not, be considered a litter. This creates a special problem when the stud fee has been set for a pup in lieu of cash. All stipulations should be made in writing, especially between friends, and cover the unhappy event of defectives. The legal, as well as good-will, ramifications of these contracts are endless.

Now that we have forewarned the reader that having one litter may not be a completely profitable and delightful experience, we can try to give a bit of help to the tenacious souls determined to carry on with the game, dreaming of the day when their "baby" takes major points in the Bred-by-Exhibitor class.

Afghan Hounds are difficult to breed with predictable results as the breed is fraught with wide genetic variability, one of its charms to the observer and its curse to the methodical breeder. The historical chapters portrayed a breed of multiform types in Afghanistan arriving in England and America. Early abortive attempts to produce stable balanced types through close breeding of related hounds were made by some breeders. All too frequently, in America these effects faded as the breed was caught up in a constant intermixing with each new import or top show winner of the day. Many early winners would be bypassed in today's competition. It was necessary for ambitious breeders to experiment with available combinations to create flashier specimens as Show Business became progressively tougher. We have only praise for the breeders who brought the King of Dogs to its current magnificence and we are not for bringing back the "good old days" but wish to warn novices that careless missteps in breeding can throw the breed into degeneracy.

Old timers bred Afghans with an educated instinct, unconscious knowledge gleaned from many years' experience in various breeds of dogs. The novice with limited experience wisely supplants this lack of instinct with textbook study of canine anatomy, gait and genetics. When properly applied, such studies may provide short-cuts in the interminable road to successful dog breeding. We urge our readers to avail themselves of these specialized texts. The technical aspects of genetics will not be covered here, as smatterings of this complicated science of life serve only to confuse those who are not familiar with its intricate principles.

The study of genetics illustrates and explains the pitfalls of the ubiquitous hidden recessive and the value of predictable strains that breed reasonably true to type. Textbook breeding of Afghan Hounds must be approached with caution, for in this breed, it is misleading to think that most winning strains derive from firm policies of close breeding. Pedigrees reveal that many of our most successful and influential foundation hounds do not repeat a family in a four-generation pedigree, being as outcrossed as dogs can be and remain of one breed. Kennel names are not necessarily synonymous with set strains, due not only to breeding practices within the home kennel, but to the affixing of such kennel names to purchased hounds and stud fee pups. Casual reliance on kennel names as a short-cut to predictable breeding may prove a costly error. The few really closely-bred hounds in this country can be expected to breed quite true to type in both their assets and their liabilities.

The great hounds of the past deserve accolades. They proved their ability to hold their own with dogs of all breeds in top competition. Nevertheless, many show type and temperament faults were transmitted by these very popular studs. These hounds were fortunate in having overwhelming virtues that outweighed their faults in the eyes of judges. Problems plaguing even some of the greatest Afghan Hounds and certainly not limited to any one breed were general unsoundness of leg with turned-out front feet and cow-hocked rears, often hidden under leg fur. Some heavily-coated bodies sadly lacked the strong bones, deep brisket, or shoulder angulation that the short-haired Greyhound must exhibit to avoid severe penalties. Coarse heads and weak or "plain" muzzles lacking in distinctive chiseling have been transmitted by popular studs, outstanding in other departments. Serious problems of body/leg ratio imbalances have persisted to this day. Surface improvements in temperament have possibly been the greatest gain in the breed, other than the highly coveted coat. Despite the fact that they harbored such "faults," the great ones stood out brightly and were constant challengers for top awards. In explanation, judge "Cissy" Froelich of the Elcoza kennel said, "Many of the old Afghans had that great quality that I call 'dash' that makes you look a second time . . . that 'I'm the grandest tiger in the jungle' look of long ago . . . which few Afghans of today possess. Today there are so many gorgeous animals in the rings. Judges have a much harder time than years ago, when one could easily pick the 'best.' We must breed good ones just to keep going. . . ." But we can only obtain fine Afghan Hounds from sires and dams who, in combination, possess superior qualities themselves. Recognition of these qualities on the part of the breeder is the very first step. Virtues cannot be assumed on the basis of a pedigree full of champions. Almost all modern Afghan Hounds, good or poor, have pedigrees rich in titled ancestry. A mediocre dog or bitch from the most imposing background of royalty is the unfortunate result of the undesirable aspects of the pedigree coming home to roost. Quality must be in hand to be transmitted. Acquiring and maintaining the best in the breed calls for a mixture of unrelenting vigil and the weeding out of inferior specimens (plus the unending generosity of Lady Luck).

Decisive proof that quality begets quality is supplied by our own Afghan champions. Through the years from 83% to 95% of all Afghan champions have come from champion sires. This is a remarkable percentage. The only early non-champion sire of great note, with ten champions to his credit, was Westmill Omar. Many of the other early non-champion sires of champions were imported hounds, valued for very special characteristics. Recent significant non-champion sires are Akaba's Royal Blue and Ben Ghazi's The Silver Shadow, both exceptionally fine hounds kept from impressive show careers by puppyhood injuries. Two others are Coastwind the Hermit and Mecca's Shoe Shine Boy. These remain the "exception that proves the rule."

At first glance, the dam's side of the ledger is different. In the 1930s and 1940s, only about 30% of champions boasted champion dams. But, in many cases, such dams were of acknowledged quality, lacking only a point or two of finishing. Seasonal coat drops interrupted many a fine bitch's show career. Some bitches, such as the lovely Far Away Loo, were selected exclusively for their brood bitch potential. Ku Mari Khyaam of Arken had a crippling injury that prevented her from being exhibited, but her quality was obvious. Admittedly, there were many cases of stock improvement breeding of a mediocre bitch to a top sire that did produce some fine specimens.

As competition broadened, the percentage of champion dams also increased. By 1960, 53% of the newly titled dogs were from champion dams. By 1963 only 7% of the champions listed could not show at least one champion parent, with the great majority having two of them. Certainly we do not mean to imply that all pet hounds lack quality, for this is not true. Many successful breedings were made well before one or both promising parents had achieved their titles. We are saying that only the experienced breeder, well aware of what they are doing, has the right to experiment with untested and unproven quality.

There are two key words to be used in deciding whether a bitch that is not pleasing the judges at the shows should be used for breeding. These are "sound" and "type." A bitch that is unfashionably small, but within the Standard, with only moderate coat and an indifferent show presence but without any serious structural faults, can be an excellent brood bitch when bred properly *if* she is really sound (meaning that her legs and gait are strong both coming and going) and "typy" (meaning in this instance, that she has a good head shape with an "Afghanish" look). It is preferable that such a bitch should also have a broad loin; an asset to rear quarter gait and the easy carrying and whelping of puppies. A very feminine bitch, short of superficial dramatics, is a far better potential brood bitch than the drippy coated, faultily constructed showgirl that finds favor in the eyes of careless judges.

As a firm rule in breeding, it is absolutely essential that at least one of the two prospective parents excel in soundness and in type or the offspring deserve to be nonentities regardless of their superficial attributes. The assets of both prospective parents must greatly outweigh their liabilities and such liabilities must never be duplicated. The fond owner who foresees fine puppies resulting from two mediocre dogs, on the chance that both hounds will throw only their best qualities, is forgetting the law of averages and indulging in the saddest type of wishful thinking.

The most unforgivable error made in Afghans is in breeding primarily for coat, whether for color or for quantity. Such grievous mistakes are testimony to a lack of knowledge of hound structure and the mesmerizing effect of constant ringside comments on coat and color, promoting a completely false sense of Afghan Hound values. We warn the novice that it is far easier for any loser to alibi that the judge didn't like his hound's color or that his dog didn't have enough coat than to admit that his dog lacks brisket or has poor shoulders and crooked legs.

Ch. Crown Crest Tae-Joan (Ch. Taejon of Crown Crest ex Ch. Egypt's Echo of Crown Crest), dam of 15 champioins. Bred and owned by Kay Finch.

Holly Hill Indus (Ch. Moonshyn of Moornistan ex Ch. Samaris of Moornistan), dam of 16 champions. Bred and owned by Sue A. Kauffman.

Ch. Hope (Ch. Taejon of Crown Crest ex Ch. Kandorissa of Aldachar), dam of 13 champions, bred by Kay Finch, owned by Charles Costabile and Kay Finch.

As the writer of a circulated pamphlet on Afghan color, one of the authors can testify to the horrible emphasis on breeding for certain colors after receiving blueprints of pedigrees projected well into the future to be checked as a basis for setting specific color strains in Afghans completely irrespective of the suitability and structural quality of the dogs involved.

The great race for coat, begun in the 1920s and never dropping momentum, has plunged many breeders into a frightening trap. In 1931 a champion English bitch of most ungainly proportions was described thusly: "Her marvelous coat makes her an outstanding Afghan." Little else about her could be complimented. While some judges are blinded by such drivel and by great hollow surplus coats, wise and dedicated breeders are not, and it is only through their insistence on retaining Standard ideals and quality beneath the fur that has kept the breed from degeneracy. Knowing that such heavy coat factors have stemmed from their breeding, owners of many full-coated hounds have cried bitterly as the trend to the great coat engulfed the breed. To these dedicated breeders, coats were not ultimate ends but means to more graceful quality hounds. They never wanted to see the "coats wear the dogs." One of the most established breeders, Mrs. Drinkwater, wrote, "Regarding coats, some of the early hounds had very little indeed and one would not like to go back to those days, but I think now we have too much and have lost the lovely saddles and angularity of line that was so typical." Impressionable judges and unthinking breeders do not seem to know when enough is enough and are methodically covering the outlines of the Great Hound. Novices must beware of breeding great coat to great coat without deep concentration on the bones beneath them.

Only when information is available on the dogs listed, are pedigrees useful. Almost all breeding represents a certain amount of covering-up of the faults of one parent with the virtues of the other. Awareness of such covered-up areas prevents the next breeder from backsliding into the same pit the former breeder arose from. For this reason even the darkest-eyed dog, a product of a dark eye-light eye complementary breeding in the previous generation, is a poor bet for eye-color improvement when bred with a light-eyed bitch.

Any dog that is double-bred (from both sides of the family) for any specific asset has twice the chance of passing the virtue intact to a large number of offspring. For such clues the novice must rely on opinions from older experienced breeders better acquainted with the dogs listed on the pedigree. It is a wise move to get as many such evaluations as possible. The novice will soon discover that even the great hounds had their gallery of critics seated right across from

Ch. Khayam's Kism of Scheherezade (Ch. Sasha of Scheherezade ex Ch. Bletchingley Sahari of Scheherezade), black masked red bitch, dam of 11 champions. Bred by Lt. Col. and Mrs. Wallace H. Pede and owned by Dr. and Mrs. Doyle N. Rogers.

the rooting sections. A verdict from the detractors leaves them wondering how the poor dog ever won a blue ribbon in a single entry class. In counterpoint, the boosters infer that the dog was just slightly less than perfect on his very worst days. The truth falls in between. Investigation of old photos help and would be more valuable if so many of the hounds were not stacked into their best, but not necessarily natural, positions. Some photographs are retouched, adding qualities not evident on the living model.

To recapitulate, mating Afghan Hounds under optimum conditions, as in any type of livestock, consists of putting together a pair of nearly perfect complementary specimens, from related backgrounds of nearly perfect hounds. But only the naive believe that such optimum conditions are readily available. Most every breeding is an experiment to be carefully planned, executed, and analyzed. To inbreed, outbreed or line-breed depends on the strong and the weak points of the dogs involved and whether a stable and desirable family background for line-breeding can be found. As long as dedicated breeders continue to breed the best to the best with their eyes focused directly on the Standard, chances are that top quality Afghans will continue to emerge.

In addition to structure and the many external niceties required of show dogs, temperament must also be carefully considered. A dull and stupid hound in a handsome, well-coated shell is certainly no more typical of this bright and lively breed than the shy or nasty dog.

203

Twelve-weeks-old puppies.

Selecting Puppies

The Afghan Hound puppy is a delightful ever-changing creature and a challenge to the most experienced breeders. The younger the pup, the greater the perplexity. The buyer who is determined to have a winning show prospect has no choice but to buy a nearly full-grown pup with proven merit under respected judges and over respectable competition. Even such a hound can suddenly throw his coat or be unresponsive to his new owner. Buyers, not adverse to a bit of a gamble and confident that with the proper upbringing a well-bred pup goes a long way, may prefer to pick a less expensive younger pup who can grow up with the family.

Prices are not a certain guide to the pup's quality. Popularity of the color and the reputation of the parents will make a difference as will the practical desire of the breeder to retain or dispose of the pups. Pups, being the enigmas they are as to future potential, are not easily priced in any from-good-to-bad order. The cheapest pup in a litter of high quality may be a better bargain than the most expensive pick in a mediocre litter. An astute buyer who moves very slowly, learning as much as possible about the breed and the breeders as possible before making a purchase, may well find a bargain.

For the novice, the best guides to the probable adult appearance of the pups, within limits, are the parents of the litter. It is not

204

necessary that they be titled champions if they have proven quality. It certainly is against the law of probabilities to believe that pups will be any better than their combined sire and dam. Beware of pups whose parents are hidden away for any reason. The bitch will not be in her best coat, but this makes it easier for the buyer to see her basic structure and her temperament. It is absolutely necessary to know the Standard before buying puppies, if only to tell whether the parents really pass muster.

All Afghan puppies are born squat-nosed, short-legged and smooth-coated. Signs of differences among siblings, other than in size and color, can be very subtle. In a litter with a wide range of from-poor-to-good pups, even the observant novice with an eye for a dog, can see the better ones at a glance. A uniform litter, either all good or all bad, is more puzzling. The novice must rely heavily on the breeder's word for clues, but would do well to take another experienced breeder with him to view the pups. Whether the visiting breeder cares to pick other people's pups or not matters far less than the fact that his presence may be helpful in giving the buyer an objective view of the whole litter.

Any buyer should be on the lookout for clean surroundings and healthy pups that are lively and friendly when wide-awake. He is also within his rights to ask to see charts of growth gains and evidence of supplemental food consumption in the way of meat. Beware of the large litter of eight or more pups unless positive proof is given that these pups had supplemental rations from the beginning. Few pups can overcome a poor nutritional start. By seven weeks they should be practically or completely weaned and on a good high-protein diet which, incidentally, is expensive and the reason why pups cannot be sold for pittances. Be suspicious of the pup that does not eagerly eat solid food by seven weeks. This does not refer to the period of adjustment when a pup goes into a new home, often temporarily affecting the appetite.

By seven or eight weeks, the pups should be well up on their feet, not down on their pasterns and hocks. Bodies should feel sturdy, not bony or ridgy, but also not covered in heavy fat. Avoid the pup who shows fear reactions and shakes badly when picked up.

Birth size itself is no gauge to adult size but, coupled with advances on weekly weight charts, may prove a fair indication. There is no size disqualification in the breed but a wide range among individuals does exist. Unduly coarse and puny animals are equally undesirable. A buyer would do well to take clues from the parents here. Avoid the gross bitch or the puny male as possible signs of undesirable extremes.

Check for bright clear eyes of small size. Don't assume that dark-eyed pups will stay that way. Most all young pups are dark-eyed and the few that show early lightness will probably turn yellow.

Heads can be puzzling. First, unless at least one of the parents had a really lovely well-chiseled muzzle, there is little chance of finding one in the litter. Not much can be seen on forefaces at an early age, but they should have good depth, with a pronounced Roman bump across the top or the nose will finish flat or dished. Length means very little and comes with the development of the permanent teeth. Decidedly domed occiputs, well-pointed at the rear of the skull, are good signs as are flat inconspicuous zygomatic arches. To indicate refinement, the skull should have a look of greater depth than breadth to it.

By three months, the deciduous teeth are widely spaced and should be slightly overshot (uppers protruding a bit) at this age for even adult teeth spacing. Any sign of an undershot mouth (lowers protruding ahead of the uppers) usually worsens.

Tails should begin to show some curl by eight weeks, especially at chow time. Some have good rings already. Beware of the really limp tail or the one that flops loosely on the back.

Unfortunately, experiences with specific lines of Afghans cannot be carried confidently over to unrelated breedings. Some "families" tend to early leggy development, filling in breadth later. Others portray early heavy body development in broad chests over temporarily bandy legs, bringing the Bulldog to mind. A few hounds grow slowly and evenly, but even this is a worry to some breeders who, from good experience, fear the perfect miniature adult type, as such pups often complete their growth too early and are undersized. The hound that goes through one annoying stage of imbalance after another is usually the large, awkward, fast-growing pup whose parts just can't seem to catch up with each other.

Experienced breeders pick up a seemingly shapeless pup to assess neck and shoulders. The broad, flat shoulder should be oblique and placed well behind the neck. Breastbone and rib cage should be large and well-defined. The lifted head must show early length of neck if it exists. Such long necks thicken with fur and fat and get lost for a while, but usually reappear in adults.

Rear legs should be very wide-spread, well-bent at the stifle and the eight-weeks pup should practically waddle when seen from the rear. As legs lengthen, the tendency is for angulation to decrease. If shoulder and rear quarter angulation is not in hand on a young pup, it never will be. Rear quarters can be forgiven for being slightly higher than the shoulders as the tendency is for rear quarters to drop when the pup is more mature. Loin should be short. Feet must be huge if the puppy is to grow to a respectable size.

Joints of the legs must be quite knobby and obvious. Ears should be broad, long and as low-set as possible. There are times when nice ears appear perched on top of the head, later to drift back into place. At three months, the ears should be longer than the muzzle, but will soon be passed by the lengthening snout.

To the experienced eye, style and stride is one of the best evidences of quality in a young puppy of ten to twelve weeks. It is well to find them at least partially leash trained by this age. The most promising Afghan pup will show its fine heritage through a naturally erect body and head carriage, and a free-moving, trotting gait with feet properly lifted and well-placed. The gait should approximate that specified in the Standard, with the rear legs hitting about where the front feet have left. Any interference of the rear feet with the front, causing side-stepping, is an indication of permanent gait problems. We are discussing a highly changeable ratio of body-length to leg-length on stride but, somehow, at about three months they often line up like they will in adulthood.

As the dog is seen coming and going, any deviation from a straight line is to be avoided, unless there is an obvious and temporary reason for such misalignment. The legs are hinged and jointed to reach the ground from their attached positions on the body. Hence the male with the broad rib cage that needs growing into may pass a period where his still short legs are on the bandy side. The narrow-chested pup whose feet turn out will only get worse.

Coat is the first thing breeders and buyers attempt to assess, both as to color and quantity. The heaviest-coated puppy will be well considered, but many a real bargain in Afghans has come with the nicely formed puppy who looked to be short on coat. A shiny appearance is undesirable; coats should have the look of dusty velveteen pile. Each breeder has his own signs of coat prediction. Some check for curling hair along the backs of the front legs. Others look for thickness on the pasterns or across the nape of the neck, by ruffling the hair backwards. There are those that swear by profuse face hair and monkey whiskers. These theories are just great as long as they work. The entire scope of Afghan coat is too variable to fit any one gauge. Some breeders have pups that are practically smooth-coated at six months of age, but are still confident that they will develop fine adult coats as did their parents before them. Other breeders look with horror on such pups, as their line of pups tends to great fuzzy fur jackets at this age, obliterating all but the tip of the nose. But the latter owners know well that these are puppy coats and not positive indications of adult quantity either. Two well-coated parents generally produce reliably coated offspring. If the parents exhibit two different types of coat textures and come from two different growth pattern calendars, the results are far less certain. Some heavy-coated males are strong at producing well-coated sons but poorly-coated daughters. Scanty-coated parents can be expected to produce more of the same but as long hair is known to be recessive to short hair, there is a chance of an occasional well-coated specimen cropping up unexpectedly. Don't rely on it, though.

Breeders prefer not to see the Afghan Hound develop a complete saddle before it is a year old. Precocious development is rarely a good sign in Afghans. The yearling should have a good thick coat, a a mixture of puppy and adult fur, plenty of facial hair, and a ready-to-emerge saddle lurking as coarse short hair beneath the longer fur. It is well to check the extent of such coarse fur by ruffling the fur backwards, for wherever such short hair can be found on sides, pasterns, and hocks, there is a possibility that the dog will become smooth-coated in these areas, temporarily or permanently. A bitch that does not have her first season until well past her first birthday is also giving a welcome sign, as the largest coat drop often comes with that first real season. To some extent, coat will come and go, rise and fall, all during the hound's life.

The looks of the pup are not all of the story. He must adjust to the world of his owner and other people. The Afghan puppy should be very outgoing as he is certain to gain dignity and reserve in adulthood. He is exceptionally quick to react to stimuli; a necessary trait in the wilds where a split-second delay in reaction can mean sudden death. But beware of the skittery, over-reactive pup who just might be neurotic and untouchable when adult. Much of his future mental attitude will be due to his environment, but some of the germs are planted at birth or in the nest. The big dull sleepy boy may be storing all his energy for growth and should not be ignored.

Finally, never be ashamed to give in to that immediate magnetic rapport that flashes between some people and certain puppies. These instinctive reactions often signal compatible personalities, so important for the enjoyment of the dog as a life-long companion and worth far more than all the blue ribbons in the world.

Color Breeding

The nature of Afghan Hound color is of great fascination to many breeders. Its transmission has long been considered a bit of a puzzle. This is not because it is in any way unique in canine coloring, but because no other long-haired breeds are allowed such wide latitude in coloration. In the surprisingly wide spectrum of Afghan colors and color combinations, somehow ordinary dog colors tend to look very different on this breed with its long sweeping side-coats and

Note variety of colors in this three-weeks-old litter. *Arthur L. Child photo*

contrasting close-haired saddles and muzzles. Long hair tends to diffuse coat colors and allows a noticeable incomplete domination of different genetic factors that produce many subtle unmatchable tones. There is unwarranted stress on Afghan Hound color both inside and out of the rings. The Standard embraces all but white markings. But, as the quiet iridescence of some shadings and the brilliant flash of other hues has lured many fanciers into the tribe, such color concern is understandable.

Afghan Hounds occur in greater or lesser numbers in all common canine colors except liver-brown. Hair color is the result of expression, or inhibition, of pigment supplied by two different forms of melanin. Phaeo-melanin can form only red-cream (tan) color hairs. Eu-melanin, a further step in oxidation, produces a sepia so dark as to make hairs appear black to the naked eye. Singly, or in tandem, these oxidates underlie all dog colors. For example:

1. **Solid Black**—all eu-melanin hairs.

2. **Red** (also called fawn, sable, apricot, etc.)—majority of phaeo-melanin filled hairs, but able to co-exist with eu-black hairs commonly found on tips of ears and scattered down the backline.

3. **Black-and-Tan**—a distinct division between eu-melanin and phaeo-melanin hair controls at the skin level. This pigment spread conflict in melanins ranges from the small black saddle seen on many Beagles, to an animal that, at first glance, appears to be solid black with a few tan hairs in the classic sites of underbelly, tips of feet, anus, and as dashes over the brow.

Color in dogs is far from a simple case of dominants and recessives. The above three base-colors are subject to added drastic changes by

209

Ch. Akaba's Royal Gold (Akaba's Royal Blue ex Ch. Akaba's Brass Bangle), black mask cream, dam of 11 champions. Bred by Lois Boardman and owned by Dr. Gerda Maria Kennedy.

Ch. Crown Crest Sancy (Ch. Crown Crest Dhi-Mond ex Ch. Hope), black mask silver bitch, and Ch. C.C. Vegas Ghamblr of Belden (Ch. Crown Crest Khanazad ex Ch. Crown Crest Safari Sand Star), black mask silver dog. Sancy was dam of 11 of the 23 champions sired by Ghamblr. Both bred by Kay Finch and owned by Leo D. Goodman.

Ch. Delhi Downs Bathsheri (Ch. Dureigh's Golden Harvest ex Delhi Downs Koh-I-Nana), black masked red bitch, dam of 6 champions, bred by Elsie S. and Jack L. Roth, Jr., owned by Delhi Downs Kennels (Norman Kattleman and Bernard W. Mansfield).

action of other genetic factors acting alone, or in conjunction with each other. This will be seen as we discuss individual final colors and their changed form.

At birth most Afghan Hound pups are some shade of mahogany. This is due to a common overlay of blackish guard hairs that will probably disappear in the ensuing months. Only an experienced breeder can predict the future color of such bronze pups, as the darkest of them may well become the lightest-colored when grown. It is the hair color that appears next to the skin at about six weeks that will be of real value, and which can best be seen by ruffling the coat backwards along the sides of the pup. Some pups are born without the guard hairs. This calls out the color immediately, but not necessarily permanently, as some of these darken and others lighten in time.

Hairs constantly grow, age and replace themselves. As the sidecoat lengthens and matures it also tends to lighten, both through fading and by a reduction in pigment laydown at the cellular skin level. The wild-agouti gene also produces a special lightening effect by interrupting pigment laydown at time phase intervals (as with wolves) producing light-dark-light-dark banded hairs, or those with full color only at the tips. Incoming new hair tends to be rich in fresh pigment and so counteracts fading with deeper tones. The coarse, close saddle and muzzle fur, so different in texture from the side-coat, remains full-colored. Blacks tend to "sunburn" or gray, reds turn creamy, and creams fade to white as the coat ages, until periods of re-growth reverse the fading process. The old adage, "You can't tell the color of an Afghan until the day he dies" covers these ever-changing effects.

At the time of whelping, novice breeders have become alarmed by the appearance of pups with pink noses and footpads. This is very common, indicating incomplete pre-natal development of pigment in the extremities. In most instances, the black color replaces the pink within a few days (some solid creams furnishing exceptions). More perplexing to breeders is the appearance of any white-markings on the feet and muzzle of the newborn. By rights, all such white-markings bring suspicion of the presence of mis-marking genes, but their occurrence is very common and experienced breeders know that white feet and barely visible bits of white above the nostrils will probably fill with color later. The line of demarcation between temporary white tips and true "mis-marks" is a tricky border dispute.

The most important base color in Afghans is the red as it has always been the most widespread color of the breed, giving it the heaviest genetic frequency. In the scale of powers the black is

Ten-months-old black-masked red male.

dominant over the red but of less importance as black genes are comparatively rare in total Afghan population. Black, being dominant, requires at least one black parent (see blue or cream also) in order to produce black offspring. The B-T (black-and-tan) pattern is more common than the black, but less than the red, and recessive to both the other base forms, meaning that the B-T must be transmitted by both parents to produce visual B-Ts. Such single B-T genes can be carried recessively for many generations before meeting their match. Hence, the occurrence of B-Ts from any breeding should not be surprising.

The common red in Afghans is well known in the world of dogs, being genetically similar to the shades called sable in Collies or fawn in Great Danes and Boxers. The dark masking found on the muzzle of most red Afghans is the result of a separate additional marking gene of a dominant type. This masking gene is very widespread in the breed, but one parent at least must be masked to produce masked offspring. Invisible masks can be worn by black-masked *black* dogs. The effect of the masking gene may be limited to just a few dark hairs around the lips or extend as dark pigment running well above the eyes. It is interesting in the U.S.A. that the mask factor is uncommon in Borzoi, Greyhounds, Whippets and Saluki.

212

The tints of cream or silver, with some exceptions (see cream or blue) are merely let-down shades of the common red, whether seen on the black-masked cream, as the pale background of a brindle, or on the ivory feet and underbody of the light-pointed B-Ts. This reduction of red pigment is due to a specific paling gene that, for some strange reason, limits its effects to the base red hairs, having practically no effect on any black hairs in attendance. As the paled forms are recessive to the full darker reds, such genes must be acquired from both parents.

The permanent retention of a goodly number of blackish hairs (sabling) on the various shades of red-creams is not uncommon, producing extremely dark saddles and black tails, often shading over parts of the shoulders and body. This heavy sabling is particularly evident in certain strains of Afghans.

Brindles are base red animals with a superimposed dark striping over the lighter background due to another specific genetic effect, dominant in type. This calls for at least one parent to have the visible brindling phenomenon to produce brindle offspring. (Again, as with masking, brindling may exist but not be visible on a black dog, there being no available light hairs for contrast.) On a B-T patterned dog, the brindle effect can only be viewed on the light

Four-weeks-old black-masked silver male.

213

points of feet and face. These two overlay features are due to distinctly different genes, but can occur simultaneously on one animal.

Brindle is the most variable of all Afghan colors. The dark striping can be so extensive that the dog is mistaken for a true black hound. Or slight dark markings on a gold dog can be so light as to escape detection and yet blossom out into full stripes in the next generation. Afghan brindles frequently appear more mottled and blotched than clearly striped due to the diffusive effects on long coat. Many so-called Afghan brindles are nothing more than heavily sabled dogs mis-labeled brindle. The base red visible as background between the dark stripes varies as with red found anywhere else according to the paling genes present. The dark overlay is affected by the same factors of dilution that govern any black hairs. (See "blue.")

The true solid dominant black is an uncommon color in the breed, but when present it conceals all other forms of coloring recessive to it. Most black Afghans are heterozygous for the color (have just one gene for black and one gene carried recessively for either red or B-T). Dilute shades of black, called Maltese Blues, are the rarest of all the Afghan colors. The true blue dog (not to be confused with blue-brindles) is genetically black, with a coat that has been diluted from black to gray by means of the Maltese Blue dilution factor (that restricts its effect to black pigment of the coat and ignores the red areas). Such blues occur in shades from deep slate gray to a pale dove gray that can be taken for white. This Maltese Blue dilution gene is recessive to the fuller color and must be supplied by both parents. As this same gene will effect black hairs on any color hound, it is present in a double dose in the gray-masked red hound (when the hound is born gray-masked). It turns the B-T to blue-and-tan. Dark striping on brindles is similarly affected.

While the Maltese Blue gene is detected at birth because of its gray-blue cast, another gene also produces blues of a slightly different type. This graying gene (most common in Kerry Blue Terriers) is a progressive deterioration of black, bringing premature graying to a hound born jet black. Some graying is evident by the dog's first birthday and may continue until the hound is three years old. This graying gene, unlike the Maltese Blue, is a dominant factor and need come from one parent only. Black-masked reds who turn gray very early may well harbor this gene. Both types of blue-grays have been unconsciously selected and often intermixed by breeders striving for the illusive blues. A word of caution for those anxious to dabble in blues in hopes of setting a strain of this color. In Afghans

Am., Aust., Nor., Swed., Fin., North and Int. Ch. Tanjores Domino (Xenos VDOM ex Tanjores Senorita), imported blue and cream dog with "domino" pattern, owned by John and Cynthia Guzevich.

it is a highly frustrating experience. The necessary factors are quite rare and very difficult to control. There is a distinct danger of blindly sacrificing total quality for color as there is in all deliberate color breedings. Even under the most carefully controlled conditions, breeders hoping for blues often find themselves getting poorly pigmented creams and whites instead (see "cream"). Remember also that the blue genes only succeed in making the more common black-masked stock turn gray bearded and ancient before their time. There is great charm and unusual beauty when the blue factors occur on brindles, B-Ts and blacks. Fortunately, they do turn up as natural happy surprises, remaining the rare gems of the Afghan spectrum.

The emergence of *domino* as a color-term dates from the importation of Ch. Tanjores Domino, but as a genetic pattern it is as old as the breed itself. Called "grizzle" in Salukis, and "cap" in some other breeds, it was known as reverse-masked in Afghan Hounds up to 1958. The pattern, characteristically, presents a peculiarly light-colored foreface, setting off a darker tone widow's peak at the forehead, with the short-haired saddle interspersed with light and dark hairs giving the effect of a much darker coat than the long side-fall of hair. Ch. Tanjores Domino sported, in tone, a dazzling silver foreface and long-coat, with slate-grey head-marking and saddle. The same pattern occurs in any color, and color combination, except solid black. Genetically these are un-masked dogs of red or black-and-tan basic colors, changed by the agouti-gene that interrupts pigment entrance into the hairs in time-phased arrest, together with the countershaded ventral-lightener gene that makes the foreface, throat, underbelly, inner legs and feet of the wolf much lighter than the rest of the animal. In other words, domino appears clearly related to the wild color.

The *cream* Afghan Hound is difficult to discuss and assess, for such hounds genetically may be any one of the three primary base colors, despite not having a single black hair visible in any part of their coat. This phenomenon is due to a "restriction factor" that positively prohibits the appearance of black hairs in the fur. Such animals are born sans dark guard hairs, remaining clear cream to white throughout their lives. They are never black-masked but frequently are reddish on the muzzle and ear fringes. This restriction factor is recessive and must come from both parents. Two such creams, regardless of their true genetic base colors, can produce only more such creams, but when the double restriction factor is broken as in mating with any full-color dog with black hairs in its coat, the true hidden base color of the cream can be released to their offspring. These self-colored creams were once far more common than they are today and responsible for many surprises when bred to black-masked reds, such as the occurrence of black or blue pups when least expected. Such experiences lead to the widely-held belief that there was just no accounting for Afghan colors. These same creams are apt to thwart schemes for blues by cropping up through a re-pairing of recessive restriction factors, so closely woven into much blue and black breeding. The ivory hounds are very lovely in themselves, and show off a good eye and a well-chiseled head to great advantage, but they have a slight problem, sometimes only seasonal ("winter nose") in a lack of jet black nose and eye rim pigment. This may appear as pinkish-grey and is a minor fault in a Standard which calls for a black nose.

The white Afghan is somewhat the same story. Most whites are either pale gray or pale cream animals due to a piling up of paling and dilution factors, plus the aforementioned "restriction factor." But it is certainly conceivable that some of our pure whites are just one big spot caused by the extreme forms of the "spotting genes" known to exist in the breed. White spots (mis-marks) are due to a specific recessive and predictable multiform gene that allows absolutely no pigment into portions of the skin, leaving it transparent (pink) with colorless (white) hairs growing from the areas. These spotting effects increase in intensity from the extremities inward. Going down from the dominant full-color form (with no white on the animal anywhere), the mildest form of spotting consists of white

216

toes and a breast locket, so common in the breed that it attracts no attention. In a stronger dose, there will be one or more white feet, a white tail tip, and possibly a definite "blaze" on the muzzle. A stronger dose of the spotting genes produces white climbing up the legs and circling the neck in the "Collie collar" pattern. The obviously spotted parti-color animal ranges from this stage to a piebald appearance with remaining splotches of color on a large white background. Most of these white-splashed Afghans are mercifully put down at birth or not used for breeding. However, extremely white-spotted animals may reach the other end of the stick in appearing a solid white color. This is frequently seen in Borzoi and the white Collie. Any traces of actual color would be found around the ears and near the base of the tail but, if cream in tone, it would go unnoticed. Such a white lacks proper pigmentation and, together with parti-colors or blazed hounds, constitutes "mis-marks," undesirable according to the Standard. All other colors are perfectly permissible.

Ch. Stormhill's Who's Zoomin' Who (Ch. Pahlavi Puttin' On The Ritz ex Pantastic of Stormhill), black mask red bitch, multi BIS winner. Bred and owned by Dave and Sandy Withington Frei, Stormhill Kennels. Handler, Sandy Frei.—*Lindermaier.*

Ch. Makarabi's Joniboi—"Korla"—(El Khani Sahm-Ba ex Dakar's Fiesta Parade), black mask red dog, bred by Betty McCargar, owned by Edward M. and Trudie Gilbert. Korla appeared in the movie "The Maltese Bippy" (1969) with Rowan and Martin, in an episode of the "Here's Lucy" TV show with Lucille Ball, and in various magazine advertising displays.

9

Care

THERE are excellent pamphlets and books devoted entirely to the care, breeding, and raising of dogs. These belong in every dog owner's library and we shall not attempt to abbreviate them here except in regards to the peculiar needs of the Afghan Hound.

Written material concerning the acts of mating and whelping is necessarily averaged from the reproductive cycles of all breeds. Such mid-point charts cannot be expected to fit precisely all Afghan Hounds. In reproductive activity there is considerable, perfectly normal variation. Owners, determined to rigidly follow the "book," rather than observe and keep notes on the cycles of their own bitches, may find themselves unable to gain issue from their hounds.

The majority of Afghan bitches commence their first season between 9 to 12 months of age, but variation, ranging from 6 to as late as 18 months remains within the normal range. Bitches should not be bred at their first season, particularly if they are less than a year old at the time.

A fair number of Afghan bitches do follow the book, coming into season regularly every six months, being ready to be bred on the 10th to the 12th day, and completing their season in approximately 21 days, but many more do not. Once-a-year seasons are not unusual, harking back to the primitive dog habits, nor are cycles of 9 to 10 month intervals. A few bitches really confuse the issue by flaming into season more than twice a year. By making notations on the backs of pedigrees or on health charts as to the exact onset and duration of each season, fairly regular cycle intervals for each bitch should reveal themselves.

Lengths of heats also vary. At the extreme, a rare bitch may have to be mated before the end of the first week; others have produced issue from breedings on as late as the 21st day. Such tendencies may be familial. Obviously this variation brings confusion in ascertaining the precise day for conception, and such bitches must be watched extra carefully to prevent unwanted matings.

The actual behavior of the dog and bitch remains the most reliable sign for optimum mating periods. The male will certainly coax the female long before she is "ready" and she may tease him in return, but she will not stand still nor hold her tail aside. During such test runs, the hounds must have room for wide maneuvering as a resentful harried bitch will snap at the male.

The physical signs are quite reliable when properly read. The bitch's vulva swells noticeably, emitting a bright red discharge at the onset of the season. Fastidious bitches, however, clean themselves constantly, often hiding early traces from unwary owners. The discharge continues and the bitch's changing scent will attract the males but she will repel any serious advances. At the time of acceptance by the bitch, there is a definite lightening of the discharge to a pinkish-yellow; and the vulva will be somewhat softened. The bitch can be assumed to have passed her season only when all discharge has completely stopped and the swelling disappears whether she has been bred or not. The owner who is unable to interpret the signs of the estrus cycle may wish to have a veterinarian make smear tests for advancing ovulation.

Forced matings, desire-attracting drugs, or artificial insemination for reluctant breeders, runs counter to selection for natural reproductive vigor in the breed. In breeding, as elsewhere, the Afghan retains an independent spirit, occasionally determined to choose their own mates by refusing to have anything to do with the suitor offered by their owners. It is certainly advisable to put a maiden bitch to an experienced stud, an allow them ample courting time well before the day of mating. Conversely, a calm matron is always an asset to an over-anxious untried male.

In breeding, as elsewhere, the Afghan retains an independent spirit, occasionally determined to choose their own mates by refusing to have anything to do with the suitor offered by their owners. It is certainly advisable to put a maiden bitch to an experienced stud, and allow them ample courting time well before the day of mating. Conversely, a calm matron is always an asset to an over-anxious untried male.

At mating time, a non-slippery ground surface should be provided (not linoleum). If the bitch is frightened or the male unpracticed, seek help from an experienced dog breeder. Breeding plans have been thwarted and potential brood stock ruined by human bungling. Forcing a bitch to be bred before she is physically and psychologically ready, just because it is the 12th day can do long-lasting harm. If the bitch is fractious, but not utterly unwilling, she can be held for the male by competent persons. A soft bandage should be tied about the muzzle of the bitch to prevent fear-biting. She will also need lavish reassurance in words and pats to calm her maiden fears.

The breeding of persistently unwilling bitches is not to be encouraged. They frequently make indifferent mothers, and may possibly be illustrating an innate reproductive weakness. We might warn novice owners that Afghan bitches are quite inclined to scream at the time of actual mating, shattering the nerves of the unprepared and sending the neighbors dashing for help. It is a blood-chilling, semi-human scream, unmistakable to the experienced. Once the animals are "tied," the cry simmers to a moan or mutter, and fades away entirely.

The "tie" lasts for a few minutes or as long as an hour. Fertile breedings can occur without a tie but are very rare. During the tie the male may wish help in lifting his hind leg over the rear of the bitch until the two are standing back to back. The bitch should be held and soothed until the tie is naturally broken. If she tries to dash off, the helpless male can suffer real injury. Bitches are not vindictive during the tie and can be unmuzzled at this time. Offer water to both parties.

Afghan bitches usually settle down and follow the book along the usual pattern of embryo development. Jot down the date (or dates) of mating to gauge the expected whelping time. Weigh the bitch at mating time and measure her circumference just past the last rib. The first definite signs of pregnancy appear about the fifth week after mating in the form of a sudden and definite jump in weight and girth. Keep weekly records of measurements.

Top physical condition of the bitch-mother cannot be overstressed. The poorest start on any breeding program is an unfit dam. A sickly bitch, one that is infested with parasites, or one that is weak-muscled from lack of exercise should not be used for breeding. Any bitch, seven years or older (five years if she has never had a litter) is a breeding risk and breeding should be under a veterinarian's supervision. Overweight bitches should be trimmed to normal weight before breeding, as obesity contributes to infertility as well as whelping time difficulties. Thin bitches should be medically checked for predisposing causes. Any brood bitch benefits from a complete physical check-up before the mating time. If not done before the breeding, it should be done right afterwards (this is too late to call it off should complications be diagnosed). Infestations of parasites,

Ch. Dynasty's Kristol Klear
(Ch. Coastwind Obsidian ex
Ch. Dynasty's Kristol Pistol),
bitch, bred by Nora Jane
Dodson and Frederic Alder-
man, owned by Kaye Greenly
Gorman.

Ch. Elmo's Tutankhamun
(Ch. Scarabet Majic Maverick
ex Ch. Shikari's Tosca Blue),
blue dog, BIS winner. Bred and
owned by Peter Belmont, Jr.,
Elmo Reg.

even mild ones that do not normally bother the bitch, will interfere with optimum embryo development. A firm program of exercise and weight control should be instituted and carried to the wire. Only walking exercise is advised as the bitch grows heavy with whelp the last three weeks.

Only normal quantities of food are required by the bitch for the first four weeks of pregnancy—assuming that the bitch consumes a highly nutritional diet, including real meat and vitamin supplements regularly. From the fourth week onward, the diet should be bolstered gradually in both quantity and quality. The need for added assimilable calcium rises greatly in the pregnant bitch as puppy bones are being formed. Veterinarian-prescribed special prenatal supplements, rich in calcium and iron, should be given to all in-whelp Afghan bitches. The gradually increasing food amounts should contain, in addition to added kibble, concentrated proteins and minerals as found in meat, eggs, fish, cottage cheese, and powdered milk.

During the last four weeks the bitch usually gains in girth rapidly with an average litter (five or six pups). The embryos can sometimes be felt, like soft walnut-sized balls, moving in the abdomen. However, the Afghan bitch has a deep and cavernous chest and can be rather difficult to follow through pregnancy if she has a small litter tucked well under the ribs.

Full-term puppies emerge from the 58th to the 65th day as well as on the celebrated 63rd. General signs and needs of whelping time are well covered in the books. One often observed sign is when the Afghan bitch, who has eaten ravenously for the last few weeks, suddenly loses either her appetite or her dinner. Another reported indication is the bitch who *shivers* uncontrollably for several hours. When any suspicious signs appear, rectal temperature can be taken. The normal temperature is 101°; the bitch's temperature will usually fall below 100° within 12 to 24 hours before the litter arrives.

From the first sign of straining or labor, the bitch should be watched unobtrusively by an attendant who is prepared to call a nearby veterinarian for help if necessary. The most common source of trouble is *uterine inertia* whereby the bitch is unable to properly contract the uterus and expel all the puppies. We do not want to be alarmists but this problem is to be anticipated in out-of-condition bitches and has complicated what appeared to be healthy situations. Today's bitches lead entirely too sedentary lives for their own good. More than two hours between pups can be an unwelcome sign of possible difficulties, especially if there is straining by the bitch. When the litter has finally arrived, we advocate calling the veterinarian to give the dam a post-natal injection containing pituitrin to contract the uterus and expel any remaining afterbirths or late puppies and anti-biotics to ward off infections. In this breed it is not easy to be certain that the last pup and afterbirth have arrived, and late-comers are not at all unusual.

Most Afghan dams do a creditable job of bringing pups into the world once the initial fright of having the first-born subsides. An age-old instinct tells them what mothers of all mammals have known since the advent of the species, but these messages are not spelled out in great detail and can get slightly garbled in translation. A bewildered dam might spend so much time cleaning the rear end of the pup that she neglects to bite the sack off the head and start the breathing. This is especially true with breech births, where the dam is not sure which end is which. If pups arrive in too quick a succession, a harried mother may not finish cleaning one pup properly before the arrival of another. There is a question as to whether to allow the bitch to eat the afterbirths or not, and it really does not matter greatly. They no longer furnish the only available nourishment for the bitch as they did in the wilds but it is believed that they do stimulate the flow of milk into the nipples and the bitch should be allowed to have at least one if she desires it.

A bowl of milk and a nutritional concentrate such as meat soup should be offered to the bitch during the whelping hours. When all the puppies have arrived, the bitch may have to be led, forcibly, outside to relieve herself, as she will regret leaving her newborns for even a few seconds. Ignore the loud protestations and hope the neighbors know you are not torturing her.

A word of caution at whelping time concerns umbilical hernias which occur in Afghans frequently enough to deserve mention. Some experts claim they are inherited. Others blame predisposing causes such as inept dams and short umbilical cords. A few bitches insist on pushing newborns around by their cords, and other dams draw their pups close to the side of their teeth and bite the cord right next to the pup's tender navel. In such cases hernias are quite apt to develop. Many owners try to sever the cords for the dam to reduce this problem. These hernias are more of a nuisance than a serious injury. Inconspicuous bumps can be left indefinitely, but large bulges should eventually be surgically repaired. Most veterinarians do this for a modest fee.

The number of puppies born to one Afghan dam can be a problem. Litters of up to 12 pups are not uncommon. This is entirely too many pups for one dam to feed without seriously tearing herself down. She will manage for the first week or so, but pups grow at an amazing rate, ever expanding their capacity and needs for milk. If such demands are not fully met, the pups' growth will be retarded.

224

In large kennels "foster mothers" (bitches of any breed that are giving milk) are used, but foster mothers are not easily located for the home-bred litter. As the usual number of good milk-producing faucets is 7 or 8, this is as many pups as the dam should be expected to handle. Unless the owner is actually in a position to take over the arduous task of "foster mother" on a 24 hour basis, large litters should be culled to a reasonable size. It is very difficult to cull litters and no one likes the idea very much but breeders that refuse to cull on the grounds that they may be putting down the "best one" are particularly short-sighted, for in a small litter, better fed and cared for, several pups may become outstanding. In the large poorly fed litter, none may reach their potential. Culling litters is not only accepted but mandatory in many European countries where dog raising is such a fine art. In America, the decision is left to the individual owner.

A word on false pregnancies: Afghan bitches are notorious for these false alarms. They occur as frequently in bitches who never see a male during their seasons as in females who are bred but do not "take." Such bitches insist on going the full route of preparing for whelping, milk production, etc., but do not produce any pups. False pregnancies cause some bitches to eat as if they were supplying a brood, gain weight, have milk in badly swollen nipples, and sustain an emotional crisis that we human beings cannot possibly appreciate as time arrives for the birth of the imaginary pups. These bitches take to mothering small animals or stuffed toys and produce enough milk to function as a foster mother. Injections may be required to relieve the milk congestion. The mild false pregnancy brings a short period of moping and slight nipple distention, but others are truly heart-rending. As it is the nature of the Afghan bitch to drop large quantities of coat towards the end of the nursing period, the bitch with the false pregnancy will do the same, to the consternation of the owner who deliberately refrains from breeding in favor of exhibition at the shows. Allowing such a bitch the privilege of one litter will not necessarily correct the false pregnancy tendency. Spaying is the only positive answer, and in the case of bitches not being exhibited nor part of any planned breeding program, such surgical action should be considered. The coat, which is greatly affected by the reproductive cycle, improves in stability and quantity with spaying. However, spayed bitches are not eligible for conformation exhibition.

The new-born Afghan Hound generally weighs about one pound. Large pups of one and one half pounds are not really uncommon. Pups from small litters tend to be larger at birth than those from the more crowded groups. For the first three weeks, the average gain is about a pound (or a little more) per week. By the 21st day, the pup's eyes are well open and unclouded, and the puppy senses are responding in a decisive manner. This is the time to introduce some solid foods. From this point onward, with the inclusion of some solid food in the diet, the weight gain jumps to about 2 pounds per week until weaning time. A range of approximately 13 pounds (bitches) to 16 pounds (males) constitutes good weight for the eight to nine week old pup. From weaning onward, if fed properly, the rate of gain is astonishing, with pups often weighing 25 and 30 pounds at the 12th week. Forty pounds for a good sized four to five months old male Afghan is not unusual. The weights given are from actual litters of Afghans but are only indications as different pups from different bloodlines and backgrounds develop at decidedly different growth rates.

The average Afghan reaches full height by his 11th month, but a few continue to inch slowly upward for a few more months. Full height certainly does not mean either full weight or full frame development which, in the Afghan, frequently comes quite slowly. Some yearlings are built much like the 12 year old boy who shot up to six feet while away at summer camp. The "fill-out" comes later.

The diet of the Afghan Hound never ceases to be of tremendous importance to his welfare, but it is more important in puppyhood than in adolescence. The Afghan, with his large, raw-boned frame only lightly covered with fat, requires a fantastic production of bone, sinew and muscle to support and construct his sprouting structure.

During the first three weeks of life, there is little that the owner can do to nourish the pups excepting to keep the bitch-mother stuffed with high quality foods, calcium supplements and plenty of fluids. The bitch-mother will eat from two to five times her normal amount while nursing. The owner can, however, clip the tiny razor sharp toe-nails of the pups on the second or third day after birth, and again every few days as they become repointed. The dam who is gouged by puppy talons soon becomes reluctant to expose herself to nursing pain. The Standard says nothing about dew claws, but it is wise to have them removed on the second or third day; it is a simple surgical procedure and will cause little pain or bleeding. They become a nuisance when left to grow and are far more difficult to remove at maturity.

Supplemental feeding of solids is best begun during the third week. As in the pediatrics wards, there is some question about the nutritional value at such an early age, but the consensus of opinion is that while not much more than milk is easily assimilated at this tender age, the body is becoming prepared for advancing textures

Ch. Coastwind Antiophe (Ch. Coastwind Obsidian ex Coastwind Ajuga), bitch, multiple BIS winner. Bred by Coastwind Kennels and owned by Jay T. Hafford and Tom Morehouse.

and tastes. If no adverse reactions are seen, continue to expand the quantities. The very act of offering food to pups at this age sets up an important rapport between puppy and human, of greater value than its use in the digestive tract. The emphatic importance of this early man-dog relationship is discussed in *The New Knowledge of Dog Behavior* by C. J. Pfaffanberger; one of the truly important dog books.

With bitches' milk being the nutritional mainstay of pups until they are six weeks old, first supplemental foods should be a mixture of scraped meat (canned baby meats are good) or lean hamburger, warmed to room temperature and mixed with equal parts of cottage cheese. To this, add a bit of powdered vitamin supplement and some form of calcium. Let the pups lick bits of the mixture off the ends of your fingers. Soon they will eagerly lick it out of the bowls.

Not all forms of calcium are equally assimilable by the dog. The preferred form is *dicalcium phosphate* with added viosteral. This can be purchased as a complete mixture in pill form or as less expensive dibasic calcium phosphate power (obtainable by the pound from the druggist) used with any brand of cod liver oil. Those who are able to find a fine steamed bone meal (in feed and grain stores) have an even cheaper substitute for the dicalcium phosphate. The addition of cod liver oil is of special value for winter litters or in areas where pups cannot readily soak up quantities of daily sunshine. When using the handy bulk dibasic calcium phosphate pow-

Stormhill puppies.

der, begin with one half teaspoon per pup, with a scant one quarter to one half teaspoon cod liver oil. As the pups readily accept the solid foods and consume ever increasing quantities, raise supplements gradually to a maximum of one rounded teaspoon of calcium and one teaspoon of cod liver oil (by about 12 weeks) plus some all-purpose vitamin of the pet type.

We do not recommend pablum or any cooked cereals for early supplementary feedings as they are primarily carbohydrates and do not fill the puppy needs for bone-building materials. Only when pups are taking copious amounts of milk from the dam, plus a good quantity of meat and cottage cheese ration is it time to add any additional "filler" foods. A commercial "puppy kibble" or whole grain unsweetened cereal, such as shredded wheat softened with warm water or milk, can then be added to the meat mixture.

Young pups should be offered solid foods two or three times a day until they are weaned. These feeding times are marvelous opportunities to discover and note individual personalities in the pups. The dam must be watched carefully as she may think the food pans are for her rather than for her kids. She may be getting multiple rations but will try to steal the pups' food if not discouraged.

It is acceptable to allow the pups to sample some of the dam's food if she does not object. Such activity should be supervised to prevent the bitch being cheated of her food or irritated with the presumptuous youngsters. A sense of adventure and enthusiasm for various foods should be encouraged in young Afghan Hounds to prevent them from becoming excessively finicky or demanding at a later date.

228

Attempts at weaning the pups should be made by the sixth week, through offerings of milk (whole, canned or powdered) between each meal of solids. Pups should be gaining weight rapidly at this point and eating ever-increasing amounts.

There are several systems of feeding growing and grown dogs, and we immediately state that if it works for you and your dog, don't change it. However, proper feeding of the Afghan Hound, especially the finicky small eater, is a loudly sung problem of many owners, warranting a few words over and above that listed on the backs of the kibble sacks.

Some misguided new owners decide to feed their hounds those wonderfully convenient, but expensive, cans of dog food that need only be opened and spooned into a pan to be eagerly gobbled by their tail-waggers. We must say, emphatically, that canned food is absolutely wrong for Afghans. Such foods are up to 80% water, actually starving the Afghan with the small stomach, by filling him with water-expanded food when he needs concentrated nourishment. Afghans, erroneously fed in this manner by well-meaning owners, can be seriously malnourished. When taken off the canned food diet and given a good grade of concentrated kibble, they soon consume far less in volume, are much less expensive to feed, and rapidly prosper in condition. An exception to the canned food ban is the canned meats (horsemeat, chicken, liver, and beef) which can be used in place of fresh meat as an additive to the kibble.

Self-feeding, a much talked about method, consists of making dry kibble available for dogs to eat at will. A drawback to self-feeding among Afghan Hounds is that long-eared hounds chew their ear fringes to pieces if not fitted with "snoods" to hold back ears at meal time. An additional disadvantage is that added meat, cottage cheese, supplementary vitamins or fats cannot be left out for fear of spoilage. A combination system, with the dogs having one wet meal including all additives, combined with self-feeding for the remainder of the diet, has been found useful by some owners, primarily for puppies and non-show dogs. With liquid absent from self-fed kibble, it is of the utmost importance that water bowls be constantly refilled, or be of the automatic waterer type.

A good grade of kibble will make up the majority of the dog's diet. Do not be misled by amounts suggested on the package. Few Afghan Hounds eat anything like such quantities (except growing pups that pass a stage of seeming bottomlessness). The quality commercial kibbles have been scientifically improved and tested in recent years, but there is some variation from brand to brand in protein type and amount, fat content, added vitamins and minerals. Ingredient analysis appears on each package. Due to individual reactions among dogs (and owners), it is reasonable to experiment with several quality brands before settling on one. Take careful notice of the different levels of palatability, signs of weight loss or gain, amounts of kibble the dog eats before slowing down and becoming indifferent to the feed, and both the quantity and quality (firmness) of the residual fecal material formed.

Most Afghan Hound breeders find that some additional protein source, such as meat (up to 20% of the total meal) is often beneficial to the Afghan Hound. Substitutes for meat, where added protein or taste-tempting additives are desired, are cottage cheese, egg yolks, fish or poultry. In the last two, all splintery bones must be removed or the food should be pressure cooked.

The "semi-soft" package foods are exceptionally palatable to most Afghan Hounds, and are a quality product, but expensive to use as a diet mainstay. Their greatest value is that of a "pick-up" meal to be used in travelling, for show purposes or vacationing. Not only are they easily obtained at any market, but their taste appeal keeps dogs from going "off their feed" away from home. Remarkable benefit comes from minimal residual "stools" resulting from change in water, environment or excitement. As some adult Afghan Hounds reject all unfamiliar food in periods of stress (such as travel or being at strange kennels), many owners introduce semi-moist foods in the form of "tidbits"—on occasion—to puppies and young dogs at home.

As substitutions for meat (or in addition to it) other excellent sources of the needed protein are egg *yolks,* cottage cheese, fish and poultry. In the latter two foods, all splintery bones must be removed.

A life-long use of a vitamin supplement is well-considered by most Afghan owners. Such all-purpose pet vitamins plus the aforementioned dicalcium phosphate mixture and cod liver oil are especially essential during the growth period of the dog's life, up to 18 months of age. Although the hound may have gained full height by the tenth month, considerable cartilage will fill into solid bone long afterwards.

Afghans prefer their food slightly on the dry side rather than mushy. It is difficult to get them to eat more than one meal a day past 10 months of age, but try to keep them on two meals per day for as long as possible.

Fats are very important to the diet and the Afghan with so much coat to nourish needs as much or more than average breeds, calling for additives of suet, bacon grease, or special oils. One is as good as another. The use of a fatty hamburger cuts down the need for additional fats.

230

In cases of serious weight problems, a veterinarian should be consulted immediately. Not only is he prepared to find the underlying causes, but he has specially prepared diets to recommend. Veterinarians, however, admittedly have far more success with the overweight dog than the underweight ones.

If simple excess weight is the problem, the most obvious solution is less calories and more exercise. Caloric reduction is accomplished by cutting back on the kibble, and substituting some added lean meat. Bitches tend to fat far more often than males. For the ravenous hound, cottage cheese can also be added. Raw carrots are a marvelous edible that allows chewing but does not turn to fat. We heartily recommend giving raw carrot pieces to young pups as chew-toys. They aid in teething problems, supply roughage and are a good substitute for real bones, so taboo to the show Afghan Hound whose leg coat must be protected from accidental gnawing.

The underweight dog must be considered from several different angles. First, an accurate diagnosis must be made as to whether the hound is seriously thin or not. A healthy, active pup, growing very rapidly, in the all-legs stage, appears terribly slender in a normal developmental stage. Before becoming distressed, owners should check the weight and appearance with a knowledgeable breeder who can give an opinion on the dog's gangliness.

If the dog is a good eater, an ordinary diet, enriched with extra fats and a highly concentrated type of kibble should suffice. Two or three small meals a day rather than just one large one is a help if the dog will eat them. A bedtime bowl of milk adds calories.

Most underweight Afghans are that way because they use up a great deal of nervous energy and are finicky eaters, somewhat of a curse in the breed. The first step here is to make certain that the dog is not ill or wormy. It is then absolutely necessary that the owner take over the diet planning for the dog and not be tricked into letting the dog make the decisions. Finicky dogs quickly learn that their small appetites distress their anxious owners and take advantage of this by refusing to eat anything but table scraps and favorite cuts of meat. Any meat fed to such spoiled dogs must be so very well-mixed into the kibble that it cannot possibly be picked out independently.

There are meats other than steaks that tempt the appetite. Chicken is one of the best. Poultry bones must be removed or pressure cooked to a soft state. The vertebrae bones in a young chicken, however, are not dangerous. Some dogs show a decided preference for liver or heart; both being very nutritious but lacking in necessary fats. A palatable meat, very high in fat, is lamb breast, which combines well with the liver and heart. Broth from cooked meats should be mixed with the kibble for added flavor. Hamburger is excellent as is all fish. "Pet mixes" usually trimmings and meat cuts not used for humans vary greatly with the meat cutter and some are far more appetizing than others. It pays to shop around for these. Add spices and salt to cooking meats. Onion, garlic and tomato juice are great flavor enhancers. Raw meat is fine (if the dog likes it), but the difficulties of storage makes frozen meat, cooked or baked as needed, more practical.

The occasional use of fish or the addition of powdered kelp to the diet may help ward off possible mineral deficiencies in the growing hound. Owners must investigate to find the most practical nutritional foods within their own areas.

For the ill or convalescent dog, there is nothing more appealing than an easily digested mixture of chicken broth and rice. Cubes of chicken or beef bouillon are fortifiers for any meal, as in any meat gravy. Cottage cheese and canned baby foods are well assimilated by the below par system. Pork, with the exception of bacon, should never be fed to hounds.

There is always a fear of rickets in any fast growing dog who does not get the optimum diet or does not properly assimilate his food. Diagnosis of rickets is a professional matter—but spying the pup that should be checked professionally must be done in the home kennel.

Pups of all ages should be bright-eyed and, by three months of age, well up on their own feet, off the back of pasterns and hocks, carrying sturdy straight leg bones and a fairly strong topline. Danger signals are any signs of dull coat, lethargy, bent bones, and slack pasterns or hocks. Large knobby pasterns and knots like small marbles at the base of the ribs where the cartilage begins, when found in conjunction with spindly bones, may well be a sign of incipient rickets, especially if these areas are tender and sensitive to the touch. Yet, on the other hand, such knobbiness on otherwise healthy, well-developed large pups indicates desirable centers of future growth, disappearing with maturity. Strangely enough, such knobs are most often found on poor growers and the best growers, and less often on the even-growing, in-between sized pups.

Feeding the Afghan Hound should not be a slipshod arrangement. Curs can exist on any scraps and digestible diggings, but such dogs rarely achieve full size and inherited potentials. Extra thought and pennies spent on diet repay the owner in the production of a healthy, relatively disease-resistant, gorgeous Afghan Hound.

Check with your veterinarian regularly for dates to have the dogs tested for worms (a must that varies with the common parasites in specific localities) as well as inoculations for distemper, hepatitis,

Ch. Dahnwood Gabriel (Ch. Crown Crest Zardani ex El Amron Tarquin), black masked golden dog, multiple BIS winner and sire of 11 champions. Bred by Forrest Hansen and Donald McIlvain, owned by Mandith Kennels (Herman L. and Judith S. Fellton).

Ch. Mandith Salute (Ch. Dahnwood Gabriel ex Mandith Circe), black masked red dog, multiple BIS winner. Bred and owned by Mandith Kennels (Mr. and Mrs. Herman L. Fellton). Yes, it sometimes rains at shows.

and, in many areas, rabies. All records of such treatments should be noted on the back of the pedigree and given with the dog if sold.

Grooming

Concerning fur alone, a young puppy needs practically no grooming. The plush puppy coat grows thickly and quietly, standing well off the body, seldom tangling. Do not be misled by this! It is of the utmost importance that the Afghan puppy, from the age of three months onward, be groomed weekly and regularly. The prime function of such attention is to train the lively pup to submit to necessary restraints when he is still mentally flexible and physically light-weight enough to be easily managed by the owner. Regardless of coat length, the wriggling youngster must be patiently taught to stand or lie still for grooming with a stiff bristle brush. Begin by restraining him for a moment only, and, to stimulate good hair growth, give him a good brush-rubbing both with and against the grain of the fur. Most pups soon enjoy these ministrations from gentle owners but do insist on chewing brushes and being silly.

As thick woolly fur lengthens, it soon becomes evident that the brush cannot get through to the skin, necessitating a change in tools. For fast growing puppy-coats, most fanciers prefer the slicker (a wood-backed brush with numerous bent-angled metal pins set into a rubber base). When the fluff is long enough to require a slicker, it is high time that the owner learn the correct techniques of grooming in the layering method.

It is well to accustom the pup to grooming from both prone and standing positions. Finishing touches and quick maintenance brush-ups are best accomplished with the dog standing, but the under-parts that snag and mat quickly are more accessible with the dog lying quietly on his side. The key words to Afghan grooming are "from the bottom up and from the skin out." Mats form near the skin at the base of the fur and surface brushing merely brushes more fur into the clumping mats. We will briefly describe the technique of grooming the dog in a prone position. With the dog lying quietly on its side, begin with the front feet. Most all Afghan Hounds are touchy about their feet and must become accustomed to having them handled. Inspect and brush the fur between the toes carefully. Brush the fur backwards from the foot upward. Cover the back-brushed fur with the holding hand and rake down small layers with the slicker. In this manner, continue to brush back the hair working up the leg, slickering bits back into place. A large cloth placed between upper and lower leg helps the groomer keep his place on the leg and also catches loose dirt and fur. When the upper leg is completed except for the inside piece that cannot be easily reached,

234

groom the corresponding inside section of the leg nearest to the floor. Pay special close attention to the tender skin right beneath the elbows as mats form there quickly due to the gait friction of leg rubbing against the body. This is also true of the breastbone area lying in front of and between the forelegs. Such mats, not easily seen, must be felt by probing fingers but will damage both coat and gait if left unattended. Clean captured hair out of grooming tools frequently. Young pups lose very little hair, but the brushes fill quickly on older dogs.

Follow similar layering procedures with rear feet and legs, closely inspecting the inside of the groin and thighs, these spots tending to friction matting as with the elbows. In grooming the sides of the dog, begin with the base of the brisket. Pampering this lower chest fur enhances the apparent depth of chest. The fidgety pup, who is impatient with leg grooming, welcomes having body fur smoothed. Layer side fur as with the legs. If the body fur is not as dense as the legs, the less harsh bristle brush will work very well.

When tangles are encountered that resist the grooming tools, do not yank them out! Gently tease the knot apart with the fingers. Here is the successful Afghan owner's art, a skill that should be acquired as early as possible. Most felted mats found on reasonably well-kept hounds are easily pulled apart. A wide-toothed comb will find any such mats if they are missed by the brushes, and the same comb works well with fingers for separating the hairs when the mats have been reduced to narrow clumps.

Never use the scissors or any cutting tool except as a last resort. The dog that is impossibly matted should be clipped completely (and allowed to grow out evenly—which takes quite some time) or tranquilized so that he can be groomed at length without suffering. If it seems that a few cuts would save the coat, *snip with the grain of the fur but never across the hairs.* Such clips separate the fur into smaller knots that can be worked apart with the fingers.

The Afghan Hound should never be allowed to get into this condition. This generally happens when one is left in a kennel with no care, or improper care. Every attempt should be made to break felt mats, or knotted balls with the fingers. If this cannot be done, cut into the knotted balls with the grain of the coat. Do not cut them out! Then continue to tease them apart with the fingers and a wide-tooth comb.

Most pups adore having their ears, topknots and throats brushed. Fluff the topknot in every direction. Tenderly comb the earflaps and valuable ear fringes. Slicker thoroughly behind and underneath the ears, a prime spot for undetected mats to form during the change of coat.

For even the heaviest puppy plush the slicker plus a wide toothed comb, both used in the layering technique, are the only tools needed —until the puppy-fluff has fully developed and begins to loosen. By 10 to 18 months of age there should be some intermixture of puppy and adult coat, turning some youngsters into animated brier bushes and others, with the more draping texture, into walking dust mops.

The era of the dropping puppy coat is undoubtedly the most horrible of all grooming periods in most Afghan Hounds' lives. The owner who lives through this phase with a really heavy coated hound can take it easy from then on. Handfuls of fur come out with each combing. If this loosening fur is not brushed out immediately (daily) and faithfully, it will tangle and form felted mats and then hard knotted balls that cannot be removed except surgically. However, it is for this reason that it is said "the Afghan does not shed." He loses hair like any animal, but it stays near the body, clumping with other hairs, rarely falling on furniture or clothing. The red alert is up when the slicker becomes plugged with hair unusually often or when the short-haired saddle begins to emerge. Grooming must be intensified. During the emergency period, the slicker is the preferred tool but get a new one as bent-over out-of-line pins do more harm than good.

This crucial coat-change period varies greatly from dog to dog. It may be passed in a month or linger for a half-year or more. Daily exploratory checks with the fingers, in the guise of petting, find fresh mats in lieu of full groomings. Habitual behind-the-ear scratches, which the dogs love, and chest attentions between the front legs will find the felting hair knots before damage is great. On the rear of the dog, check loins and inside of thighs. Thick quantities of fur often drop from feet, pasterns and hock fronts during coat-changes, requiring localized extra brushing. When the smooth short-haired saddle has cleared the full length of the back, the worst is over. There will be intermittent periods of coat growth spurts and drops but once the puppy coat is out, a thorough weekly grooming keeps most hounds in handsome condition (barring jaunts in weed laden fields).

Do not shave a saddle onto an Afghan Hound. Use your natural bristle brush to brush out the loose long hairs. This hair can be easily brushed out when the short saddle coat is underneath. Some dogs have produced a clean saddle at six months; others wait until they are two years old. Remember what the Standard says: "The Afghan Hound should be shown in its natural state; the coat is not clipped or trimmed . . ."

The adult coat, longer and usually far silkier than puppy fuzz, is less suited to the slicker as the sharp pins can rake the skin and tangle the fur if not handled expertly. Different thicknesses and textures of Afghan coats do necessitate individual tools and some grooming experimentation with each dog. The awesome kit of combs and brushes carried by the seasoned exhibitor is bewildering to the novice but is a case of the right tool for each dog. As a general rule, for most adult coats, a good stiff bristle brush and a wide-toothed comb are recommended. The same "from the bottom up" technique is an absolute necessity. All brushings must be done with long smooth strokes, layer by layer, with no flicking motions that cause the hair to twist and tangle on itself.

For the exceedingly heavy, long, durable coat that defies bristle penetration, a Poodle pin brush can be substituted. This good-sized oval brush contains long straight metal pins set into a rubber base. The pin brush does not give the smooth finish that many owners desire, but is efficient and relatively quick for home maintenance. A final surface touch-up with bristles or slicker gives polish.

During grooming, close attention should be paid to the skin beneath the fur. Check ears for any form of matter and clean them with baby oil or alcohol only if dirty. Long eared dogs such as the Afghan Hound are especially susceptible to ear infection. Do not use any liquids in the ear such as the commercial dog ear cleaning fluids. Whenever the ear gets wet inside, dry it out. If ears have a dark red exudation especially with a foul odor, get veterinarian aid immediately. When brushing feet, check for small mats that cause sore spots between the toes as well as burrs that might be caught under the foot between the pads. If toenails appear long and sharp, have them trimmed before the quick grows out too far. Neglected toenails cause the toe-arches to break down, a problem with old or very lazy dogs and those with no access to rough hard ground surfaces.

If rashes are seen on the skin, get help immediately. Many fanciers have home remedies for mild skin eruptions, alcohol, antiseptic powders, etc., but the novice should not experiment with skin symptoms as the Afghan Hound can ruin his coat with frantic chewing and scratching in an unbelievably short time. An injection from the veterinarian will put a quick end to the inflammatory state, and professional treatment will seek the roots of the trouble, be it diet, allergy, or parasites (the most common being fleas, often difficult to detect on this thick-furred breed).

Bitches are prone to lose coat with each season regardless of the loving care given to their fur. Some drop much more than others due most probably to hereditary factors. The large coat drop that comes with the very first season, usually timed to occur with the puppy-coat fallout, is generally the worst that will be experienced.

When bitch-coats are at low ebb, brush frequently to stimulate the regrowth. Most unspayed bitches tend to be in or out of coat all their lives.

Males have less extreme ups and downs, but do have lusher coats in some parts of the year than others (not necessarily coordinated with the weather). An adolescent male coat of some skimpiness is not unusual, following the puppy-drop. Those that expect a full-length drape to magically supersede the puppy fuzz are in for a disappointment. The magnificent draping of a full-blown champion takes time. Ear fringes, for instance, may take years to gain reputable length despite protective "snoods" and tender grooming care. Illnesses that include periods of fever or the use of anesthetics may cause a coat drop of a temporary nature.

Caring for the Afghan's coat is not really such a chore if a particular person, place, and time are designated for the job. No Show Coat or even handsome pet coat will last on hounds that suffer through spasmodic slap-dash attentions. Such neglect only results in stubborn dogs who detest being groomed and cut-up, jagged, ugly coats, ripe for immediate re-tangling. The fancier who is unable or unwilling to give constant attention to the Afghan coat has taken on the wrong breed.

There are tricks-of-the-trade used by professionals that give coats an extra brilliance at the shows, arousing the curiosity of the novice. Much of this sparkle comes from pure undiluted cleanliness. Show dogs are bathed from one to three days before the show, depending on the type of fur and the color of the dog. For the best-behaved coat, many show dogs are constantly brushed while drying after the bath. A gentle human shampoo that gives a glossy sheen is used or special pet mixtures that are a far cry from cheap flea soaps. Liquid shampoos are diluted with water and placed into a squeeze bottle for easy application. Fly away coats are given creme rinses. All soaps or detergents are scrupulously rinsed off the dog.

At the shows commercial spray conditioners help last-minute smoothenings, and are doubly important as cleaners when shows occur too frequently for in-between baths. Baby powder which tends to separate the hairs is used on some light-colored coats that tangle quickly. Such powder is brushed out before the dog enters the ring and is of little value on dark colored dogs as it dulls the coat color. Dogs with extremely dry coats are occasionally oiled, but all such oil must be washed out completely before the show date as the oily or dirty coat will hang in lank strings.

The professional applies know-how to moulding the coat, through controlled brushing, to enhance the best possible lines of the hound. The heavier dog benefits by being brushed smooth to minimize

238

bulk, while the refined hound takes a bit of extra fluffing. Some hounds are flattered by topknots that hang forward, while others are enriched with full sweep of clear muzzle. Brisket hairs should be carefully combed to emphasize depth of chest. The bend of stifle on rear leg is accentuated with forward brushing, but at the hock the fur should flow backwards to indicate low hock-points and large feet. Wide fluffing of foot fur to the front and sides increases apparent size. Skimpy hair under brisket and on feet detracts from the line of a well-endowed hound.

From the front of the Afghan there should be a columnar look from leg to floor. If the coat is scanty or bunchy at the elbow line, careful brushing might prevent the coat from indicating a fault that does not exist under the fur.

Such tricks can never make a poor dog into a good one (and will not last in the wind or high motion) but can easily make a small point difference between two dogs of similar quality. Cleanliness and careful grooming have tipped many scales in producing greater visual impact on the judge's eye.

Ch. Bletchingley Sahari of Scheherezade (Eng. Ch. Horningsea Sheer Khan ex Ch. Bletchingley Zelda), black mask golden bitch, dam of 8 champions, bred by Mrs. Peggy Riley (England), owned by Lt. Col. and Mrs. Wallace H. Pede.

Ch. Fox Run's Phoenix (Ch. Kabik's The Challenger ex Ch. Fox Runs On and On and On), black and silver dog, BIS winner. Bred by Lynn Mercer and Colin Stees. Owned by Lynn and Jamee Mercer and Colin Stees. Handler, Lynn Mercer.—*Kernan.*

Ch. Lipizzans Big Red Machine (Prince Bearnhardt of Lipizzan ex Huzzah Rubiyat of Lipizzan), black masked red dog, multi Best in Show winner. Bred by Vicki Smith Zayac, and owned by Mr. and Mrs. H. Rubacks. Handler, Ralph Murphy; judge, Kay Finch.   —*Jill.*

10

Exhibiting

"A Show Dog is essentially a production to delight the eye, a presentation, as is a piece of theatre . . . The stars in the heavens are not more numerous than good prospective Show Dogs that have been ruined by poor management."

C. Bede Maxwell

OF the annual crowd of Afghan Hounds which enter the show rings, only a few fill the judge's eye, outstanding with power and pride, sparkling in a well-kept, immaculate coat that accentuates the hound's courtly manner. Too many others, often of no less basic structural quality, are practically ignored by the judges. Their puzzled owners are blind to the obvious, unaware that their hounds fail sadly in coat condition, musculature, or ring demeanor. To a marked extent, the difference between the "eye-catcher" and the "also-ran" is a man-made commodity known as conditioning. Proper conditioning of the show dog allows him to take his starring role as a proud and able color bearer for his breed.

An early decision faced by many a novice giving the Show Game a whirl, is whether to hire a professional handler or go the route himself. The amateur owner may well make a few bumbling efforts at showing his own dog, only to have a kindly onlooker, sensing greater potential in the dog than the handler, suggest a professional be hired.

This decision hinges on clear-cut practical principles. Undoubtedly, the pro can take a dog of reasonable quality and present it with the skill of many years' experience to quicker success than the shaky novice. If the owner's primary aim is to boast of one quick champion—hiring a competent handler is probably the most practical solution, but the owner with a yen to be a part of the breed, do some breeding and exhibiting of offspring after offspring, must weigh the expense of the hired professional against future aims. And there is as much knowledge of the breed to be gained in the ring as from without. As in most sports, the thrill of competition keeps the owner-handler going. The smart handler knows that the judge cannot fully disassociate the dog from the handler. Therefore, he must always keep his team sharp.

The challenged, able-bodied fancier concludes that the pro had to learn once, and while the training period may cost their dogs a few wins (and it probably will), they are making an investment in skills for the future. This trend of thought is bolstered by the knowledge that most of the top-winning Afghan Hounds have been owner-escorted past the best that the Professional Handlers' Association had to offer.

The rivalry between professional and amateur is in the main synthetic, too often a sham excuse for being beaten. Confident owner-handlers take no part in this type of buck-passing. It is the contrast between awkward bumbling and skilled guidance that is real and painfully apparent in many classes. The thoughtful owner will neither curse the pro nor use him as a whipping boy but, instead, courts and learns from these dedicated people who have made showing and winning their vocation.

Showing dogs has different implications in different sectors of the United States. On the heavily-populated coastal regions, exhibiting dogs is a semi-regular weekend diversion for those who have dogs and will travel, but in the interior, show day is long-anticipated with breath held for fear the dogs will be out of coat or the bitch will be in season. At the highly competitive coastal shows, exhibitors are forced into greater awareness of maintaining hounds in peak condition and become sensitive to when they are or are not ready to win. In all cases there are times when the owner knows full well that the hound should be left home temporarily, but succumbs to Entry Blank Fever. As such dogs are actually being exhibited for fun and experience, the owner should never resent losing to dogs obviously more ready on that day.

Novices should contact the local show-giving superintendent, obtain a copy of the AKC Rules Applying to Registration and Dog Shows, and request that their name be placed on mailing lists for the coming shows. The ambitious fancier would also do well to join the nearest regional club devoted to his breed and the nearby All-

Breed Club. In this manner, he can become informed of Sanction Matches and Training Classes.

Preparing the Afghan Hound for exhibition begins in early puppyhood. The first steps consist of raising healthy, outgoing puppies. Diet and early socialization have been covered elsewhere in this book. Refer to *The New Knowledge of Dog Behavior* by Clarence Pfaffenberger for information on the importance of early socialization.

Leash training is commenced by the ninth week of puppyhood. Not a severe routine of heeling calculated to win obedience degrees, but a simple accustoming the puppy to leash restraints. This can be a trying period for both the puppy and the inexperienced owner. Most Afghan Hounds stubbornly consider freedom one of their inalienable rights. The timid owner who encounters frantic resistance to such early training is usually conned into dropping the subject, with the misconception that it will go easier in a few months. He is in for a rude shock. Afghan puppies only grow larger, stronger, more determined, and voice louder protests. It is better to carry it through when the pup is young.

Occasionally some pups adapt to the leash without protest, but they are the exception and are usually bitches. Most pups, finding themselves on the end of a leash for the first time, will do one of several things. They will scream in anguish. This convinces the neighbors that they are being brutally attacked. It is calculated to shrink the handler into invisibility and force the matter to be dropped. Puppies use this trick to the hilt. The youngster may buck like a rodeo stallion, hurl himself into the air, head over tail, always fighting the lead. This is an encouraging sign. Most will lie down and positively refuse to budge, screaming at each touch of the lead.

Individual pups demand individual attention and solutions. A few general solutions follow. Use suitable equipment. A light-weight, puppy-sized chokechain (about four inches longer than the circumference of the pup's neck) and a ribbon-weight leather lead. Some pups respond best to the gentler show lead.

Ignore the screaming completely, with a word of explanation to the neighbors, and trade brute force for a little canine psychology. Leash training is an understandably frightening experience for a tiny pup. Not only is his precious liberty being challenged, but he is being dragged away from his siblings, his home and security. For this reason, try carrying the pup to the far end of the yard and work back towards the house and kennel. Tidbits may help as encouragements, but are usually ignored in the early days of stress.

Standard obedience methods of giving small jerks that tighten the collar and the immediate release of tension are called for. Never use steady strangling pulls. This only makes for a bull-necked, uncontrollable hound. Keep training lessons very short, a minute or two for the first few days, and for every inch of progress give liberal praise.

A basic method is to train the dog to come to the handler as a first step. When the pup, finding himself on a leash, lies down with resolute immobility, walk in front of him, stoop or sit a few inches from his face, and call his name while accentuating the call with a positive jerk on the leash. The pup comes, or is dragged, those few inches to lavish praise and sympathy in the trainer's arms. Repeat the performance. Always use an encouraging tone and positive jerks. Move slightly further back from the pup each time, forcing him to advance. This method keeps the pup on his feet a good bit of the time, half the training battle. Some pups respond far quicker than others. This is not seemingly correlated to either intelligence or obedience aptitude.

When the pup unhesitatingly and gaily runs to the handler at the sound of his name and a slight jerk of the leash, it is time to begin to encourage the dog to heel at the handler's side. At this point, specialized show-training comes into play.

The successful show dog moves with great style, unafraid, head and tail high and proud. The style of the dog's heeling is far more important than how close he hugs to the handler's knee. The show dog must be discouraged from sniffing the ground, a great natural temptation. This is best achieved by the handler who sets a brisk pace, with "come-along" jerks. Do not give the pup time to stray towards nearby bushes or ground scents. Encouraging words and, perhaps tidbits, help alert the pup and keep him prancing near the handler's side. Animation and even silliness, such as the pup taking the leash in his mouth, is welcome at this age. Do not attempt to correct the puppy lunging with any severe methods. The very young pup soon learns where the end of the leash is. Most handlers use the obedience trick of making swift turns of directions, away from the puppy, to subtly correct puppy lunges. Such turns, with attendant jerks of the leash, inform the pup that if he doesn't keep an eye on his master, he just ends up facing the wrong direction and no one gets anywhere on these fascinating walks. Lunging is a serious problem on the powerful untrained *older* dog, and must be corrected drastically and immediately. Some breeders have success in taking an older well-trained dog along on these walks to give example and assurance to the pup. It is worth a try if the older dog approves the plan.

Pups are always kept at a *trot* when leash trained. A leisurely stroll with pup ambling along, nose to the ground, neck hauling on

Ch. Egypt's Echo of Crown Crest (Ch. Felt's Thief of Bagdad ex Big Carmelita), silver blue bitch, dam of 10 champions, bred and owned by Kay Finch, Crown Crest. Shown as a puppy at top, and as a champion below.

the leash, can be harmful to show dog posture. A spirited gait, with flickings of the chokechain under the chin, promotes high head carriage, and glimpses of objects in the distance keep it there. Any dog, properly trained with love and patience, delights in these educational walks.

A word of warning to the novice who has observed Afghan Hounds being "strung up" in the ring (with taut leash held overhead). This is not for most Afghan Hounds. It is a method of forcing the dog to hold its head high, a cruel restraint that pulls the front legs off the ground, preventing the natural free-swinging gait of the breed. Most Afghan Hounds, once well trained to the leash, move far better and with a natural, proud head carriage on a loose lead. A professional handler, given an ill-trained hound to show, has little choice but to employ such high-handed methods. It is definitely not to be emulated by the novice! When the pup has agreed to accept reasonable leash controls in exchange for the enjoyable training jaunts, he is ready to widen his circle of friends.

The normal Afghan puppy illustrates great gaiety and friendliness. But, in adulthood, a very real sense of reserve and aloofness comes over these hounds. Most mature Afghan Hounds give overwhelming demonstrations of affection just to their owners and special chosen friends. The unwary owner who presumes the puppy personality to be a permanent part of the dog's nature, may be in for quite a shock at the later date. Suddenly, at a show or circumstance where the owner expects to show off his gay inimitable puppy, the hound may show a new and frightening face. Such reactions vary from a frantic reticence at being touched, to cringing panic or aggressive uncontrollability. This dog is only demonstrating his awareness of being in strange surroundings. While such reactions cannot be considered actually abnormal, they most certainly are undesirable and have been the ruination of many a show dog.

To understand or to cope with such reactions, it must be realized that Afghan Hounds in their natural semi-wild state must have an aggressive curiosity. But this curiosity must be well-tempered, connected to a trigger-quick, glandular mechanism that controls the dog's lightning fast advances and retreats. This is the essential life-saving and life-taking device of the guard-and-hunter hound. In urban surroundings, the hound may suffer from a glandular over-secretion and frustration. He no longer has a natural channel for such defense and attack impulses, and is given no program to help him identify friend or foe, although he strongly senses that both exist. Undirected glandular impulses confuse the dog to the consternation of his perplexed owner. Owners tend to ascribe such unreasonable reactions to the hound which has been mistreated or over-disciplined in the past. Strangely enough, the very opposite is more often true. Hounds that are victims of over-protection by zealous owners tend to associate owner with "friend" and everyone else is suspect. Certainly there is great temperamental variation among the hounds, but the Afghan Hound as a breed is noted for its marked aloofness and tendency to be a "one-family dog." Controversy as to whether really unstable temperament is inherited points up the fact that we are dealing with a bundle of precious instincts in an unnatural environment of fences and forbidden temptations. Some hounds are far more adaptable than others. Those that cannot cope with their environment may be breeding risks, and pass on their own neurosis.

Canine tendencies can frequently be rechanneled. The owner can deliberately widen the hound's circle of accepted friends in this civilized world by exposing the hounds, from puppyhood onward, to people who are kind to them. Trips to the veterinarian for shots should be counteracted by joyful excursions elsewhere, or the dog is to be forgiven for suspecting that all men have needles behind their backs.

In the home situation, the pup does not show these symptoms, appearing bold and fearless until something disrupts his secure routine such as a trip into the world of men and dogs. The longer such hidden symptoms are unsuspected and undetected, the slimmer the chances of cure. Afghan Hounds are quite capable of changing personalities well past their second birthdays. It is an interesting fact that the Afghan Hound who has led a somewhat more nearly natural existence, having been allowed a certain amount of field hunting experience, often gains a quicker differentiation of safety and danger, friend and foe, than his hot-house brothers.

It is not unusual for the Afghan Hound to have an inherent dislike of being touched by strangers and instinctively draw back from the offered hand. But the show dog is required to allow strangers to examine teeth, body, ever-touchy paws and rear quarters. Under training conditions, the show dog learns to suffer such touches without question. Hounds prosper from trips around shopping centers, or from Sunday afternoons in the park. People are always curious about the breed, wanting to feel the soft hair and the aristocratic snout. The owner will welcome these attentions from strangers and kindly insist that the pup stand for them. A long dry spell between such early social training and adulthood can bring renewed reluctance at being handled as this instinct is not far beneath the surface in many Afghan Hounds.

Dogs learn through imitation of other dogs. Hounds brought up near a suspicious older dog which tolerates advances from no one but his owner often behave in like manner. This goes on for generations. A friendly brood-bitch is a great asset to a show kennel, teaching her pups to view the human race kindly. The matron that gives even a small portion of the soul-bursting welcome, generally reserved for loved ones, to visiting people-friends in sight of the imitative young pups does her owner an invaluable service.

Having older hounds as instructors is a mixture of assets and liabilities. A jealous stud may bully the youngsters. Caste systems are quickly assumed in dogs. Some pups are intimidated into subservient roles. Such attitudes carry over into the show ring. The underdog may act defeated before he begins, or take out his frustrations on small dogs. If two or more hounds vie for attention, the solution is to take them out independently whenever possible. It is also helpful to have individual cages or quarters as a sanctuary for the antagonists. The youngster who accepts the background, or wants to be alone, is demanding special attention away from the pack.

Car sickness is a by-product of fear and nervous reactions. The happy hound, taken on regular rides from early puppyhood, is rarely bothered by the malady. The usual reaction to the dog who upchucks on rides is to leave him home. This is precisely the wrong approach. Car sickness can be cured by the owner who takes time to acclimatize the hound to car riding. Begin with no more than one city block and gradually increase the riding a block at a time to trip status.

There are some who may not connect all this talk of training and re-training with blue ribbons for their dog. It can only be said that bold natural assurance, the basis of a true King of Dogs attitude, is the essence of showmanship and is a commodity most winners have in rich supply.

The importance of powerful musculature on a show dog is often overlooked. Many hounds that look like first place winners when standing still, drop right out of contention after being gaited across the ring. Without engaging in a prolonged discussion of type versus soundness, our working definition of soundness follows: A sound dog is one that strides forward with obvious purpose and strength, without wavering or weaving, shuffling or slipping; a dog in full command of his muscles, able to change directions in a split instant without being thrown off balance, illustrating absolute coordination between all moving parts. Admittedly, there are anatomical faults that prevent such achievements. But many more hounds are unsound in gait due to underdevelopment or incorrect development of musculature because of their sedentary life, so different from the natural routine of the hounds in Afghanistan.

Muscle development is a continuous process beginning the mo-

248

Am. and Can. Ch. Oranje Wilhelmina (Int. Ch. Xingu van de Oranje Manege ex Int. Ch. Icarie van de Oranje Manege), bitch, breeder/owner Lila Stafford Wadsworth. Completed Championship at 10 years and 7 months.

Ch. Surya of Ahmir (Ch. Akaba's Brass Cinder Feller ex Pinecrest Posha), bitch. Bred by Sandy Arkin, owned by Al and Pam McQueen. Completed Championship at 10 years and one month, after two litters.

249

ment the pup stirs in the embryo, continuing throughout the life of the animal. As soon as pups are able to stand on their wobbly feet, they spend their waking time in rough-house push and shove play with their siblings. From their owners, they ask only a little attention to their diet and increasing space as they double and triple in size. As soon as one pup leaves the nest for a new home, often becoming an only pup, opportunity and desire for the important muscle building play is greatly diminished. Some hounds, naturally more excitable than others, compensate for a lack of sparring partners with wild dashes over the furniture at the sound of the postman, milkman, or a cat next door. Such jousting lacks in enduring intensity and is understandably discouraged by the lady of the house. The foolish owner who attempts to rear Afghan Hounds in crates or tiny pens must make very definite provisions to counteract the effect of such a restrained unnatural life. An Afghan Hound is not necessarily unhappy in a limited space as long as he is with loved ones (proven by those raised in garden apartments), but rarely are such dogs well-muscled and good movers.

Deliberate muscle formation can be implemented by owners in several ways. When possible, run two dogs together of a companionable age. Have sufficient space for reasonable romps. A long narrow run is better than a short square section. Uneven terrain or hillsides are marvelous. These hounds are remarkable at turning, dodging, and climbing, but need some length of ground in order to stretch their legs and work up full tilt speed. On flat ground, stairs to leap or man-fashioned obstacles are beneficial. Large wooden crates, tractor tires, etc., make fine doggy jungle gyms. The one-dog owner must contrive play periods for his pet. Balls can be thrown for the dog. Most Afghan Hounds will chase a ball but, unfortunately, few will retrieve it. The game is worth the try and good for the owner's waistline. Tug-of-war is marvelous for developing a strong cord of muscles from jaws to paws. Pieces of tough leather, rug, or towel remnants are lasting. Tugging games are doubly valuable as they can be played indoors with a minimum of furniture interference. The only dog owner will wisely visit other dog-owning friends with his pup as often as possible for invigorating romps with canine pals.

The growing dog does not play every minute; in fact, most of the daylight hours are napped away. Until the puppy is well over six months old, a few minutes of controlled trotting on a leash plus a bit of full-tilt running and dodging once or twice a day, is sufficient for average muscle-building activity.

Lagging muscle development is the curse of all large breeds. The largest, longest legged, and most highly angulated hounds go through prolonged periods of unsteadiness. Some never learn how to stand properly on their underpinnings. While young, immature hounds can be expected to have loose muscles, the judge and ringside jury rightly penalize hounds of all ages until such weaknesses have been overcome. Mother Nature would be no kinder. In her realm, only the fittest can survive. Some highly excitable hounds do have a muscular self-stimulation that keeps them constantly tense and fit, while the relaxed lazy ones need special encouragement to get them moving.

As the hound approaches his first birthday, and need for muscle tone increases, some owners look to roadwork for magic answers. While undeniably useful for certain dogs, under certain conditions, we must caution against its being indiscriminately instigated without careful analysis of the precise needs of the dog on the day. The Cardinal rule is: *No Owner Should Ask, or Expect, a Dog to Do Anything On Lead that It Cannot Already Do in a Well-Coordinated Manner Off-Lead!*

Dogs of all ages should be carefully studied during free play, with special attention to the pose, and the gait, that the dog assumes *naturally* when alert to some special sight or sound. The resultant tensely controlled posture is the *best* that dog has to give at that time of his life. Exhibiting should be a capture of such poses and action, in a conditioned manner for the Show Ring. All apparent lacks in gaiting *off lead* must be carefully analyzed as to probable cause before corrective action can be considered. Just as proper roadwork can help a good dog to become better, it can make a faulty one worse—by setting wrong muscle patterns.

There is a long trip from puppyhood to maturity in Afghan Hounds. Particular attention should be given to whether observed problems might, in fact, be growth related. Many adolescents, especially large and fast-growing males, trot awkwardly—or prefer not to trot at all—during a period when gangly legs are disproportionate to central body length. If such dogs are forced into roadwork, or show-trot training, they frequently develop compensations which may become permanent habits. During this period such dogs show a decided preference for a canter, or pace, in lieu of free trotting. The pace (an ipsilateral, rather than contralateral, action) is the choice of Afghan Hounds that are ill-proportioned, young, old, or tired— while it is the natural gait in some breeds. While less tiring, and less precarious in leg-timing, the pace is not an agile gait and is to be avoided in the Afghan Hound showring. The dog with a preference for pacing can be snapped out of it, usually, by quick sideways jerks and a speed increase—but if its choice is due to physical imbalance (possibly temporary) the dog will retaliate by crabbing (sidewinding) or inventing even more bizarre timing solutions that are more easily avoided than cured.

The training mode for dogs with temporary proportion imbalances is a concentration on a loose-lead stylish posture within the non-damaging speed of a fast walk, or a trotting figure 8. Here side-winding becomes part of a circle—reversed in its other half—with the outer leg always taking a longer stride than the inner. This avoids setting bad patterns. Thoughtful use of circles, and figure 8's, is also useful as part of recovery treatment for dogs that have had leg injuries.

If roadwork is decided upon for timing and toning, the proper speed depends upon the dog and what is expected of the method. For the dog that naturally trots in a straight line, with head and topline in reasonably correct alignment, a speed of 5 to 10 miles per hour is a good rate. Hindlegs should set down short of forelegs, and the joints show good pickup and putdown flexion, with no crabbing or shuffling. If properly executed, the trot speed may be increased. Crabbing must not be allowed to persist. If remediable, reduced speed may help; acceleration will only increase the problem.

Roadwork is always an education for the person in charge. As dogs become tired their weaknesses become apparent by magnification. Heads will be thrown forwards and down, and backs buckle. Tired rear legs tend to stagger and shuffle. Forehands become labored, as shoulder-tops begin to bob badly and elbows move from side to side as much as smoothly forward. Pastern action becomes sprung rather than powerfully springy. On scantily coated dogs attention should be paid to the shoulder-upper arm joint for clearer understanding of basic dog gait. It is probably the topline that gives the broadest messages. Weak, or tired, backs sag between shoulders, roll over, dip, or conversely roach. A correct topline remains level and seemingly weightless.

The dog which handles its back and front well, but tends to shuffle in the rear, may benefit from trotting up inclines (never down them) or over surfaces so uneven as to force the dog to lift his feet higher. Swimming, or running on the beach, in or out of the water, can do no harm, and might do much good—provided the dog can swim and then get out of the water (swimming pools).

Careful observation of the dog tells when to go further, or quit for the day. If the legs are tired, but endurance is the aim, a quickened change of pace, into a canter/gallop, often refreshes the dog-spirit and brings different muscle groups into major play. This should be followed by walking, or slow trotting, as a cool down period.

Improvement in timing or strength cannot be expected to appear in a matter of days. Video tape taken of the dog at the instigation of the program, repeated in three month intervals or less, is a good way to check for wanted (or unwanted) changes. Remember that Afghan Hounds are not mature until three years of age. Those gawky ones with good potential show brief flashes of brilliance but more often seem like a lost cause from day to day. Many such males, with mental and physical maturity, suddenly put it all together in sustained form. In truth, roadwork given without an eye to the immediate showring, but in conjunction with a general program of health conditioning, will have beneficial results on both mind and body of the dog, just as does any sensible form of exercise.

A word of caution. Never work dogs during the heat of warm days. Take advantage of cool mornings and sundown. Do not allow overheated dogs to become chilled, nor let them have more than a couple of swallows of water for at least an hour after the run. Check feet carefully for stones, burrs, cuts, or sores.

Not all exercise is good exercise. Some postures are detrimental to proper muscle development, especially in the long rear quarters. Pups should not be encouraged to stand on their immature hind legs for any length of time. Jumping is also taboo. The upright position puts undue strain and the young dog's full weight on cartilaginous bones and joints, promoting cow hocks as the dog turns his hocks in for better balance of the weight. The pup who loves to stand on hind legs, jumping up and down with excitement, front feet propped against the fence for a better view of the outside world is doing his legs a great disservice. Another form of damaging play is that resorted to by Afghan Hounds reared in confined spaces such as small pens or on balconies. To get exercise in such limited areas, hounds will take to wheeling and spinning around on their hind legs from a crouched position. This does the rear legs no favor, and can produce a semi-crouched gait as well as cow hocks.

No owner need become frantic everytime he sees the dog standing other than squarely on all fours but, if the dangers are in mind, the pup can be discouraged from turning harmless intermittent acts into firm damaging habits. A change of yard shape or fence type may get to the trouble.

The showdog must be taught to take, and hold, a show stance calmly and without slouching when viewed, or examined, by the judge. The correct stance is dictated by the natural character of the breed—and the attempt of the handler to make each individual dog conform, as nearly as possible, to the portrait painted by the Standard.

Placing the dog into a show stance is called stacking. Refer to the drawing in this Chapter for the correct Afghan Hound outline when stacked. Front legs are to be parallel from elbow to ground—as viewed from either front or side. Feet point straight ahead. If the dog stops correct *do not fiddle with his legs*. The most obvious mark of the

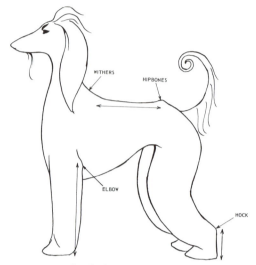

WITHERS

HIPBONES

ELBOW

HOCK

Stacked Afghan Hound.

nervous amateur is constant over-setting of parts. If the dog stops
with one, or both, front legs out of line, correct with a minimum of
motions. Adjustments are made most inconspicuously from the
inside of the elbow. Pushing the elbows out slightly tends to turn feet
in, and vice versa (tribute to the importance of correct ribcage form).
Badly twisted legs cannot be corrected past a point and should bar the
dog from high winning. A dog put off-balance by stacking will tend
to put his feet right back where they best bear his weight, albeit
crookedly. When setting the dog it is wise to keep one hand under the
dog's chin for control. Reassuring finger-scratches on the throat help
relax fidgety hounds.

Back (topline) should be as level as possible—from withers to
hipbones (refer to Chapter 7, Conformation and Official Breed
Standard, for discussion of level vs. flat). As the levelness of a table top
is governed by the lengths and angles of its legs, dog toplines change
with re-positioning of underpinnings. Correcting the topline that
tends to flow uphill towards the croup is done by spreading the
hindlegs wider apart, or placing them further back. (Note: It is better
to let immature youngsters stand high in the rear than to pull their
legs into non-balanced positions out behind them.) Downsloped
toplines call for reverse adjustments. A sagging back is bad, but can
result from boredom as much as poor musculature. Either may
benefit by a brisk tummy-scratch, an excited word, and a brisk turn
around the handler, especially in long-lasting classes.

Hind legs are correct when hock-lengths are perpendicular to the
ground and parallel to each other in all views. Adjust hindfeet by

254

picking up the foot from the point of hock, but do not expect any dog to sustain uncomfortable, or unbalanced, stances.

Unfortunately, the Afghan Hound ideal portrait has been, at times, subject to a number of powerful vagaries of fad and fashion. Some have come and gone, while others persist, despite being in greater, or lesser, conflict with the word—and intent—of the Afghan Hound Standard.

One controversial point in the stance revolves around the tail. Since the disapproval of Venita Vardon Oakie in 1940, breeder-judges have deplored the lunacy of handlers propping up the Afghan Hound tail. Judge Cy Rickel has stated, "Basically, an Afghan Hound can show tails if it is a good Afghan Hound, far better than any handler can pose it. . . I do not know where or when this procedure started but, if it continues, it is certainly going to ruin tail carriage in Afghan Hounds. . ." Nevertheless, other judges and the majority of modern handlers have insisted on perpetuating this silly custom. The Standard says nothing about the tail being raised except "in action." There are grounds for suspecting that some handlers have used this trick to slyly foreshorten a long backline, which it does, or to minimize other unflattering effects. One owner freely confessed to holding an Afghan's tail "to keep the darn thing from wagging all the time." But, in the main, it is a frightening case of follow-the-leader. The tail that is flagging naturally at any point from the level of the back upward should most certainly be left alone! The low tail, or the unfortunate, tucked tail, must be left to the handler's discretion. If the tail must be propped, the handler does well to keep a wary eye on it, for unhappy tails can do some weird humping from the point of contact to the tip. A tail pushed too high can spoil a good topline.

In the late 1960s, and through the '70s, in frantic attempts to display a more spectacular-appearing animal, handlers began to train, and force, dogs into silhouettes that covered far more ground than is correct for the square, firm-based Afghan Hound. This was done by hand-placing the dog's hind legs further and further behind the dog—at the cost of the integrity of the dog's back and muscular joints. Aided by a flowing coat, the new stance gave an illusion of rear-quarter angulation, but was, in fact, open extension (a straightening), rather than flexion of the hind leg behind the hip joint. In result the weight-bearing role of the hindlegs was forfeited. Sensible and strong animals fought this by rolling back from the forelegs, to better distribute weight, or repeatedly attempted to bring one, or both, hindlegs forward to regain proper four-square balance. Through the unthinking selection of dogs with hyperextensible ligaments, and any number of reprehensible training methods, dogs that would accept that posture were developed. That this style was in serious conflict with both the tenets of the Standard, and the best interests of the dogs and their inner structure, was blatently ignored due to the success it had in the show ring, until older and wiser judges began to scream "Enough of this."

Damage incurred to the resiliency of the musculature became quite evident at a loose-lead trot of controlled speed, and from the fact that toplines in the breed became the disgrace of the gazehound family. For a while handlers covered this by pulling the hindlegs even further out from under the poor dogs, and moving from the breed's traditional collected trot to one of flying extension, in which momentum took the place of coordination, and flash took the plce of honest trotting gaits.

Placing dogs' hindlegs well behind the hip-joint came into further conflict with the Standard by putting the dogs onto their tip-toes— creating faulty tiny feet. More importantly, with part of the body weight off the hindlegs, the center of gravity is forced forward into the shoulders, throwing terrible stress into withers and forelegs. This causes the withers to rise as the shoulder-upper arm joint must become rigid like a column—contributing to the much criticized high withers and straight shoulders that became endemic in the breed. By stretching the ligaments along the spine, it also broke down toplines. In trying to outdo other exhibitors in creating the most spectacular outline—at all costs—this type of mindless stacking moved from the innocuous, to the seriously damaging, in the 70's. Happily the screams were heard. The 80's has brought some reversal to the trend, with return to respect towards breed outline integrity.

In show training it is vital to consider the developmental age of the dog. Young pups should be introduced to basic loose-lead leash-training (of typical obedience class type), the word "stay"—for a few seconds duration—and to being touched on all parts of their bodies. That is all. Intelligent use of canine behavioral knowledge demands socialization and the constant awareness of positive habit developments. For instance, affectionate scratching under the dog's chin promotes proud head-bearing; petting on the top of the skull brings a submissive appearing dropped foreface. The aim is to interlace wanted response with the dog's sense of pride and enjoyment. Countless potential show dogs have been lost by unsuitable training methods that engendered resentment, rather than enthusiasm, for the game. Many sensitive gazehounds go through stages of frightened rebellion. If patiently allowed to explore each new surrounding in ways that allow them to let inate curiosity help them overcome an inner resistance to new conditions, they may develop real confidence in time. Adolescent dogs present the same range of problems as hormonally-confused human teenagers.

Ch. Driftwood's Sea Farer (Ch. Zorro's Intrepid ex Zorro's Get-Away, CD, LCM), bitch, bred by Rita A. Figg, owned by Fred and Rita A. Figg.

Ch. Elmo's Pajourah (Ch. Coastwind Graffiti ex Khamelot's Portia Panache), self-masked cream bitch, bred by Peter Belmont II and Gordon B. F. McDowell IV, owned by Susan Bahary Wilner.

Ch. Zafara Odetta (Ch. Mecca's Falstaff ex Ch. Coastwind Ouija), bitch, bred by Bob and Bobbi Keller and Coastwind Kennels, owned by Al and Pam McQueen.

Mock judging situations, such as handling classes, and Puppy Matches are useful for exposing young dogs to strange hands, novel terrain, unexpected noises or other animals. They provide insight into the animal's development physically and mentally. Should the youngster prove jumpy about novel experiences a gradual relaxed exposure may make a big difference. The over-aggressive youngster should be given the discipline of obedience training techniques, before it becomes a serious danger to itself and others out of uncontrolled exhuberance. But the object should be to *control*—not break—high spirits.

In both gaiting and stacking, every hound will vary in its individual needs. The true secret of properly presenting a dog is in knowing the dog's assets and liabilities—knowing just where the dog does or does not come up to the ideal Afghan Hound image. Remember, the ideal image is presented in the Standard. Know it. The judge has less than three minutes per dog; therefore, it is a case of accentuating the positive and never drawing attention to the negative.

The beautiful movement of the Afghan Hound can only be shown to advantage in an adequately sized ring. It is felt that an indoor or outdoor ring should be at least 30 feet wide and 50 feet long, and under no circumstances be less than 30 feet wide and 40 feet long. Smaller rings can make a good Afghan with good movement look bad because he can't hit his stride. All show-giving clubs should provide rings of this minimum size for the Afghans. If they do not, Afghan judges and exhibitors should insist on it.

There are two distinctly different phases to gaiting, that done in a circle in which the judge is watching the side gait and the overall balanced picture of the hound, and the coming-and-going gait done with the individual examinations. There are different stories to be read here. In the circle, the length of stride, power of drive, and lack of interference is most easily viewed. The skillful handler, long before entering the ring, will have ascertained the most flattering speed for his dog in the big circle. The handler, with the ground-swallowing gaited hound, would be foolish to allow a "mincer" set the pace for his dog. There is no rule that says the fast dogs must stay behind the slower ones. But such maneuvering must be done with courtesy, not in rude drives that force other dogs against the fence or by allowing a fast dog to trod on the heels, or nip the rump, of the dog in front of him.

This large circling is vitally important in the initial impression the judge gets of the hounds and, right then and there, some of these dogs will be mentally picked as winners. The remainder of the judging is a comparison of these dogs against the others. The novice,

Ch. Holly Hill Desert Wind (Ch. Kabiri of Grandeur ex Ch. Samaris of Moornistan), black mask apricot dog, multiple Best in Show winner and sire of 22 champions. Owned by Mrs. Cheever Porter. *William P. Gilbert photo*

unless finding himself in the position of leader, should follow the pace set for him without trying any tricks and concentrate on alerting the dog to run gaily with head and tail high.

Once the judge has signaled the line to stop, he will examine each dog individually. This is the second of the elimination rounds taking place in the judicial brain, the first being the impression gained in the circling. The wise handler will not permit his dog to slump while the judge is examining other dogs before him or after him, for the judge constantly looks back and forth, making mental comparisons of this and that. Don't spoil a first impression by letting down in the line. The dog which will not stand still can be quietly moved around the handler from time to time and reset. The bored handler, gazing off into space while his dog takes on a sloppy stance, is throwing away his chances.

As the judge approaches the dog, step back, but do not drop the leash. The judge may ask, "Show me the bite," or "Does he bite?" and should be listened to carefully. He may want to inspect the dog's teeth personally, or prefer to have the handler show the bite to him.

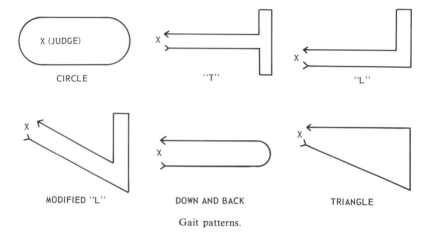

Gait patterns.

As a general rule, handlers always keep the dog on the left side, but the paramount rule is to see that the dog is invariably between the judge and handler. The owner pays his fee to have the judge look at the dog, not at legs or trousers. This takes a bit of maneuvering around the dog on the part of the handler at all times. In this matter, the novice would do well to study the methods of the professional handler.

When the judge has checked the dog's structure to his satisfaction, he will send dog and handler to the far end of the ring to see the dog's gait, this time with the emphasis on the coming-and-going aspects. Judges vary in their opinions of how best to view the gait and the size and shape of the ring must also be taken into account. There are several standard patterns, and attention to the dogs gaited previously gives the handler a fair idea of what will be expected of him. Follow the judge's instructions carefully. Some of the common gait patterns are shown in the drawing. These should be practiced with the dog always between the handler and the judge, entailing a bit of hand-switching and dog-turning for smoothness. As a breed noted for surefootedness, the hound that makes the smoothest turns wins the merit points. The fumbling owner who throws his dog off stride on the same turns earns demerits.

Take the dog back and forth in his best gait speed unless instructed by the judge differently. On returning to the judge, the dog may be sent out again with instructions to go faster, slower, or perhaps in a different pattern. The judge is usually not trying to find faults at this point, but looking for a special factor in the gait, or possibly giving the dog a second chance to get its tail up or move in a straighter line. Judges usually sense when a dog is not in his best stride and, if time permits, will often give the exhibitor a second chance.

A precious moment of great importance occurs when the dog returns from gaiting and stops in front of the judge. Here is the instant that the pro takes full advantage of. He will stop his hound and immediately alert the dog, knowing that the judge is carefully taking in the hound's natural "expression" at this moment. The Afghan Hound who stops dead true and looks the judge firmly in the eye improves his odds considerably. Such dogs are "asking for the win."

Once all the dogs in the class have been examined and the necessary comparisons and re-gaitings accomplished, the judge may have all the dogs make one final great circling. When the final decisions have been made the judge will mark them in the Judges' Book and hand out ribbon awards accordingly.

Ribbons will be given the first four placings and the other dogs are excused from the ring. Recipients of the ribbons customarily thank the judge, and all first and second place winners are to stand by for possible further judging.

Training for show requires regular training sessions at home or in a handling class. Handling technique can be improved by having a friend take movies of your handling. Run the film slowly and study your technique. Improve your weak points.

Exhibitors frequently stand around to ask the judge about his placings after the breed has been judged. There is no rule against this, and occasionally really useful information emerges. Many judges prefer not to be put on the spot. Others have been embittered by quarrelsome losers to the point where they doubt the innocent intention of any questions. Some just do not remember the dog in question. This is a great pity in our breed where helpful and honest comment is golden treasure for the sincere but bewildered novices. The breed would stand to benefit immeasurably from extra time and effort donated by the breeder-judge in helping the novice better understand the breed and the dog beneath the fur coat.

The optimum impact any dog can project is, in reality, that excitement and balance that it shows *naturally*—off lead—when alerted by a living sight or sound. It is up to every would-be handler to brand that impression into their own mind with the aim of bringing it into the ring in a captured form. No more tragic mistake can be made than to lose sight of the individual Afghan Hound's own potential, in the aim of working towards the re-creation of a photo, or living facsimile of some differing dog—no matter how much admired. A copy can never be better than second rate. Individuality is one of the hallmarks of the breed. It must not become a case of which dog has the least faults, or the greatest resemblance to some remembered winner—but, instead, a case of which dog displays the most positive breed-essence in its own right.

Ch. Concert's Firebird, U.D. (Ch. Rujha's Rigoletto De Concert ex Rujha's Susahra), bitch, owned by Dr. and Mrs. Franklin, trained and handled by Mrs. Joycelyn (Joy) E. Franklin. First champion with a Utility title in Afghan Hounds.

11

Obedience

OBEDIENCE TRIALS first became recognized by the AKC back in 1936 after having been held previously in Europe. According to the AKC rules and regulations, "The purpose of Obedience Trials is to demonstrate the usefulness of the purebred dog as a companion of man, not merely the dog's ability to follow specified routines in the obedience ring." Degrees of Companion Dog (C.D.), Companion Dog Excellent (C.D.X.), Utility Dog (U.D.), Obedience Trial Championship (O.T.Ch.), Tracking Dog (T.D.) and Tracking Dog Excellent (T.D.X.), can be won by all successfully competing purebred dogs.

The gazehounds as a group were rather slow to warm up to the idea of obedience work for formal degrees. A view of them as royal independent hunters did not fit the framework of subservience that has falsely colored the concept of obedience work. Not until Afghan Hounds fell into the hands of owners with previous solid dog training experience did members of the breed appear on the title lists. The concept of obedience as a competitive sport in which a dog with a conformation fault could excel played no part in the early days of the breed. Of the 16 Afghan Hounds to make the C.D. degree up through 1948, eight were conformation champions, with several of the others "pointed." Owner attitude alone made the difference.

Ross Hamilton's Doreborn's Kamu was the first Afghan Hound to hold a C.D. degree. The year was 1939 and by the end of 1940, the dog was a C.D.X. He was followed by Mrs. Hovey's Ch. Harisun, C.D. Late in 1940 Elizabeth Whelan, who had previous successes in gaining obedience degrees for her willing Shelties, determined to put her Afghans through their paces, but found them quite a different breed: "When I started Maharanee on simple heeling and sitting, she was not the least bit interested and absolutely refused to sit—although I am certain she knew what I wanted her to do . . . After several weeks of doing nothing, I decided to try her again. Much to my amazement, she heeled and sat beautifully on the first try. She had discovered that when she did something well, she was praised, and she loved that . . . Afghans never forget a thing they have learned, but one has to be very patient with them in obedience work." Miss Whelan's Maharanee retired as Ch. Maharanee of Arken, C.D.X., and her Ch. Mogul of Arken, C.D., was a famous Best-in-Show hound of his day.

The number of obedience titled Afghan Hounds has been small and in sharp contrast to the high percentage of the breed shown in breed competition. Wild tales of the breed's untrainability due to stupidity emanated from outside the breed, and super-intelligence from within the breed, by those who see "The Afghan" as something well apart from "dog." A pervasive belief, that like oil and water, obedience and conformation do not mix, frightened the timid away from obedience work along with those who neither had the time, nor cared to take the time, to investigate the aspect properly.

Concerning the Afghan's temperament and intelligence, there is much that needs saying. Trainers that want a high-scoring dog that performs like an automatic machine are certain to come away disappointed and oftimes resentful of the Afghan. These hounds are highly individualistic, but most of them retain a great sensitivity and stubborn sense of independence, being determined to make the final decisions. In other words, they must come to accept and to want to do the things that are asked of them. This insistence is a perfectly natural attitude for any hound whose function in life was to use *his own wits* in tracking down and overcoming treacherous wild game. Unlike many other breeds, at no time has the Afghan been bred for any form of mental subservience. For this reason they can be most exasperating to train, but a constant and fascinating challenge to the understanding owner. These breed characteristics are also noted by the professional dog trainers. Mrs. Frank Burger, who has a group of Afghans in her famous circus act, has this to say: "At present we use about 20 dogs in our act, 8 of which are Afghan Hounds. They are very difficult to work with as they are strong-headed and will only learn a trick when they are good and ready . . . However, once they learn a certain trick, we never have any trouble with them. It takes about two months to train a Terrier or Poodle, but the Afghan about one year. They are intelligent and independent and bribery will get you nowhere with Afghans . . . They are trained to skip double rope, a three round boxing match, cake-walk dance and about a dozen other tricks. They attract a lot of

264

Suzon, skipping rope in Burger's Performing Animal Revue.

High jump with Farouk, nine months.

Tut and Rajhah, the world's only boxing dogs.

attention wherever they have been shown and we're very proud of them." Mrs. Burger has also confessed to having rather disliked the stubborn hounds on first acquaintance, but once she understood them they became her favorites.

Each Afghan has its own idiosyncrasy on what tricks it rebels against, but as an overall breed characteristic in the C.D. training, it is the "recall" that is the most troublesome; the Afghan by nature being a bit resentful of having to be told just when to come and when not to. Away from obedience areas, the fact that the Afghan hates to come when called is common knowledge. This command is best learned at a very early age, before the dog ever learns the meaning of unadulterated freedom.

Among C.D.X. Afghans, the most challenging phase is certainly the Retrieving, an act evidently alien to the Afghan's nature. Teach-

265

San-Dhi's Kuza Nama of San-Dhihi, C.D.X. (dog), earned C.D.X. in three consecutive shows, average score 193 plus; owned and trained by Mrs. B. V. Houtsma.

ing this requires a saint's patience until the day when the Afghan finally accepts what seems to him a highly ridiculous act. You can practically hear them say, "You can put that thing in your mouth if you like, but I am certainly not going to put it in mine." From Betty Whelan's time until today, trainers wail about the vexation of convincing the Afghan that he should take and hold a dumbbell in his mouth. But all say that once the hounds accept this basic idea, teaching them the remainder of the retrieve is easy. All Afghans adore the hurdle work. In C.D.X. training, Virginia Withington found the long sit one of the toughest tricks for her dogs, and finally concocted a pulley tied-to-a-tree technique to prevent a dog from always lying down the moment she went out of sight. Afghan trainers become highly resourceful in pitting their wits against their clever Afghans.

Neither the age of a dog nor of its owner is a necessary deterrent to obedience training. Charlotte Gilbert when just 13 years old trained her Afghan, Valair Ditto of Dido, obtaining the dog's C.D. in three straight shows. And while it is true that most young Afghans are far too unsettled to take formal training seriously, Jean Givens (15 years old) set a new record for precocious learning in the breed when her personally-trained Firishta of Kubera gained a C.D. when just seven months and one day old. Among the older hounds one of the authors' own bitches, Ch. Sultan's Cuttingadido, C.D., began her formal obedience training as a five-year-old granddam, to dispute the "you can't teach an old dog new tricks" theory.

In the '50s a surge in obediencee interest was sparked by the unforgettable appearance of Virginia (Gini) Withington with the delightful Koh-I-Baba. He was the first Afghan Hound to become a U.D. dog. Baba's titles were not easily won as he was a born clown. His titles remain a tribute to the understanding persistence of his owner. Always a favorite with a crowded ringside, Baba was a ham, considering the audience reaction as a clue for him to ad lib. His favorite attention-getting device was an unorthodox method of coming into heel by hurling himself skyward, spinning in mid-air with fur flying, to land slightly out of kilter, next to his red-faced mistress. His sedate expression innocently asked, "Well, what's everyone laughing about?" Gini was accused of deliberately teaching Baba this method of coming in, but the truth of the matter is that she would have much preferred a more orthodox approach. While the rule book was not so specific as to make Baba's unique style formally unacceptable, stuffy judges were unamused and strongly penalized the degree of landing kilter. Points lost sometimes meant the difference between winning a "leg" and having to try another day.

In 1959 two other dogs crashed the tough U.D. barrier, those being Tazi Jini Mabat and Ivardon Tufon Khan. Dr. W. H. Ivens, Jr., was co-owner of Ivardon Tufon Khan which was trained and shown by Rose Thompson.

Within Southern California the success of Gini in combining show and obedience work in the glamour dog brought a narrow surge of obedience trained Afghan Hounds among friendly competitors with pedigree-related dogs. Another Virginia, then Mika, took her BIS Ch. Desert Chieftain of Mikai through basic work to his C.D. This brought a rash of Mikai dogs based in different parts of the country onto the C.D. rolls. To a marked degree the obedience titled dogs reflected pedigrees stemming from breeders with positive attitudes towards this type of challenge.

In the mid-'60s the separation between obedience and conformation became more positive as an either/or action. It was not absolute. Joy Franklin put an early C.D. on her Concert's Firebird, and then added the conformation title. Not at all content with small laurels the dog went on to achieve the high honor U.D., to become the only Champion/U.D. titlist in the breed.

The joy that obedience brings to the dog, as opposed to the boredom of the showring, was amply proved by Lee Whitehouse's High Life Zareef of Camri. The handsome Zareef began as a show dog winning points easily, but hated the tedium of the ring. He solved the problem by developing a psychosomatic limp in a hind leg. After a number of embarrassing excusals for limping, and a battery of tests that disclosed no reason for it, the dog was pulled from competition— lacking only the second major. Having previously obedience trained their non-show female, the Whitehouses exposed Zareef to the sport, which he took to with pleasure and no limping. His C.D. was quickly obtained. A knowledgeable dog friend happened to visit the home and was surprised to learn that the handsome dog was not yet finished. On hearing the story of the persistent limp he suggested an experiment. The dog was entered in the next large-entry show. But this time he was groomed off the grounds, taken into the ring on a choke-chain and leather lead and given the commands "heel" and then "stand." Happily fooled into enjoying himself, Zareef was chosen BOB from the classes and became a new champion. This is one of many instances in which obedience training saved a dog's conformation potential, rather than costing it. Owners would do well to investigate the psychological advantages of coursing and obedience before dismissing either out of hand.

The first steps to the successful training of Afghans is to understand the breed nature and then to properly assess the temperament of the specific dog under training. The big brash hound takes far firmer handling than the over-sensitive hound who panics at the sound of a cross word or a strong jerk. It is certainly advisable to take the dog to formal training classes if possible, but several Afghans have won degrees based on training hints found in books. The texts written by Blanche Saunders or W. R. Koehler are the most popular. Afghan owners should avoid any obedience classes run by rigid teachers whose methods are inflexible and not geared to the individual dog. Cruel force will not work with Afghans. These sensitive hounds respond only to kindness, understanding firmness and great patience. They will turn sullen, mean, or hopelessly frightened if bullied in any way. Trainers must realize that the Afghan often goes through periods of vacillation as he accepts and then rejects training dogma before finally becoming a reliable worker. He is only making up his own mind about the worth of these things, and testing his owner's reactions rather than witlessly accepting commands. Very few Afghans are ready to compete for their degrees in any reliable manner at the end of a ten-week course.

A sensitive insight to the nature of the Afghan is provided in *Challenge for Angel* by Francis Priddy. This book is a teen-ager's story but is for both those who have and those who have not had the joy of training the unpredictable Afghan Hound. Miss Priddy has trained both her Afghans in obedience: Shah, a clown; Satin, a good worker. Shah's counterpart in the book is Shazam or "The Abominable Snowman."

The best working Afghans are the ones which enjoy obedience work and associate it with praise and fun. The breed does have a weakness for tomfoolery while working. This should be ignored rather than actually squelched to retain a certain amount of gaiety in the dog's work.

By the '70s the rise of a special sort of owner eager and able to combine obedience work with coursing degrees, often in addition to conformation, was evident in various geographic niches. Those whose primary interest fell in the coursing activity are mentioned in

Indrani, C.D.X. (Ch. Tarylane's Mr. Wonderful ex Princess of Grandeur), bitch, eleven years old and still working in Obedience. Indrani was a Canadian champion. Bred by Jean Bernstein, owned by Natalie Waznys.   —*Photo, Jimmie.*

the Coursing Chapter. Others moved from a primary base of obedience work.

In Texas, Roger and Johanna Tanner spearheaded triple-duty activities with their own enthusiasm, helpfulness and the success of Ch. Xanadu's Xixith, C.D., F.Ch. Known affectionately as Breezy, this daughter of Champions Akaba's Royal Flush and Xanadu's Sweet Xephyr helped to entice southland admirers into all phases of Afghan Hound activity. The Tanners are totally sold on the all-purpose Afghan Hound, plan their breedings to this end, and happily infect others with the same virus.

Shelley Hennessy heads the achiever parade combining obedience and coursing with conformation compatibility in Ohio. Her articles in breed magazines have been inspirational to other fanciers. The proof of her pudding lies in her dogs. Ch. Chaparral Soylent Blue Ro-Jan, C.D.X., also holds the ASFA F.Ch. title. Soy was the first Afghan Hound to be so titled and is now working on the coveted U.D. at nine years of age. Never content with the laurels on any one dog, Shelley has a yardful of F.Chs. and C.D.X. dogs, some of whom are well on the road to their conformation titles as well.

In Colorado Julie Roche has done an outstanding job in bringing out the full potential of Ben Zari's Dusty Dawn, now a U.D. and LCM. Better known as Sirsa, this bitch nears her conformation title with BOBs to her credit. Her obedience scores have been astonishingly

Alexander of Hamilton, UD (Duke's Devine Delivery ex Doupnik's Chocolate Doll), dog, bred by Barry S. and Orvilla Doupnik, owned by Michael and Elaine Hamill. Alex is enrolled in Therapy Dogs International.

Ch. Chaparral Soylent Blue Ro-Jan, C.D.X., F.Ch. (Ch. Dureigh's Ro-Jan of Ebonwood ex Dark Secret of Dureigh), dog, bred by Janice B. Wargo, owned by Shelley Hennessy.

Personality Plus, Ch. Kismet's Jaccala, CDX (Ch. Remus of Azad ex Ch. Kismet's Princess Samantha), dog, bred by Shirley and John Handley, owned by W. S. Cook III and P. L. McNeil.   *—Fox & Cook PhoDOGraphy.*

high taking her to the top of the charts for sighthounds of the period. No automaton, but a dog with a mind of its own, Sirsa learned quickly but embellished her work with such acts as deliberately going over the Utility jump several times instead of just once. Her favorite heart-stopping trick was to dash up to the broad jump, stop dead in her tracks, and when the crowd was sure she couldn't make it, leap straight into the air and clear the jump by several feet. There is no doubt she loved the gasps and applause. Taking the urban Afghan Hound's versatility one more step Sirsa serves as ambassador through performances at schools for normal and handicapped children.

Sheila Grant's Bo-Rene's Cameo Sasha, C.D., T.D., LCM, leads the multi-title parade in the Pacific Northwest. Interestingly, for the first two years of her life, Sasha was taught never to chase *anything*. Yet, at her first sight of the "bunny" at a lure course, as a two-year-old, she knew the difference and became an accomplished lure-courser almost overnight. As the second Afghan Hound in history to achieve a Tracking title, Sasha confirmed the Afghan Hound's ability to easily follow a spoor. The biggest obstacle, naturally enough, Sheila reports, was in getting her to *smell*, rather than look, for the object. "We had to resort to tricks such as hiding the glove in deep crabgrass, in holes, etc." and when found, Sasha indicated the item's position in an Afghan manner—front down and fanny up in the air. In common with the report of most all the serious Afghan trainers, Sheila admits, "In training Sasha, I have found that one must take a different approach than with other breeds. Force is *out!* I must make her believe that the current activity is what *she* wants to do." Clearly, training the Afghan Hound, whether in obedience, coursing, or for conformation is best done in a joyous cooperative partnership, not as a master/slave relationship.

Based in Louisiana and specializing in obedience work, Windsor Forest's Brandy has a record that is not to be ignored. Racing through his C.D. requirements, Brandy became the youngest Afghan Hound to obtain his C.D.X. (at 17 months), and as similar prodigy in earning his U.D. before his second birthday, it took only 10 months from C.D. through U.D. Only owners who have attempted the U.D. training can appreciate this feat. Possibly the most remarkable fact is that his owner/handler, Les Johnson, had never previously trained a dog.

Up in Massachusetts, Elaine Hamill took the first dog she ever trained, Alexander of Hamilton, all the way to U.D. by the time he was three years old. Alex earned his C.D. in four trials, C.D.X. in four trials, and his U.D. in eleven trials. He loved to show off and go to the shows. Since his U.D., Alex is enrolled in Therapy Dogs International (TDI). TDI is described in the February 1982 *Pure-Bred Dogs— American Kennel Gazette*. Alex through his jumping and retrieving

Ben Zari's Dusty Dawn, UD, F.Ch., LCM (Ch. Ben Haasin's Czar Illya ex Oromeo Zamara, CD, F.Ch.), bitch, bred by Pamela B. Simmons, owned by Julie Roche. "Sirsa" is AKC pointed with multiple BOB's and is the first Afghan Hound to earn O.T.Ch. points.

provides therapy for troubled children and the elderly at hospitals and nursing homes. All this came about because as a puppy Alex broke collars and leashes and would make a run for it. After obedience training he could be trusted to walk off lead. His favorite reward is a long walk—food never worked as an incentive for Alex. In the 33 years since the first U.D. Afghan Hound, Koh-I-Baba, only 17 Afghan Hounds have earned the U.D. title. To date only two dogs have earned a T.D.: Ch. Vinroc's Country Girl, C.D.X., T.D.; Bo-Rene's Cameo Sasha, C.D., T.D., LCM.

272

Another title that is starting to receive attention is the TT which is awarded by the American Temperament Test Society, Inc. (ATTS, INC.), 13680 Van Nuys Blvd., Pacoima, CA 91331. They regularly hold Temperament Evaluations in various parts of the country. Dogs must be at least one year of age and be presented in good condition. The scoring and passing of the dogs is the consensus of three nationally registered Testers officiating simultaneously. Dogs passing their tests earn their TT.

The test simulates a walk in the park with the dog on a loose lead. During the evaluation the dog's canine behavioral response to stimuli resulting from interaction with its daily environment is uniformly tested. The environment consists of strangers in non-threatening situations; sudden non-threatening stimuli; a threatening stimulus; a sudden visual stimulus; unusual footing in the field; a potentially threatening situation; a threatening situation. The TT indicates that the dog has sound temperament and is therefore a useful tool for accomplishing some long term goals for breeders.

The long years of the breed in America have only served to prove the astute observations of Mary Amps who repeatedly stated that Afghan Hounds must live as partners with their loved humans, as when relegated to the kennel they become disobedient or half-developed. There are many cases of insecure or difficult hounds who were duds in the show ring until their self-confidence was bolstered by the proof of love and attention gained from obedience training. The only conflict between the two trainings is the temporary confusion that can be caused by expecting the dog to sit when brought to a halt in obedience work. But patient owners find that these intelligent dogs quickly differentiate between the demands of the chokechain collar and the light leather show lead. All other phases of obedience training are assets to a show dog, especially the "stand for examination." Owners who do not wish to chance confusion may prefer to concentrate on one form of training at a time and schedule obedience and then conformation aims accordingly.

Whether formal obedience is attempted or not, all owners would do well to remember the words of Lt. J. T. Sharkey who trained Afghans successfully in the service, when he wisely pointed out, "There is no such thing in civilized life as an untrained dog. That idea is a fallacy. Every domestic animal is a trained animal whether he has acquired good habits or bad; and whether he has come from the alley or from a fine home. Every dog is either trained or he is a wild beast . . . The habits he has formed alone from puppyhood, plus those he has been helped to establish, have been his training up to date."

273

Ch. Yantra Mojou Jabbar, LCM (Yantra Baksheesh Camino Real ex Ambrosia Baksheesh), black and tan dog, bred by Clark and Linda Melrose, owned by Michele Giasone and Gail Phelps. Top Lure Coursing Afghan Hound 1981.

12

Coursing and Racing

DOWN through the centuries the Afghan Hound's existence was fostered by man's need to obtain game for sustenance, to protect his flocks from marauders, and eventually by his more sophisticated activity, the sport of coursing. Westerners entering Afghanistan stumbled onto a professional hound breed highly revered for its successful labors. In *Hounds and Dogs* Mary Amps reported: "They (the hounds) are both trained to hunt deer and wolves and also to course hares and foxes. In fact anything that will bring grist to their owner's mill. Incidentally they act as watchdogs also . . . In Afghanistan the hounds never show the slightest tendency to chase the innumerable sheep, cattle, camels and donkeys scattered over the countryside. They are thoroughly trained from puppyhood what to hunt and what to leave alone." Present day notes on training the Afghan Greyhound from a Middle East newspaper give a seldom-read story:

". . . They are trained for coursing and hunting from the age of two months; the 'prey' used for training is generally the 'Jerboa' or 'Khanay' as it is called. With spades and picks in hand, the trainers take out the budding hunters early in the morning and proceed toward a line of 'Karez' wells, where the Jerboas commonly congregate and have their warren or holes. Soon after reaching the selected spot, the spades and picks begin to fly and, lo, a jerboa pops out like a kangaroo, which it resembles. The excited puppies tumble over each other in an attempt to catch the leaping rodent, but generally fail to do so and return after a few moments with tongues lolling and sides heaving. This is kept up day after day until the pup is one year old, when it is 'matched' with a more mature and 'seasoned' dog to chase the real game, i.e., wild hares . . . It is comparatively easy to catch hares in summer because they feed on green grass and plants and, therefore, are 'heavy,' but few dogs can grapple with the 'autumn' or 'winter' hares which, by feeding on dry grass, are as lean as a fine thorough-bred in racing 'form.' The owners fear most the hare with one ear standing and the other lopping down; such a hare is called, in Afghan parlance, a 'Chot-Khafi.' This is considered to be a 'mean' hare, which may break a young Greyhound for good. The 'break' occurs when a Greyhound pursues the hare or gazelle with intense concentration and uses every ounce of strength in its body; a time comes when the dog has had enough and something snaps inside him. He gives up the chase and lies down, but cannot get up; in other words, it is crippled forever and is ruined as a hunter . . ."

Afghan Hounds have hunted a fantastic variety of game if all reports can be believed. An incredible experience of big-game hunters with Sikh Indians and Afghan Hounds on a safari in the African bush country of Tanganyika in search of the fierce East African leopard was reported by Bob Wales in a letter published in *Kennel Review* magazine, September 1948. He observed that the Sikhs ran a brace of males after the leopards, males being of superior strength. The men and dogs hunt the beast using native drum corps to unnerve the leopard, forcing him from his refuge in the trees. As he forsakes the protective branches the hounds take over: "While moving under full speed, one of the dogs lunges and seizes the leopard's neck on one side while on the opposite side the other hound streaks in, slashing with flashing fangs, ripping and tearing out the leopard's jugular vein." Mr. Wales mentions that the hound's hunting methods are instinctive rather than the product of any human training. The dogs are not held on leashes while hunting, but permitted to range free, ". . . ever alert and ready to pursue and bring their prey to earth." In the past few years there have been reports of the farmers of Kenya, Africa using the Afghan Hound to hunt predatory jackals. (This practice has been deplored by the English Dog Press as jackals are considered to be dangerous spreaders of hydrophobia.)

The Afghan Hound's reputation as a canny and powerful hunter followed him out of the East, but direct purebred associations with the chase have not been well established in the Western world. In England and elsewhere, where hunting or coursing was permitted, the desirability of obtaining "a little bit of the Afghan" was readily accepted. In 1911, with the great Zardin's memory still bright, Mr. Dunn put his red Afghan Hound, Baz, to Capt. Ellis' purebred Greyhound bitch, Explosion, in an honest effort to improve stamina and soundness in competition Greyhounds. In describing Baz, which was a sturdy 26 inches tall and weighed 62½ pounds (having a 32-inch girth), Capt. Ellis wrote: "(Baz) has a strong back, short coupled with splendid legs and feet . . . The dog himself has a peculiar look. He has a hairy coat, long face and ears, and a peculiarly gentle expression which made Mr. Dent remark, '. . . All you want is an organ to make you complete.' " The bitch, Experimental, resulting from the mating was most handsome but utterly smooth-coated, easily taken for a prize-winning Greyhound except for droopy ears and a trace of ring tail.

In these United States a confusing pack of varying local and state laws govern game hunting with dogs. (Hounds that not only seek out but kill game are taboo in many areas.) In certain states hounds are deliberately used to kill predators such as wolves and coyotes for bounty. Such game hounds are carefully bred for their job, go unrecognized by the AKC, and frequently show a strong dash of European gazehound influences. Braden Finch wrote of an early attempt at predator hunting with Afghans in a 1948 magazine wherein he stated, "But when the Afghan came to the United States a scant score of years ago, it was to work for his living, like any other immigrant. He was imported to rid a Missouri farm of coyotes! And it is recorded that one pair of these powerful speedy hounds within a few months cleaned the coyotes out of one entire Missouri county."

For many years the hounds were used on jackrabbit and coyotes in New Mexico. Miss Amelia White (Kandahar) tells, "My kennel manager, Alex Scott, used to take the dogs out hunting. They had their own system, hunting in couples. One knocked the quarry down. The other went for its throat. Very bloodcurdling and effective."

Jackson Sanford gave added details on hunting with Afghan Hounds in America in the '30s (via the 1965 *AHCA AFGHANEWS*). Contrary to reports of Afghan Hounds working in pairs, or packs, in Afghanistan, he found the breed "highly individualistic, and not at all inclined to work in concert in the field." His observations encompassed hunting rabbit, hare, fox, puma, lynx, house cats and domestic poultry—with or without human encouragement. "A good hunting Afghan will chase or stalk and kill any game that will give him a run, and some that will not." However, he concluded that just being a purebred Afghan Hound was far from enough to insure either

Ch. Hullabaloo's Tiger Rag, "blasting out" of starting box, owned by Betty and Earl Stites.

J. Barry O'Rourke photo

Crown Crest Behapi Goluki, racing in the first annual races at Santa Barbara in 1960.

Santa Barbara News-Press photo

success, or attempt, at hunting. "Of ten males put to the test (with luck) one will develop into a real hunting Afghan. Of bitches and puppies I have one thing to say—the game is not worth the candle." He found the best "to have the ability to climb a vertical rock face (as probable) heritage from the breed's experience in the mountainous regions of Afghanistan" concluding, "The best hunting Afghans appear to descend from the dogs of those regions."

In a scene familiar to all who have observed free-running Afghan Hounds on variable terrain, Sanford described, "In any kind of country, the opening move of the experienced hunting Afghan is a race to the nearest rise of ground. In this he does not dawdle; the young, inexperienced, or never-to-be hunting Afghan may violate this rule, but the genuine article goes flat out. Gaining the crest of this objective, the dog comes to a standstill. The head goes up, the tail down, while the eye scans the country roundabout. Sometimes, to improve the elevation of the eye, the dog will rear up on the hind legs, balancing himself apparently by means of pawing or boxing motions of the forelegs. He may hold this attitude for quite a little while, often taking a few steps without coming down on the forefeet." Once game is seen, close enough to be worth the chase, unparalleled agility becomes the Afghan Hound's special weapon.

In considering the descriptions of Scott and Sanford it must be remembered that they spoke of a transplanted breed, with freshly mixed pedigrees, at most several generations from native hunting stock. Studies of wolf packs illustrate how much a family learning tradition of older animals teaching youngsters (by example) enlarges cooperative aspects and innate factors. Scott and Sanford were observers of foreign dogs in short-term randomized situations. Sanford's own lack of appreciation for hunting potential of either puppies or bitches betrayed short-sightedness, and consequent inability to develop an American hunting strain in the breed. His was an overview of free-ranging individual dogs that stalked, chased, followed and (when lucky) killed whatever happened along. This is a far distance from the selected, trained and pack-related hounds of Afghanistan.

Rather than using Afghan Hounds for general field hunting in America, fanciers have preferred to cling to remnant beliefs in the breed's functional ability through ordered racing or lure coursing activities. The first recorded Yankee attempt at organized Afghan Hound racing was on a Greyhound track over homemade brush hurdles concocted by Shaw McKean and Bayard Warren in the 1930s. Seen as a little too spectacular for comfort by Greyhound owners, wary of vested interests, the track was quickly made unavailable to the longhairs. This stumbling block reared time and again in the spotty history of attempts to put Afghan Hound racing on a regular footing.

The prime instigators of more recent Afghan Hound track racing were Earl and Betty Stites who, in 1958, with the aid of Wendy Howell (fancier of show and racing Whippets) developed makeshift racing equipment in northern California. They were excitedly joined by your co-author (Conni Miller) and other local fanciers, to make racing a quasi-regular activity of the Northern California Afghan Hound Club. Every race date was an experiment with new ideas for wheels, boxes, muzzles and protocol. No attempt was made to collect times or to assign titles, although by elimination, the faster dogs worked up to challenge each other. That some dogs were "naturals" and others could be "developed" with training became apparent. There certainly were some—in both sexes—"not worth the candle." The sight of youngsters who, when tired of running, simply stopped in the middle of the track and sat down, eliminated any fear that some dog might run itself to death, as a few Greyhounds have done.

The move to southern California by the Stites spawned the Orange County Racing Assn. Shortly before that date Bill and Gini Withington and Dick and Georgiana Guthrie, inspired by the Stites' race movies, formed the Afghan Coursing Association in the San Fernando Valley. The word "coursing" had been carefully chosen, not as an indication of open field hunting, but to circumvent the hostility of groups who feared the word "racing" might reactivate commercial dog racing in the State. Actually nothing could have been further from the aims of those owners who only wished to run their urban-raised hounds not for prizes or money, but for the stimulation, conditioning effects and joy of watching flying hounds with fur streaming after them. Certainly there was understandable pride at owning an outstanding runner. Pat Ide's Botar was consistently unbeatable from his first sight of the lure. Tragically, while still in his prime he lost his last race to an automobile, after having slipped, unnoticed, out the front door of his home.

With three active race clubs in existence in California, straight-line races after a lure, with or without starting boxes, became added attractions at several All-Breed shows. The meeting of dogs from north and south in conjunction with the then benched Santa Barbara Kennel Club show on the Polo Grounds became the highlight of the show and racing year. Excited newsletter descriptions spawned requests from Afghanite groups for details on equipment and methods from all over the United States.

Seeming to have a strong start as an added breed activity, the race mania spread through Chicago, the Mid-West, and Albuquerque. Finding, and keeping, grounds on which the dogs were permitted to run, proved the most difficult of all problems. In Massachusetts the Curnyns provided a local solution by building their own one-sixteenth mile track, complete with powered lure and starting boxes at Devi Baba.

Sadly, by the mid-60s, the steamroller of enthusiasm for track racing had run its course. Up to that point in the still small population of the breed the vast majority of race dogs doubled as show dogs at the occasional AKC events. But this was a period of marked proliferation of new AKC clubs, holding Matches and then gaining regular AKC Show dates. In result race practice schedules suffered. More and more time became devoted to keeping the dogs in superficial bandbox-pretty condition the year round. An attitudinal schism developed between exhibition and racing proponents. Despite an extraordinary record of safety, timid owners protested that racing might injure their show prospects. Somewhat more reasonably, other owners quit the races on grounds of unsuitability for mountain-bred hounds to run flat, and generally straight, distances—especially when, in match races with Borzoi, Greyhounds or Whippets, the Afghan Hounds generally brought up a game but lagging rear. These fanciers warned that concentration on competitive straightaway speed could bring about breeding practices that unwittingly sacrificed the Afghan Hound's precious maneuverability. Characteristic differences between breeds were accidentally demonstrated in a race with Afghan Hounds against Borzois, in which the Russian hounds outran the Afghan Hounds, but, in headlong flight, ran right past the lure and literally smashed into a fence shortly past the finish line. With the agile, quick stopping Afghan Hounds the barrier posed no hazard. Some experimentation with hurdles geared to the Afghan's effortless leaping ability occurred, but faded with lack of sustained organizational effort, just as did the residual flat-land runs.

In retrospect, your authors see this as the period in which the idea of the Afghan Hound as a fast, agile and well-muscled galloping animal became taken for granted as one *automatically* tied to its lineage. In result it no longer received either the consideration, or playful testing, of former more casual generations. Exhibition considerations became paramount in picture postcard photos emphasizing "showiness." That the demoting of selection for mental alertness and taut musculature was to have subtle deleterious effects on the physical strength of the breed, as a whole, became sadly evident within a decade. This was evidenced by the development of beautifully manicured and expertly handled ultra-elegant dogs—sadly unbalanced in their parts and with Silly Putty musculature from goose neck to hyperextensible hocks. No selection towards flatland speed could ever have accomplished such intrinsic breed damage.

Mr. and Mrs. Lyle Gillette, of Rancho Gabriel Borzoi fame, brought dogs to Afghan Hound race practices in the early 60s. With excited determination to preserve some semblance of sighthound functionality, but living well south of the Santa Rosa Fairgrounds where the Afghans generally practiced, they masterminded a rule-ordered open field coursing endeavor—The Pacheco Hunt Club. At the demise of organized box, muzzle and lure trials, residual Afghan Hound owners more dedicated to racing than to showing, joined the Pacheco Hunt. Janet and Gary Gustman's Afghan Hound, Sheba, was winner of the First Grand Course Mixed Stake in 1963.

Due to coats that magnetically attract weeds, burrs and loose twigs, Afghan Hound owner interest in open field coursing was sporadic. A few retired champs, adolescent stock or non-show dogs made up the faithful coursing string. Some amusing attempts at creating protective suits to cover the coat were made. A possible field clip for Afghan Hounds was considered but never really adopted. The best answer was self-discovered by an Afghan Hound who spied a rabbit and, in pursuit, plunged through a neck-high mud puddle. This plastered the dog's fur to its body. After the chase his hair dried in the warm sun and the loosened sand easily brushed out. But this was hardly a permanent answer. Within a year nearly all Afghan Hounds running in the Hunt Club were away from the mainstream of exhibition dogs, yet closely related to them by pedigree.

Ch. Wita Vail of Nightwatch, F.Ch. (Ch. Mecca's Falstaff ex Wita Rosie van de Oranje Manege), black and tan bitch, bred and owned by Denyce Verti. First dual Ch. Afghan Hound, BOB, and winner of Field Champion stake at the first Grand National Lure Course in Denver, 1975. Judges: Steve Copold and Jack England.

After consulting with the AKC on the feasibility of developing some form of coursing title for sighthounds, the Gillettes accepted the impossibility within the open field sphere. As a national body the AKC could never sanction a blood sport that was impossible, or illegal, in many regions of the United States. The Pacheco Hunt Club folded. Some spin-off of open field coursing continued in California but with a miniscule number of participating Afghan Hounds.

But the Gillettes did not long remain idle. By 1970 Lyle was experimenting with a revolutionary new mechanical lure able to dart around pulleys in some simulation of a running hare. This could be set up under controlled ground conditions in far less space than open field demanded. Thus the modern sport of Lure Coursing was born. Not only could uniform trials be held on football or other athletic fields all over the country, but in its use of a mechanical lure it gave hope for the eventual establishment of pseudo-coursing titles as an official AKC sighthound activity.

The American Sighthound Field Association (ASFA) was officially established in May of 1972 as a simulated field activity for sighthounds. From a numerically modest beginning, five trials and a total of 150 entries in 1972, Lure Coursing gained wide momentum in the following decade. In 1981, 250 trials were held with over 10,000 entries involved. In 1984, the AKC was willing to have Lure Coursing as an official AKC Field Trial activity, but due to AKC's conditions, ASFA voted down the merger. The ASFA Lure Coursing titles are worn with great and well-deserved pride.

The young sport of ASFA Lure Coursing was hastily joined by the remnants of racing and coursing Afghan Hound enthusiasts. A sideline of stalwarts already entrenched in Obedience work with the breed quickly added the new challenge. The dogs were primarily from show pedigrees of champion or near-champion lineage, but with some notable exceptions, had been retired or derailed from exhibition. Some, in fact, were rescue cases. Their owners were aggressively concerned about the mental and physical attributes of their dogs and willing to expend considerable personal energies to expanding those facets. A high percentage of ASFA-titled Afghan Hounds also hold Obedience titles.

The California Afghan Hound, Reddy to Love Thru Kindness, right off open field coursing success, was the first of the breed to become ASFA-titled in 1973. First dual show/coursing champion, in 1974, was the lovely Wita Vail of Nightwatch, from the breeding of Dutch import Wita Rose van de Oranje Manege to Ch. Mecca's Falstaff. Dee Verti's Nightwatch became happily dedicated to triple-threat all-purpose Afghan Hounds.

The first Afghan Hound to win the coveted title of Lure Courser of Merit (LCM) was Micky May, officially known as Ahmir's Silence, LCM. Micky May is owned by Phyllis Roe.

The German race champion import, Begum el Bamian, moved into northern California lure coursing in 1975, to become Grand Field Champion, and then Lure Courser of Merit (LCM)—the latter title replacing the former in the ASFA rule change of 1977. Begum astonished viewers, not only with her speed and agility, but also her differences from the show-Afghans of the day. This bitch was small, rather stocky, with a stand-offish coat and inelegant lines (by current show standards) but lightning-quick in her movements. She was, in short, everything American show-dog breeders have been moving away from, thus serving as living proof that top notch coursing character must be tested, and carefully preserved, as a specific attribute not necessarily tied to picture postcard beauty—if coursing character is to survive.

ASFA's growing pains were characterized by changes in rules,

Marietta Forrester and "Bandit" (Tamora's Image of Ali, C.D., LCM, Can. F.Ch.X, TT) receiving 1977 AHCA Lure Coursing Trophy. AHCA presenter—Lt. Col. Wallace H. Pede.

Tamora's Image of Ali, C.D., LCM, Can. F.Ch.X, TT (Ch. Nativ Dancer of Scheherezade ex Ch. Tamora's Salome), dog, bred by Hugh R. Morgan, owned by Gary and Marietta Forrester.

ground plans, member clubs and dog eligibility. They were met in the flexible spirit essential for a new sport. The addition of the LCM category has provided an orderly, but stringent, mode for the coursing cream-of-the-crop to emerge from the first title, Field Champion (F.Ch.), for tougher competition. It signifies that as a F.Ch. the dog has gone on to win at least four first placements and 300 points all from the Field Champion stakes. From its base on the West Coast, ASFA sent fast-rooting tendrils across the United States and into Canada; *Field Advisory News* (FAN) became the *Gazette* of the Lure Coursing world. As a serious new sporting activity for all sighthounds, lure coursing gives every evidence of being here to stay.

Fassl's Oh What A Girl, LCM, owned by Suzie Fassl, finished her LCM in nine trials with eight first placements and 302 points. Her record was spoiled by one ninth place. All other trials were first placements, including those for her F.Ch., and she received another first on the day after she completed her LCM.

In the three years of '75, '76 and '77, a total of 19 Afghan Hounds earned the basic ASFA F.Ch. title, 13 of which also held Obedience titles. Four of the ASFA F.Ch. went on to earn the coveted LCM, in different regions of the country. Chaparral Soylent Blue Ro-Jan, Starlane's Suni Daze, Ramu'a Khala-Tzarina and Tully's Khayam Cassandra became dual-titled ASFA F.Ch. and AKC champions. The list of F.Ch. is very long and replete with dual and triple title holders. The AHCA book, *Afghan Hounds in America,* contains a list of F.Ch.

Ambassador for Afghan Hound lure coursers has been Gary and Marietta Forrester's Tamora's Image of Ali, C.D., LCM, Can. F.Ch., TT—a black and tan, better known as Bandit. Based in Pennsylvania, and flown to many an Eastern trial success in his owner's small plane, Bandit was number 1 Afghan Hound lure courser in '76, '77 and '78. Winning the Grand National Lure Course (the Westminster and Santa Barbara of ASFA trials) proved his formidable all-breed ability. As of this writing, Bandit is still the all-time ASFA gazehound winner. Not only an LCM, he earned his C.D. in obedience in three straight shows, and his American Temperament Test Society's TT at 11½ years of age. Royally-sired by Ch. Nativ Dancer of Scheherezade ex Ch. Tamora's Salome, Bandit began as an exhibition dog that hated dog shows. At first sight of the lure, when 17 months old, life gained positive meaning for him. He instantly caught the eye of the show-set by consistently winning the specially added Lure Course at the AHCA National Specialty. Much to the breed's modern gain, Bandit and the Forresters have encouraged a number of Eastern owners to put their show-hopefuls into lure coursing trials.

Bandit and his son, Marah's Limited Edition, LCM, Can. F.Ch.X., TT, are the only two American Afghan Hounds to hold all lure

Can. Ch. Nightwatch V Onika, Ame[r?] and Can. F.Ch. (Int. Ch. Ophir vo[n] Katwiga ex Ch. Wita Vail of Nightwatc[h] F.Ch.), black mask gold bitch, bred b[y] Denyce Verti, owned by Dee Verti and Ja[n] Priddy. In one litter produced four F.Ch. Top Afghan Hound in CSFA competitio[n] in 1976/77 and first dual Ch. sighthoun[d] in Canada.

Ch. Wielki Sezlem of Nightwatch, F.Ch., litter brother to Ch. Wita Vail of Night-watch, F.Ch., first two dual champions. Black mask gold dog, bred and owned by Denyce Verti. Sire of nine F.Ch.

Wita Rosie van de Oranje Manege, F.Ch. (imported from Holland) (UICL dual Ch. Kysyl van de Oranje Manege ex Rosita van de Oranje Manege), black mask red bitch, bred by Eta Pauptit, owned by Denyce Verti. Two litters produced two dual champions plus three field champions.

coursing titles in North America.

By the end of 1983, only one dog was able to obtain a conformation championship and LCM—Ch. Yantra Mojou Jabbar, Can. F.Ch., LCM. Mojou was never trained to course. As newcomers to the breed the owners, Michele Giasone and Gail Phelps, were anxious to experience both coursing and showing. Mojou's first birthday found him placing second at the AHCA 1980 National Specialty Lure Field Trial at Palo Alto, California. This was the beginning of a successful and unexpected coursing career.

Faced with the decision to either course or show, they decided to please Mojou and course. By December 1981, Mojou was the number 1 Lure Coursing Afghan Hound. His titles included both LCM, Canadian F.Ch. and he was close to achieving a Canadian Lure Courser Excellence (F.Ch.X). Coursing gave Mojou the maturity and attitude required for success in the show ring. He obtained his Championship in just six months of showing.

As best as can be determined, the record for breeding field champions is held by Denyce Verti. Out of eight litters, four of which were co-bred, a total of 16 ASFA F.Chs. and one Canadian Kennel Club (CKC) F.Ch., three AKC Champions, one C.D., and five CKC Champions were produced. Some of these dogs and their records are shown in the photographs in this chapter. Ch. Wita Vail of Nightwatch, F.Ch., finished with all majors owner-handled with a St. Louis Specialty BIS from the Open class at 18 months of age. Vail is featured on the cover, in full flight, of ASFA's *Introduction to the Sport of Lure Coursing.*

Friend of the Forresters, Karen Wagner, smashed the separatist fence between notable show achievements and field work with Ch. Zuvenda Renegade of Esfahan, F.Ch., when this dog became the first ASFA F.Ch. to win Best of Breed at the AHCA National Specialty (1979). Better known as Razzle, he has sired both show, field and dual champions, with the notable inclusion of the 1981 AHCA National Specialty BOB, Ch. Zuvenda Razcym, now a field trial dog in his own right. Conscious breeding efforts are now being made to combine the most suitable bests in dual and triple purpose Afghan Hounds from one side of the country to the other in efforts to regain and intensify these versatile qualities within the modern American life style.

No single fact promises richer dividends for the breed than the re-emergence of fanciers determined to combine show and lure coursing efforts. That there is great benefit to be gained for the show dog in coursing is proven. Marietta Forrester reports—"It tightens up toplines and loose rears, develops chest, and most of all a positive attitude on the dog's part by giving the dog a special joy and satisfaction that seems to clear the cobwebs from the mind."

Ch. Xanadu's Xixith, C.D., F.Ch. (Ch. Akaba's Royal Flush ex Ch. Xanadu's Swe Xephyr), bitch, owned and bred by Johann B. Tanner.

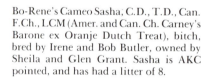

Bo-Rene's Cameo Sasha, C.D., T.D., Can. F.Ch., LCM (Amer. and Can. Ch. Carney's Barone ex Oranje Dutch Treat), bitch, bred by Irene and Bob Butler, owned by Sheila and Glen Grant. Sasha is AKC pointed, and has had a litter of 8.

Conformation titles followed coursing titles with several dualists for just the reasons listed. Commonly expressed necessities for superior coursers, such as "basic balance between front and rear," are those of value for the conformation hopeful. Owners assert that the medium angulated rear works best, with the "overdone ones—totally useless!" With a few exceptions the standard sized Afghan Hounds do better than the over-sized ones. Bandit weighed 63 pounds in running weight and stands just over 27 inches. As a controlled test of straight speed, eagerness, plus agility around twisting turns, the sport of lure coursing allows owners to observe, compare, condition and preserve much that is precious to this sightound extraordinaire.